Using Movement to Teach Academics

The Mind and Body as One Entity

Sandra Minton

Rowman & Littlefield Education
Lanham, Maryland • Toronto • Plymouth, UK
2008

Published in the United States of America
by Rowman & Littlefield Education
A Division of Rowman & Littlefield Publishers, Inc.
A wholly owned subsidary of The Rowman & Littlefield Publishing Group, Inc.
4501 Forbes Boulevard, Suite 200, Lanham, Maryland 20706
www.rowmaneducation.com

Estover Road
Plymouth PL6 7PY
United Kingdom

British Library Cataloguing in Publication Information Available

Library of Congress Cataloging-in-Publication Data

Minton, Sandra Cerny, 1943–
  Using movement to teach academics : the mind and body as one entity / Sandra Minton.
    p. cm.
  Includes bibliographical references.
  ISBN-13: 978-1-57886-784-4 (hardcover : alk. paper)
  ISBN-13: 978-1-57886-785-1 (pbk. : alk. paper)
  ISBN-10: 1-57886-784-3 (hardcover : alk. paper)
  ISBN-10: 1-57886-785-1 (pbk. : alk. paper)
  1. Dance—Study and teaching (Primary) 2. Dance—Study and teaching (Elementary) 3. Education, Primary. 4. Education, Elementary. 5. Movement, Psychology of. I. Title.
  GV1588.4.M56 2008
  372.86'8—dc22   2007046648

∞™ The paper used in this publication meets the minimum requirements of American National Standard for Information Sciences—Permanence of Paper for Printed Library Materials, ANSI/NISO Z39.48-1992.
Manufactured in the United States of America.

This book is dedicated to my parents, who encouraged me to think for myself;
to the teachers who invited me into their classrooms to present movement-based lessons;
to the students who participated in these lessons; and
to my husband Clarence Colburn, who has allowed me the space and time
to write this and other books.

Contents

Foreword: Moving, Dancing, and Learning

Sandra Minton has been presenting workshops for teachers on the content of this book for almost two decades, and I have had the opportunity to experience some of them at national dance conferences. Her presentations and workshops have been enthusiastically received by both beginners and experienced teachers. And now this book, which delineates the unique viewpoint found in Minton's work, is available.

This book is designed to dispel the myth that the mind and body are two separate entities by demonstrating how movement can be used to teach academics. While the connection between mind and body seems self-evident to some, this relationship is not readily acknowledged by those who live and work in fields that do not embrace or engage in movement. Throughout the book, readers learn to look at movement in a new way by using a step-by-step process for transforming stuff of the mind into actions and dances—a process called active learning. By using movement as an instructional tool, teachers encourage children to do something they want and love to do naturally, which is to move. While some feel that using dance as part of the academic teaching process is demeaning to the art form, Minton argues that the movement transformation process, which is at the core of this work, is actually the same creative process used in the beginning stage of movement discovery for any choreography. Both processes—using movement as a teaching tool and creating a dance—are the same in the beginning when ideas begin to emerge and transform into movement. The strength of the information in this book is also found in the connections that exist between creating movements, making dances, and many educational theories of the day, such as zone of proximal development, multiple intelligences, cooperative learning, and brain-based learning. Thus, this book weaves practical and theoretical information into one text, providing teachers with how-to information and content that can be used to substantiate the use of movement as a teaching strategy in schools.

Using Movement to Teach Academics: The Mind and Body as One Entity is written for beginners who have not worked with creative movement and dance making so they can confidently use movement as a teaching tool in their own classes. This book also provides experienced movers and dancers with many suggestions for transforming academic concepts into movement. While this book includes much practical information, it also describes education theories, relevant research, and articles written by authorities that substantiate the use of movement as a teaching strategy. In particular, the reader learns how movement-based lessons can be structured to appeal to students with a variety of learning styles (kinesthetic/tactile, visual, auditory).

Literacy is emphasized in our schools today as never before. The use of movement-based lessons provides teachers with another way to address the literacy issue. In addition, movement used as a teaching tool can connect curricula by emphasizing commonalities rather than differences between subjects. It is an interdisciplinary way to approach learning. Minton clearly presents her methodology and theoretical and practical information and provides the beginner with a step-by-step process of transforming academic concepts into movement-based lessons. *Using Movement to Teach Academics* is an appropriate text for college and university courses for prospective physical educators or classroom teachers.

Billie Lepczyk, Ed.D.
Associate Professor of Dance Education
Virginia Polytechnic Institute and State University

Have you ever noticed how you seem to remember ideas learned from personal experiences better than ideas learned from a book? The following text makes use of this human trait by using movement as a teaching tool. When students perform movements related to concepts and ideas, learning becomes more personal and concrete.

Using Movement to Teach Academics sets the stage in Chapter 1 for the remainder of the book by introducing a movement-based teaching strategy known as active learning. This mode of learning fits the natural tendency of children to want to move and play. Active learning in the form of movement-based lessons also parallels principles described in many popular educational theories.

In Chapter 2, you are introduced to the teaching tools used throughout this book. I call these tools movement components. They include direction, level, size, speed, duration, rhythm, quality, shape, pathway in space, and body position. Whether a movement starts or stops is a component, too. Following a description of each component, you will do exercises enabling you to determine how each movement component feels in your own body. Such an examination of body feelings or kinesthetic feedback is something we usually overlook in daily life but is key to using movement as a teaching tool. For example, moving forward feels different from moving backward; traveling on a straight pathway feels different from moving on a curved pathway; and making a wide shape with your body feels different from making a narrow shape.

Next, you discover how to translate academic concepts into movement using direct, literal methods and a second process that is more indirect or abstract. A direct way to translate the canopy of a rainforest into movement is to have students form a canopy-like shape by lifting and curving their arms and touching their fingertips together at the center of a circle. An example of a more abstract movement transformation is to move at a low level to represent a sneaky character in a story, while higher actions represent an honest character. Exercises are also provided to guide you through the creative movement process, so that by the end of Chapter 3, you know how to use each of the movement components to translate academic concepts into movements.

Single movements make up parts of a dance, but they are not a whole dance. In Chapter 4, you learn how to combine movements together so that they form dances. The most elementary way to make a dance is to link movements together in a series, one after the other. Other ways to create dances include text-based, tableau, established dance forms, such as ABA, and problem solving. An example of a problem-solving dance is to create body shapes that represent different geological formations on a map and place each body shape in its proper location with respect to the map. The problem to be solved is to create a dance using transitional movements that connect the body shapes. The transitional movements can trace the path of roads or rivers on the map. These and other approaches to dance making are described in this chapter, followed by exercises to help you design your own dances using concept-based movements.

In Chapter 5, movement discovery and dance making are connected to various thinking skills or tools that are described by Michele and Robert Root-Bernstein in their book *Sparks of Genius*. In this chapter, you learn how to hone such thinking skills as observing, recognizing patterns, empathizing, body thinking, imaging, transforming, abstracting, playing, forming patterns, modeling, and synthesizing. Normally, learning such thinking skills is an unconscious by-product of doing creative work, but here, you focus on the thinking tools through movement discovery and dance making. For example, when you give order to movements in a dance, you create relationships between the movements, and patterns are formed. At times, movement discovery also involves creating movements by extracting the essence of an inspiration or concept through the process of abstracting.

Chapter 6 gives you a chance to put all the skills you have learned thus far in the book to work. You begin with a set of concepts, organize these concepts into a lesson, and translate these concepts into appropriate movements. Then, you are guided through the process of forming these movements into a dance. Finally, you describe your dance in terms of the thinking skills you used in its creation.

In Chapter 7, you come full circle by returning to the initial premise on which this book is based: the connection between mind and body. Here you explore the mind–body connection from a variety of perspectives, including how the body or kinesthetic sense operates during learning and how it connects with emotion, imagery, modes of thought, literacy, and language.

Acknowledgments

I would like to thank the students from Ammesse and Remington Elementary Schools, Denver Public Schools, and the Centennial Academy of Fine Arts Education, Littleton Public Schools, who posed for the photos in this book. I also want to acknowledge Anna Newell, who took most of the photos, and Judi Hofmeister, dance and theatre teacher, Douglas County High School, and Joan Brown, former dance and physical education teacher, Denver Public Schools, who read the first draft of this text and provided suggestions. A special thank you goes to Allison Jaramillo, who allowed us to take photos in her studio, the Littleton Dance Academy, and to Judy Anderson, director, Platte Forum, where I had the chance to present my interdisciplinary dance and visual arts project with the Whiteman Elementary School students, Denver Public Schools.

CHAPTER 1

Connecting Movement, Dance, and Academics

This book is designed to dispel the myth that mind and body are two separate entities. Content illuminates the idea that the body and kinesthetic sense can be used in teaching and that many popular educational theories can be approached through movement-based lessons. To realize this goal, you are provided with a step-by-step process for designing movement- and dance-based classes while learning to look at movement in terms of its components. Once you have practiced using the movement components, you will learn how they can be used to transform academic concepts into actions. A number of concepts from different academic areas are used as examples. Because single movements are not dances, you will also learn many ways in which separate actions can be combined together to produce a dance.

MAKING THE CONNECTION: MOVEMENT, DANCE, AND ACADEMICS

Most children like and want to move, whether this movement is in the form of playing games, changing from one classroom to another during the school day, or performing tasks within a classroom, such as handing out blank paper to other students. There seems to be a limit to how long children can and want to sit or remain in one spot and stay on task. This period of time, frequently called attention span, diminishes with the age of the child, so younger children tend to pay attention for shorter periods of time. Teachers may need to use various techniques to gain or keep students' attention.[1]

The natural tendency of children to like and want to move is the premise on which this book is based. Throughout you will learn how movement and dance can be used to help students in elementary and middle school connect with academic concepts, including those from reading, writing, math, science, social studies, history, geography, multicultural studies, visual arts, and music. Teaching by using movement and dance is an educational strategy that is sometimes called active learning.

WHAT IS ACTIVE LEARNING?

Active learning contrasts with traditional instruction in which teachers do most of the talking and children remain passive; through active learning, students have opportunities to talk, listen, read, write, and reflect.[2] Active or experiential learning helps children understand and remember information. Many educators believe that children learn best when they are doing because they become engaged with the subject matter. Students who are actively participating are also more interested in what they are learning. Research shows that active learning is more effective than traditional teaching methods in providing understanding, learning problem solving, stimulating curiosity and independence, and creating positive feelings about school.[3] Active learning also assumes different children learn in different ways.[4] One way to actively learn is to learn by moving and dancing.

Active learning also uses interdisciplinary teaching strategies. In an active form of learning, children process information through oral expression or written work, but they can also make diagrams or drawings, do peer teaching, and present performances or demonstrations.[5] From this description, we can see that during active-learning students are involved with more than one discipline—in this case, reading, writing, the visual arts, and one or more of the performing arts. Throughout this book, you are introduced to many movement and dance experiences based on interdisciplinary teaching strategies.

By using interdisciplinary teaching techniques, teachers can also tap into a number of the senses to make varied sensory experiences part of a lesson. Effective multisensory instruction engages children by asking them to see, hear, touch, and move in relation to the concepts they are studying. Multisensory teaching also encourages children to be emotionally connected to what they are learning.[6] When a lesson is movement based, the kinesthetic, or body, sense becomes involved. If the movements or dances are performed to music, the auditory sense is part of the learning experience, while adding visual aids, such as pictures or drawings, incorporates the visual sense. Finally, if the movements and dances are created by the children or are from the students' cultural background, learning becomes more personal or feeling based.

We now know that active, interdisciplinary, and multisensory teaching approaches use a greater number of human intelligences, promote better retention, and inspire an inner desire to learn.[7] One reason this is true is because such teaching techniques tap into the multiple intelligences, or the many ways in which humans learn and understand information.

DANCE IS A PERFORMING ART, NOT A TEACHING STRATEGY

There are some individuals in the dance field who object to using dance as a teaching tool. This objection arises from the fact that some dancers and dance educators believe that dance should be appreciated in and of itself, and using dance to help with the academic teaching process is demeaning to the art form. The premise in this book—using movement and dance as a teaching tool—does not exclude the development of dance appreciation because the two goals can be part of the same lesson. This is particularly true when children create and perform a whole dance as part of an academic lesson or when they view videos of dances created by master choreographers as part of lesson content.

Of all the art forms—dance, music, theater, and the visual arts—dance is the least understood and appreci-

ated by the public. This lack of appreciation is due in part to the small number of dance programs that exist in our public schools. Affluent or middle-class parents can afford and frequently do send their children, particularly girls, to private dance studios, but families that are in a lower income bracket cannot afford such a luxury. This means that lower-income children receive little exposure to dance unless that exposure is provided by our schools.

In an article published in 1999, Jane Bonbright, executive director of the National Dance Education Organization, and Susan McGreevy-Nichols, past president of the National Dance Association, stated that the 1997 National Assessment of Educational Progress could not be implemented for dance because there were not enough 8th-grade students enrolled in dance education courses across the country. Although a less formal assessment was done of in-school dance programs, the dance sample was not large enough do a statistics-based analysis.[8]

In light of this problem, movement and dance used to teach academic concepts can give dance educators and other types of teachers an alternate avenue for including dance in our schools. Such lessons are based on concepts already being studied by students, providing a natural bridge between what students are already studying and dance. In my experience, students have trouble appreciating and understanding content that is not connected to their own lives. All people, in fact, learn most easily when the information to be learned can be connected to their personal experiences. Creating connections between dance and academics is also a goal of both the fifth and seventh national dance standards. The fifth dance standard states that students should be able to demonstrate and understand dance in various cultures and historical periods, while the seventh standard advocates having students make connections between dance and other disciplines.[9] Using dance as part of a lesson about Mexico would fulfill the requirements of standard 5, while a dance-based math lesson would apply to standard 7.

But why are there so few dance programs in schools? One reason is that dance certification does not exist in all the states. Declining educational budgets and the need to spend more time teaching children the basics also contributes to the low number of dance teachers, as well as having fewer teachers in the other arts. Connecting movement and dance to academics is one way to initiate dance experiences even when a school's budget does not permit hiring dance specialists. Nevertheless, the ultimate goal should be to create interest in dance and to build on this interest by developing dance programs taught by certified dance educators. Judith Lynne Hanna, an advocate of dance in education, made the following statement: "Without dance education—the wellspring of dancers and dance audiences—the field of dance is in jeopardy."[10]

Another objection to using dance in academic settings is that individual movements based on single concepts are not dance. Dancing, as the thinking goes, involves sequencing movements to produce a more complex whole, and individual actions do not form a whole dance. But let's examine this statement more closely. When movements are used to teach academics, the creative process is used to transform concepts into movement. This transforming process is also the first stage of the same creative process used to discover movement for a dance. Dance educators frequently talk about an inspiration for a dance as the starting point for creative work. In this book, the inspirations for creating movements are academic concepts. The two methods for transforming concepts into movement, literal and abstraction, are described in this text.

This book also advocates dance making, or shaping a number of single movements into dances. Once individual actions are created by transforming concepts into actions, the movements can be combined in various ways to produce dances. In this book, creating and performing a dance serve as the culminating parts of movement-based lessons. Many different dance forms are explored as a way to weave single movements together into dances.

The third reason for including dance in our schools is that learning to dance and learning to make dances can be connected to classroom learning. For example, when children learn a dance, they focus on and observe the teacher's movements. They must also remember the order of movements in a dance and the number of times each action is performed. In addition, when dance making is part of lessons, students solve movement-based problems, leading to feelings of accomplishment. Thus, learning a dance and creating one provide different types of educational experi-

ences. Sue Stinson, a well-known dance educator, commented that there may be a difference between the kind of intelligence or creativity needed to be a dance performer and the kind needed to be a choreographer, or person who makes dances.[11]

WHY USE MOVEMENT AND DANCE AS A TEACHING TOOL?

Have you ever wondered why some people are good musicians and others excel in accounting? Or why do schools teach addition and subtraction in elementary school and algebra in middle school? There are many different theories found in educational literature that attempt to explain how and why students learn depending on their age, personal talents, lesson content and organization, environment, and cultural background. Some of these theories include the zone of proximal development, learning styles, the multiple intelligences, multisensory learning, experiential or active learning, cooperative learning, and brain-based learning. Teaching that includes movement and dance connects with and supports many of these educational theories and concepts.

The Zone of Proximal Development

The zone of proximal development (ZPD) is key in the sociocultural theory put forth by Lev Vygotsky in the early 20th century. ZPD represents the space between a child's developmental level and the amount of learning that can be accomplished by students who are provided with proper teaching and guidance. It is the amount of learning possible when a child is given the right conditions for instruction.[12] ZPD means that a child's learning experiences must match his or her level of development, but this level of development can be extended if the child is given proper guidance.[13] In everyday terms, ZPD refers to the fact that students of a certain age may be able to add, but with the proper coaching, they soon learn to subtract.

The point here is that teaching using movement and dance can be tailored to meet the developmental needs of a child. While older children like to work in groups or teams to make dances, younger children are more "me" oriented and work better by themselves or in pairs. Younger students can create simple movements or body shapes in response to a particular idea. Increased socialization begins to occur because the young children are creating movements alongside other students in their class. The knowledge base of young children can also be extended by connecting movement and dance with new academic concepts and ideas.

Learning Styles

There are many ways to analyze learning style, or the preferred mode of processing information. Some authorities talk about learning modality or multisensory learning when addressing learning style.[14] The description of learning styles found here is based on the senses—auditory, visual, or tactile-kinesthetic. Auditory learners get their information orally. They also prefer to process facts individually, leading to an eventual understanding of a whole concept. The visual learner makes sense of new information by looking at drawings, charts, diagrams, or outlines and prefers to process input globally. Visual learners also use mental imagery or mind pictures to help them understand. Tactile-kinesthetic learners think concretely and understand by doing. They rely on physical interactions while learning.[15]

Unfortunately, some teachers avoid using instructional strategies that appeal to a variety of learning styles. One of the reasons for this neglect is that lessons appealing to the sense of touch or that include movement and pictures can get messy. Imagine 28 or 30 pairs of little hands all trying to touch the fuzzy leaves on an African Violet or the same number of little heads craning to see a picture. Using movement as a teaching tool can also be messy—a problem that requires added time in planning how to organize and present such lessons. Another aspect of this problem is that movement and the kinesthetic sense are often forgotten when teachers design lessons because we use our bodies daily in a functional way. This fact makes us take movement for granted, so we often overlook how movement can be integrated into lessons.

Analyzing a student's learning style can be tricky, although it is fairly easy to know when a student is having problems processing information in a particular way and narrow down a child's preferred style of learning. For example, students who cannot match colors, shapes, or sizes or who have trouble copying words from the board may have visual processing problems; those who cannot follow step-by-step verbal instructions or who are distracted by loud noises can have auditory processing problems; and those who cannot keep their hands to themselves or who crave or avoid touching things may have tactile-kinesthetic processing problems.[16]

Educational researchers have also discovered teaching that relies less on verbal instruction and more on the other styles of learning can benefit children from diverse cultures. Some Native American children, for example, are not accustomed to interacting verbally with their elders and do not respond well to class discussions. In the same vein, teachers who have taught Hawaiian children found that moving or doing while teaching worked better because these techniques were similar to the Hawaiian cultural tradition called a "talk story."[17]

Movement and dance-based lessons are a natural way for tactile-kinesthetic children to understand information. As indicated earlier, such lessons can include visual and auditory input by showing children pictures or diagrams that relate to content or by verbally describing content. Verbal descriptions and visual aids can be followed by introducing a movement or movements that transform the concepts into actions. To make sure you are reaching all the students in your class, it is best to teach to all the learning styles during a single lesson when possible.

The Multiple Intelligences

The theory of multiple intelligences (MI) is closely connected to the theory of learning styles. This Theory was originally described in detail by Howard Gardner in his 1983 book *Frames of Mind*. In its original form, the theory outlined seven different forms of intelligence. These forms of intelligence were identified by Gardner and his Project Zero research team at Harvard University. The original seven intelligences included linguistic, musical, logical-mathematical, spatial, bodily-kinesthetic, interpersonal, and intrapersonal intelligences.[18] Gardner and his colleagues have since developed other forms of intelligence, but the focus here is on the original seven.

Linguistic intelligence is related to words and language, in both its written and spoken forms. Musical intelligence can be found in the ability to play musical instruments and also in people who compose music. It is a form of intelligence based on musical components like pitch, melody, and rhythm. Logical-mathematical intelligence begins in the early years when children order and reorder objects and perform other operations on them, such as addition and multiplication. Gradually, mathematical intelligence becomes more abstract as children learn to substitute symbols for the objects.[19] They also learn these symbols can be manipulated, for instance, what the possible values of x and y are when $x + y = 10$.

Spatial intelligence is related to the ability to visualize objects, patterns, or images in one's mind and to be able to mentally modify or move these objects and patterns around. Champion chess players have a high degree of spatial intelligence because they can anticipate the movements of chess pieces across the board. To have a high degree of bodily-kinesthetic intelligence means being skilled in using the body for functional or expressive purposes. To be able to eat with chopsticks without dropping your food on the table requires a certain degree of the functional form of bodily-kinesthetic intelligence, while a professional ballet dancer has honed and refined his or her bodily-kinesthetic intelligence for expressive purposes.[20]

Gardner called the last two forms of intelligence the personal intelligences. Interpersonal intelligence is focused outward toward other individuals, while intrapersonal intelligence is directed inward toward oneself. A person who has a high degree of interpersonal intelligence easily senses the moods and feelings of others. A skilled politician or teacher has a high degree of interpersonal intelligence, as does a good store manager. Intrapersonal intelligence refers to being sensitive to one's own feelings and being able to distinguish between them.[21]

The movement-based approach to teaching concepts complements MI in many respects. When ideas are described with words, the lesson relates to linguistic intelligence, while bodily-kinesthetic intelligence comes into play during the movement portion of a lesson. When students create their own dances, they frequently visualize the dance before hand and must imagine how the dancers in a piece can travel around without bumping. If movements or dances are created individually, the work involves intrapersonal

intelligence, but working in a group to make a dance requires interpersonal intelligence. Finally, if a dance is created to music, the creating involves a level of musical intelligence. Sometimes it is necessary to count the number of times an action is performed or to count beats in the music, which touches on mathematical intelligence.

When movement is used as a teaching strategy, lessons naturally appeal to students who have a strong kinesthetic intelligence. Adding other elements to lessons, such as pictures, music, or verbal descriptions, helps students use the other forms of intelligence. In this way, lesson content allows children to process information with their preferred intelligence, and the information becomes more meaningful to them.[22]

Experiential Learning

Experiential learning is based on and involves a learner's experiences. According to one authority, experiential learning is dependent on having direct experiences with the intent to learn something. Reflection and feedback are also part of this type of learning, as is an active phase in which students do, experiment, or participate. These elements make experiential learning similar to active learning. Many believe that experiential learning is superior to other forms of learning, but such superiority is dependent on the use of skillful teaching techniques and strategies.[23] Hands-on learning is another way to describe experiential learning.

It is easy to see how the use of movement and dance can contribute to experiential learning. If children learn dances from other cultures, they are having a direct experience with the movement and music of the culture. When children create concept-based movements and dances, they are learning through direct experience or through the kinesthetic sense. They are not only experiencing concepts and ideas on a physical level but are learning what it feels like to put a dance together.

Cooperative Learning

Cooperative learning takes place in groups and is most effective when a group has similar goals and members connect in a positive way.[24] When used successfully, cooperative learning reduces competition and encourages members to contribute to a common goal. Successful use of cooperative learning is also dependent on how well teachers plan a lesson by determining and clearly describing objectives. Stating objectives is followed by designating who is in each group, outlining parameters of the problem, providing some examples of how to achieve the goal, and giving groups enough time to work.[25] Teachers should also rotate group membership and create groups that have children who are both the same and different from each other. Similarities reinforce what students know, but differences lead to new knowledge, respect, and appreciation of cultural and other types of differences.[26]

By using a team approach to create dances, students are engaging in a form of cooperative learning. At the same time, students are learning how to work with others in a way that does not lead to arguments or fights because cooperative learning means learning to compromise and appreciate differences in others. Cooperative learning is especially appropriate for older students from the 4th grade on up because primary-age children are more individualistic in how they relate to the world.

Some of the research I have done in recent years has explored the connection between participation in dance and self-esteem. In a 9-week qualitative study done with middle school students, I discovered that when the students worked in teams to create dances, they learned much about themselves and the others in their group. While many students thought dance making in a group was fun, they also discovered something about their own talents; learned that their opinion mattered; appreciated their peers; and learned how to communicate with each other.[27]

Brain-Based Learning

In recent years, neuroscientists have been studying what happens in the human brain during learning. Currently, the results of this research are being described in educational theories. Teaching that attempts to mirror how learning takes place in the brain is called brain-based learning. One neuroscience discovery that relates to education is that experience creates new connections between the neurons of the brain, so an enriched environment encourages brain development.

The specific teaching strategies used for providing an enriched environment have yet to be thoroughly tested, however.[28] Neuroscience also confirms that the brain needs to find meaning by connecting new information to knowledge and skills the brain already knows.[29]

Brain research has shown there are centers in the brain that respond to specific disciplines. We have known there are language centers in the brain, but recent research demonstrates the arts also engage specific brain areas (see Figure 1.1). Music affects our emotions because the nucleus basalis, a part of the midbrain, or upper part of the brain stem, gives weighted meaning to sounds and codes them for storage in memory.[30] Other areas of the brain help us appreciate the visual arts. In general, the parietal lobes process spatial layout; the occipital lobes respond to color, contrast, and form; and the frontal lobes determine how long we look at an artwork.[31] But what about movement-oriented art forms? Simple movements like running involve areas of the brain, such as the basil ganglia and cerebellum located below the cerebral cortex, however highly complex movements like dancing engage much more of the brain.[32]

Renate and Geoffrey Caine, two educational theorists, have consolidated the neuroscience discoveries in their brain-mind principles. According to the Caines, the brain is adaptive, so thoughts, emotions, imagination, and physiology work together, exchanging information with the environment. Second, the brain is social because the brain-mind changes in response to others. Third, the search for meaning is innate and depends on forming patterns or relationships between bits of information. Fourth, learning is both focused and peripheral, involving conscious and unconscious processes. Fifth, learning is developmental and depends on introducing certain content at specific stages as children mature. Finally, learning is encouraged by challenges but discouraged by threats because learning and emotion are connected.[33]

The use of movement as a teaching tool reflects the brain-mind principles. A movement-based curriculum is interactive because concepts are transformed into actions and social, if dance making is done in groups. The search for meaning is based on forming patterns and relationships, and a dance is made up of many patterns of movements. In addition, when concept-based movements are formed into a dance, they can be com-

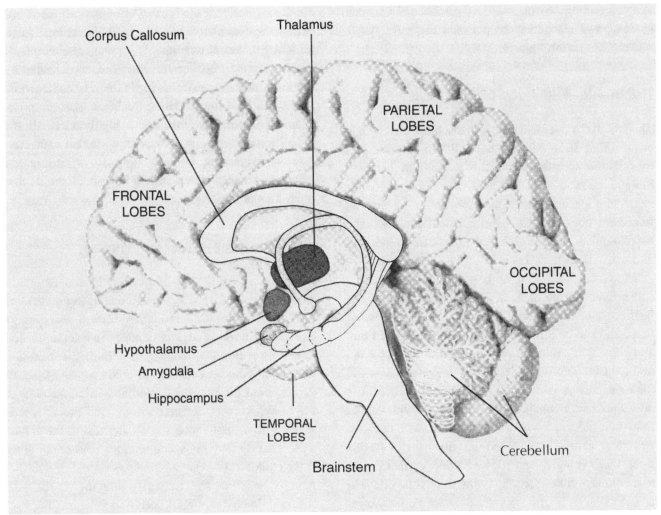

Figure 1.1.   *Medial view of brain.* Reprint of Figure 2.2 (p. 20) from *Brain Matters: Translating Research Into Classroom Practice*, by Patricia Wolfe. Alexandria, VA: Association for Supervision and Curriculum Development, 2001. Used with permission. The Association for Supervision and Curriculum Development (ASCD) is a worldwide community of educators advocating sound policies and sharing best practices to achieve the success of each learner. To learn more, visit ASCD at www.ascd.org.

bined to make sense in terms of the subject studied. For example, a rainforest grows in several layers, beginning with the emergent layer on top, followed by the canopy beneath it. In the rainforest dance, described in detail later, the movements representing the emergent layer are performed at a high level to show that it is the top layer, followed by performing actions representing the canopy at a lower level.

The fact that learning takes place in both an unconscious and conscious way is also applied during dance making because creative work involves both ways of thinking. In the first instance, movements simply appear and seem right after you have worked with a concept. At other times the creative process is more conscious because you will have to think about exactly

how to transform concepts into actions. Arranging and rearranging movements in a dance is also largely a conscious process.

It is easy to design developmentally appropriate lessons using movement and dance as well. This is done by choosing content that is appropriate for an age group and by using techniques that fit how children think and understand information at a particular age. Finally, a movement-based class can be challenging but not threatening. The right atmosphere can be created by choosing content that is age appropriate and designing classes that are structured clearly so that students know what the teacher expects. In addition, it is best to base dance making on neutral rather than personal or emotional concepts at the beginning of a class.

When a feeling of trust has been established between students and teacher, more personal ideas for dance making can be introduced.

THE BRAIN–MIND–BODY CONNECTION

The fact that movement used as a teaching strategy can be justified in terms of the brain-mind principles makes one wonder about the continuum between brain, mind, and body, if indeed such a continuum exists. Thinking about this issue inevitably leads to an important question that has intrigued scientists and psychologists for years. Where does brain-mind end, and where does body begin?

The Caines indicated the body and brain penetrate and influence each other in a reciprocal way and can be thought of as a single system. The Caines also wrote that mind can be affected by what is done to the brain and body, while mind can influence both the body and brain.[34] But what is mind? The Caines state that while the exact nature of mind is still open to debate, it is now apparent mind is more than an activity of the brain because mind works at a different level; physiology alone cannot explain and describe mind.[35] In this light, there is a growing body of evidence that points to a connection between the brain, mind, and body. In an interview with Bill Moyers, Candice Pert, who researches peptides, or one of the chemical messengers of the body, said that peptides seem to facilitate communication between cells and are found throughout the body and brain.[36] Other researchers found particular chemicals released in parts of the brain have specific functions in the body.[37] For example, under stress, epinephrine is released under control of the brain and raises the level of fatty acids in the blood in order to supply energy to muscles.[38]

Marian Diamond, who has spent many years researching the influence of environment on the mammalian brain, wrote that rabbits raised in captivity have smaller brains than those living in the wild.[39] In other words, the behaviors of the two groups of rabbits are different because the wild rabbits had to use survival behaviors—a way of reacting not needed by the rabbits in captivity.

Joseph LeDoux, a professor of neural science and psychology, has studied the connections between memory and emotion—particularly the emotion fear.

He discovered that the human brain may shape memories of fearful events in a way that affects later mental and behavioral reactions.[40] A practical example of the connection between the emotions experienced by the brain and human behavior is the effect classroom stress can have on students. Such a classroom environment causes students to be highly alert all the time—a way of being present in class that can interfere with learning because it destroys feelings of safety and security that should be part of the atmosphere in any classroom.[41]

A MORE TANGIBLE WAY TO CONNECT MIND AND BODY

There are more tangible ways to demonstrate the connection between mind and body. Several years ago, I was at a conference and participated in a session titled "The Power of a Positive Mind."[42] In this session, the presenter, Nancy Tidd, used a simple exercise to demonstrate the power of mind and its connection to the body. As part of her session, Tidd passed out a string with a small, common washer tied to the end of it. As I sat holding my string with the washer dangling at the end of it, I wondered how this simple device was going to teach us about positive thinking. In the next several minutes, though, I became a believer.

Next, Tidd instructed us to hold the string and washer up in front of our faces and think about a pathway, such as a circle or line, in which we wanted our washer to move. To my delight, I found that by simply thinking circle and by seeing that circle in my mind, I was able make my washer loop around in a circle. In contrast, thinking and seeing a straight line in my mind made my washer swing back and forth in a straight pathway. I even discovered that I could hone this newfound talent by willing my washer to move in large or small circles or swing back and forth in a long or short pathway.

As a result of this experiment, I asked myself various questions. For example, was thinking about a movement and producing it with the washer a natural human talent? In my estimation, everyone at the conference session had degrees of success with this experiment. I have also found 3rd-, 4th-, and 5th-grade students can successfully perform this exercise when it is presented as a mental focusing activity.

I believe that successfully moving the washer on the string tangibly demonstrates that there is a connection between mind and body. The washer obeyed my mental message to move in a particular way because I focused my thoughts and saw the washer moving in my mind beforehand. Put simply, I believed a particular response was possible, and this thought was transmitted by my nerve impulses from my brain to the muscles of my arm and hand. Although no movement could be seen in my arm or hand, there was sufficient muscular activity to cause the string and washer to move in a visible way. I have repeatedly tried this exercise, and the result has always been the same—the washer moves in the exact way I mentally direct it to move.

SUMMARY AND CONCLUSIONS

Dance educators disagree on the exact content of the dance curricula taught in our schools. At one pole are the purists who believe that dance should be appreciated in and of itself as an art. At the other pole are those who think dance can be used as a teaching tool to help children understand academic concepts. The view taken in this book is that dance can be used both as a teaching tool and to develop appreciation of the art form. These diverse goals can be met by presenting dance lessons based on academic content, followed by viewing a video of a dance by an accomplished choreographer that deals with lesson content, such as one that includes the creatures of the rainforest. Appreciation of dance as an art can also be achieved by having students make dances based on lesson content.

It is important to point out that dance taught in the traditional way and dance used as a teaching tool are more similar in terms of their educational benefits than they are different. First, teaching dance in a traditional way requires students to observe, focus, and remember, but learning concept-based dances uses the same mental skills. Second, dance used as a teaching tool is an active form of learning, but learning to dance and make dances in the traditional sense is also a form of active learning.

Using dance as a teaching tool addresses important educational theories, such as ZPD, MI, experiential learning, cooperative learning, and brain-based learning. A well-designed dance class based on the age of the children and the dance standards and that includes both technical and creative work addresses many of these theories, too. In dance technique class, students observe a movement demonstration, which uses visual intelligence. Later, students perform the dance movements to music using their musical and bodily-kinesthetic intelligence. A traditional dance class can also include dance making by groups of students, which encourages both experiential and cooperative learning. Finally, a tenet of brain-based learning is that meaning is discovered by forming patterns from input, and dance making involves weaving single actions into patterns.

Using movement and dance as a teaching tool incorporates the natural connections that exist between brain, mind, and body. This is true because students must recognize and understand academic concepts with the brain-mind, followed by performing concept-based movements with the body. A traditional dance class, particularly one that includes dance making, also explores the brain–mind–body connection. Initially, dance movement is discovered by moving the body, but later the movements are manipulated and arranged in the context of the dance by using the brain-mind.

REVIEWING YOUR KNOWLEDGE AND UNDERSTANDING

Now is your chance as a teacher or future teacher to connect the materials presented in this chapter to your understanding of movement and dance.

1. Describe several active learning teaching strategies, and give an example of how movement and dance can be used to teach in an active way.
2. Why do some people discourage the use of movement and dance to teach academic concepts?
3. What are some of the reasons described in this chapter for using movement and dance as an academic teaching strategy?
4. What similarities exist between an approach in which dance is used as an academic teaching strategy and one in which dance is taught as an art form?
5. Explain how you can design a concept-based movement and dance lesson that complements the ZPD theory.

6. The theories of learning styles and MI are similar in some ways. In what ways are these two theories similar? How are the two theories different?

7. Briefly explain how information from these two theories can be integrated into a movement and dance-based lesson.

8. How can movement and dance-based classes be designed to fit the cooperative learning model and be used to teach academic concepts at the same time?

9. What is brain-based learning?

10. How do movement and dance lessons used to teach academic concepts complement brain-based learning?

11. Describe one statement from this chapter that indicates the brain, mind, and body are connected.

NOTES

1. Bruce W. Tuckman, *Educational Psychology: From Theory to Application* (Fort Worth: Harcourt Brace Jovanovich, 1991).

2. Chet Meyers and Thomas B. Jones, *Promoting Active Learning: Strategies for the College Classroom* (San Francisco: Jossey-Bass, 1993).

3. Linda Darling-Hammond, *The Right to Learn: A Blueprint for Creating Schools That Work* (San Francisco: Jossey-Bass, 1997).

4. Meyers and Jones, *Promoting Active Learning.*

5. Renate N. Caine and Geoffrey Caine, *Education on the Edge of Possibility* (Alexandria, VA: Association for Supervision and Curriculum Development, 1997).

6. Edgar McIntosh and Marilu Peck, *Multisensory Strategies: Lessons and Classroom Management Techniques to Reach and Teach All Learners* (New York: Scholastic, 2005).

7. Anne K. Kanter, "Arts in Our Schools: Arts-Based School Reform That Applies the Concept of Interdisciplinary Study and Active Learning to Teach to the Multiple Intelligences" (Master's Thesis, University of Northern Colorado, Greeley, 1993).

8. Jane Bonbright and Susan McGreevey-Nichols, "NAEP and Dance: On Contextual Data, Process, and Problems in Dance Assessments, and Recommendations for the Field," *Arts Education Policy Review* 100, no. 6 (1999): 27–32.

9. National Dance Association, *National Standards for Dance Education: What Every Young American Should Know and Be Able to Do in Dance* (Reston, VA: American Alliance of Health, Physical Education, Recreation, and Dance, 1994).

10. Judith Lynne Hanna, *Partnering Dance and Education: Intelligent Moves for Changing Times* (Champaign, IL: Human Kinetics, 1999), p. 2.

11. Susan W. Stinson, "Testing Creativity of Dance Students in the People's Republic of China," *Dance Research Journal* 25, no. 1 (1993): 65–68.

12. Dale H. Schunk, *Learning Theories: An Educational Perspective*, 3rd ed. (Upper Saddle River, NJ: Prentice Hall, 2000).

13. Stephen N. Elliot, Thomas R. Kratochwill, Joan Littlefield Cook, and John F. Travers, *Educational Psychology: Effective Teaching, Effective Learning*, 3rd ed. (Boston: McGraw Hill, 2000).

14. Linda H. Wilson, *Teaching 201: Traveling Beyond the Basics* (Lanham, MD: ScarecrowEducation, 2004); McIntosh and Peck, *Multisensory Strategies.*

15. Lynne C. Sarasin, *Learning Style Perspectives: Impact in the Classroom* (Madison, WI: Atwood, 1999).

16. McIntosh and Peck, *Multisensory Strategies.*

17. Linda Darling-Hammond and John Bransford, eds., *Preparing Teachers for a Changing World: What Teachers Should Learn and Be Able to Do* (San Francisco: Jossey-Bass, 2005).

18. Howard Gardner, *Frames of Mind: The Theory of Multiple Intelligences* (New York: Basic Books, 1983).

19. Gardner, *Frames of Mind.*

20. Gardner, *Frames of Mind.*

21. Gardner, *Frames of Mind.*

22. Harvey F. Silver, Richard W. Strong, and Matthew J. Perini, *So Each May Learn: Integrating Learning Styles and Multiple Intelligences* (Alexandria, VA: Association for Supervision and Curriculum Development, 2000).

23. Jennifer A. Moon, *A Handbook of Reflective and Experiential Learning: Theory and Practice* (London: Routledge Falmer, 2004).

24. Susan Hill and Tim Hill, *The Collaborative Classroom: A Guide to Co-operative Learning* (Portsmouth, NH: Heinemann, 1990).

25. Wilson, *Teaching 201.*

26. Paul J. Vermette, *Making Cooperative Learning Work: Student Teams in K–12 Classrooms* (Upper Saddle River, NJ: Prentice Hall, 1998).

27. Sandra Minton, "Middle School Choreography Class: Two Parallel but Different Worlds," *Research in Dance Education* 8, no. 2 (2007): 103–121.

28. James P. Byrnes, *Minds, Brains and Learning: Understanding the Psychological and Educational Relevance of Neuroscientific Research* (New York: Guilford Press, 2001).

29. Elaine B. Johnson, *Contextual Teaching and Learning: What It Is and Why It's Here to Stay* (Thousand Oaks, CA: Corwin Press, 2002).

30. Eric Jensen, *Arts With the Brain in Mind* (Alexandria, VA: Association for Supervision and Curriculum Development, 2001).

31. Jensen, *Arts With the Brain in Mind*.

32. Jensen, *Arts With the Brain in Mind*.

33. Caine and Caine, *Education on the Edge of Possibility*.

34. Caine and Caine, *Education on the Edge of Possibility*.

35. Caine and Caine, *Education on the Edge of Possibility*.

36. Bill Moyers, *Healing and the Mind* (New York: Doubleday, 1993).

37. Neal E. Miller, "Clinical-Experimental Interactions in the Development of Neuroscience: A Primer for Nonspecialists and Lessons for Young Scientists," *American Psychologist* 50, no. 11 (1995): 901–911.

38. Miller, "Clinical-Experimental Interactions."

39. Marian C. Diamond, *Enriching Heredity: The Impact of the Environment on the Anatomy of the Brain* (New York: The Free Press, 1988).

40. Joseph E. LeDoux, "Emotion, Memory, and the Brain," *Scientific American* 270, no. 6 (1994): 50–57.

41. Caine and Caine, *Education on the Edge of Possibility*.

42. Nancy Tidd, "The Power of the Positive Mind" (Workshop/Lecture, Convention of the Central District of the American Alliance of Health, Physical Education, Recreation, and Dance, Fargo, ND, February 7, 2003).

CHAPTER 2

Introducing the Learning Tools

After reading the first chapter, you may be wondering how you can transform academic concepts into movement. The first step in this process is learning to look at movement in terms of its components. These components are the building blocks used in the movement transformation process. An example of one of the movement components is direction. Another movement component is speed or timing. Many may think that a step-by-step exploration of these components is not necessary. I have found, however, that even experienced movers do not all look at movement in the same way. In addition, some readers are not experienced movers and will welcome a detailed description of these components. I have found that experienced and less experienced movers overlook the many ways movement can be analyzed. Our society takes movement for granted because it is a utilitarian and sometimes unconscious aspect of life.

We use movements on a daily basis to accomplish many tasks without thinking about how they feel in our bodies or what they look like. I am sure you have climbed into and out of your car many times, but you probably never think about how these movements feel in your body or how they look to an observer. For this reason, movement components, such as size, energy, and speed or timing, are described in detail so that you can understand these components and use them to analyze and create your own movements. Such a detailed analysis of the movement components helps readers understand movement in the same way, so that, hopefully, all are on the same page. Once you have become comfortable with the movement components, you will be able to use them to transform academic concepts into actions.

FAMILIARIZING YOURSELF WITH THE MOVEMENT COMPONENTS

There are 11 essential movement components. They include direction, level, size, speed or timing, duration, rhythm, quality, shape, pathway, position, and starting and stopping movement. Immediately following the description of each is a set of step-by-step explorations. Thus, you read about a movement component and then have a chance to physically experience it in an individual and personal way. You can also use the same explorations with your students to help them experience each of the movement components.

What Is Direction?

Direction is where in space you move a part of your body or your whole body. Direction can also refer to where you face your body. In dance, this movement component is described with eight basic directions that relate to the center of your body—forward, backward, side right and left, and four diagonal directions (front right and left diagonals and the back right and left diagonals; see Figure 2.1). These eight basic directions, which are important in some ballet training systems, can be represented by drawing a cross with an *X* marked over it. It is also possible to describe the same eight directions by relating them to a square or rectangular room. For instance, if the wall you face is front, then the wall behind you is back, and the two walls at your sides are sides right and left. In addition, the four corners of the room mark the outermost points of the four diagonal directions.

Figure 2.1.   The eight basic directions can be represented by drawing a cross with an X over it. Photo by Anna Newell.

Let's look at how direction relates to your movements. You can easily move one body part, such as an arm, to the front, back, and from side to side in relation to your body's center. You can also move one arm in all four diagonal directions. In addition, it is easy to move your whole body in all eight directions. Finally, it is possible to face your body in each of the eight directions without moving from a single location.

This analysis becomes more complicated if you describe the direction of your movements with respect to the walls of a room. When you use this orientation, movements performed in a forward direction reach or travel toward the wall facing the front of your body. Backward or side-to-side movements, on the other hand, extend or travel toward the other three walls. But all of these directions are relative because they change if you face a different wall of the room (see Figure 2.2). If you change the facing of your body so that the side wall of the room becomes front, then the placement of each of the eight directions changes, too. Now, if you reach or move forward, you will be reaching or moving toward the wall that was formerly at your side.

Exploring Direction

Now, you will have a chance to move and explore the movement component direction and see how moving in different directions looks in a mirror.

1. Decide which wall of the room is front. Then, reach one arm out from the center of your body

Figure 2.2.   Facing in different directions changes the orientation of all eight directions. All of the dancers are reaching forward in relation to their bodies but facing different directions. Photo by Anna Newell.

   in each of the eight basic directions: front, back, side right, side left, and the four front and back diagonals. Did you find that reaching in some of the directions was more natural or normal than reaching in other directions?

2. Stay in one place and practice facing your body in each of the eight directions. Which facing do you think makes you look strong? Which facing may appear weak or make you look anonymous?

3. Return to the original frontal orientation, and move your whole body in each of the eight directions using a simple walking step. Was it easier for you to move in some directions in comparison to moving in other directions?

4. Finally, change your orientation in the room so that you are using a different wall as front. Then, try reaching, facing, and moving your body in each of the eight directions again. How did you feel about changing your facing and repeating the same actions? Was it confusing for you to use a different wall as front?

What Is Level?

Movements can be performed at high, middle, or low levels or at all levels that fall between. When you move at high level, you travel on the balls of your feet or propel your body upward into the air. When you move your body at middle level, you move as you do in daily life with the soles of your feet rolling from heel to toe through a flat position on the floor. Sometimes actions, such as walking at middle level, are called pedestrian movements. Moving at low level, on the other hand, requires traveling while bending your knees to some degree. I think you can see that there can be many degrees of bend or flexion in your knees, producing a number of different low-level movements. In some low-level actions, you bend your knees slightly, while in others, you squat down close to the floor. You can even assume a very low level by sliding your prone body across the floor on your stomach.

Exploring Level

1. Return to the same front facing you used in the first exploration in the previous section. Again, reach one arm out into the eight basic directions, but as you do this, change the level of your actions (see Figure 2.3). Does it feel different to

reach forward high in comparison to reaching forward middle or forward low?
2. Travel around your movement space in any direction you like. As you travel, try moving at each of the three levels: high, middle, and low. Which movement level seems most comfortable to you? Can you describe how moving at each level looked in the mirror?
3. Now, face your body in at least three different directions, and move in these directions at three different levels. Were you able to move continuously in one direction and then in another direction, or did you have to stop at some point or points?

What Is Size?

Size simply refers to the bigness or smallness of a movement. In this sense, you can perform the same movement repeatedly but change its size each time you repeat it. A forward-pushing movement performed with one hand is a simple movement, but it is possible to do this same pushing action in a large, medium, or small way (see Figure 2.4). If the pushing movement is

Figure 2.3.   Each of the dancers is moving at a different level. **Photo by Anna Newell.**

Figure 2.4.   Each pushing action is of a different size because the dancers' hands have moved to a different distance from their bodies. **Photo by Anna Newell.**

performed in a large manner, you push your hand as far away from the center of your body as possible. If you push using a medium-size action, you push your hand only half as far away from your center. A small-size push means that you push your hand a very small distance from the center of your body. The small pushing movement would look more like dabbing.

Exploring Size

1. Pick a simple everyday action that can be performed while you stand in one spot. Some examples of such actions are waving, picking up an object, or combing your hair. Then, experiment with the size of this action so that you perform it as large as possible, as small as possible, and what you think is a medium size. What size feels most appropriate for the action you chose to perform?

2. Now, try traveling with a walking step. First, see how large you can make your steps. Second, continue to walk, but make your steps as small as possible. Finally, walk using steps that are medium in size. How did each way of walking feel in your body? How did each type of walking look in the mirror?

3. Try walking throughout your movement space while you continually vary the size, level, and direction of your steps. What size, level, and direction of walk do you prefer?

What Is Speed or Timing?

Speed or timing is how fast or slow a movement is performed. Usually the speed or timing of a movement is described by using the terms *fast*, *medium*, and *slow*. There are, of course, many variations between these three arbitrary speeds. Let's return to the movement example of pushing. You can push repeatedly using very fast, medium, or very slow actions. For example, it might take a few seconds to perform a fast push. In comparison, doing a push of the same size or length could take a minute or more to perform if the action is done extremely slowly.

There is a close relationship between the relative speed of a movement and the number of times it can be repeated over a specific period of time. This statement means a fast pushing action can be performed more

times in a minute than a slow push of the same size. The same comparison can be made for movement size because you can repeat a small movement more times within a minute than you can perform the same movement in a large way during a minute.

Exploring Speed or Timing

1. Use the same everyday action that you used in the first exploration of size, but play with the speed or timing of this action so that you perform it as fast as possible, as slow as you can, and at a tempo that is somewhere between these two extremes. Was there a speed or tempo that was easier or more normal for the performance of this movement? Try the same exploration using another common action.

2. There are many ways you to travel across space besides walking. Some of these other modes of travel include running, hopping, jumping, sliding, skipping, leaping, and galloping (see Figures 2.5, 2.6, and 2.7). These traveling actions, including walking, are called locomotor movements.

Running is similar to but faster than walking, and unlike walking, there is a point at which both feet are off the ground. In a hop, you go into the air and land on one foot, while jumping involves leaving the ground and landing on two feet. A slide is actually a gallop performed to the side rather than to the front, but in both a slide and gallop, one foot chases the other as you move into the air and back to the ground. In a leap, it is im-

Figure 2.5. *The dancer on the left is landing from a hop, and the dancer on the right is landing from a jump.* **Photo by Anna Newell.**

Figure 2.6. The dancer on the left is preparing to slide, and the dancer on the right is in the aerial part of a slide. Photo by Anna Newell.

Figure 2.7. The dancer on the left is preparing for a leap, and the dancer on the right is landing from a leaping action. Photo by Anna Newell.

portant to take off from one foot and land on the other foot. When a leap is viewed from the side, the center of the body follows an arc or over curve in space. It is also possible to leap to the side.

Choose a locomotor movement that you have not explored previously. Then, perform this locomotor as fast as you can. Was there a limit to how fast or slow you could perform the locomotor?

3. Walk around your movement space, changing direction as you travel. At the same time, see if you can do a simple everyday action such as waving, picking up an object, or combing your hair. Once you have practiced doing both of these movements at the same time, begin to vary the speed of your actions. For example, try doing the everyday action slowly while you travel rapidly across

space. Were you able to do this, or did you have a problem? If you had problems with this exploration, why do you think this was so?

What Is Duration?

Duration is how long a specific action is performed. Light travels at a speed of 186,000 miles per second, but it can travel at that speed for a duration of 1 second or for a duration of 1 year. In the same sense, you can walk around a space for a duration of 2 minutes or 1 hour. Although the speed of your walking may be the same for the 2-minute or 1-hour period of time, the duration of the activity has changed. It is easiest to understand the movement component duration if you think of doing the same action repeatedly. Thus, you can repeat a pushing action over a short, medium, or long duration of time.

Exploring Duration

1. Return to the same everyday action you used when exploring movement size. This time, play with the duration of this movement by repeating it for both short and long durations of time. Does it feel different in your body to change the duration of this repetitive action?
2. Pick a new locomotor movement from the section titled "Exploring Speed or Timing." Now, perform this new locomotor movement repeatedly. Is there a limit to the duration or number of times you can repeat this same action? How did it feel in your body to perform this locomotor movement repeatedly? How did the repeated action look in the mirror?
3. Perform the same locomotor action you used in exploration number 2 above, but this time, perform it for both a short and long duration. Did performing the locomotor in these two ways feel different in your body?

What Is Rhythm?

Many pieces of music have an underlying beat or pulse. You can establish a basic pulse by clapping your hands or tapping your foot on the floor at evenly spaced intervals. Performing movements this way creates an even rhythm because all the movements are performed for similar intervals of time.

A different type of rhythm is created if you move at different speeds in relation to the pulse beat. Omitting some pulse beats can also create a different type of rhythm. Thus, if you move on counts 1 and 3 of a four-beat measure but remain still on counts 2 and 4, you create another rhythm. A more complicated rhythm is produced by moving two times on count 1, once on count 2, remaining still on count 3, and moving once on count 4. You can reproduce this rhythmic pattern in movement in the following way: count 1 (move twice), count 2 (move once), count 3 (remain still), count 4 (move once). The last two rhythmic patterns described are uneven. Figure 2.8 is a diagram of these three rhythmic patterns.

Exploring Rhythm

1. Look at the bottom row of dashes in Figure 2.8. It is a diagram of an even rhythmic pattern. Sometimes we call such a rhythm the pulse or underlying pulse. Clap this rhythm followed by traveling across space by using evenly spaced running steps. How did this type of rhythm feel in your body?

2. Next, look at the top two rows of dashes in Figure 2.8. These two rows of dashes are diagrams of uneven rhythms. Count one of these rhythms and then clap it. Next, see if you can duplicate this rhythm by moving one body part in space. How did performing this rhythm with one part of your body look?

3. See if you can move through space so that the timing of your steps copies the same rhythmic pattern you used in number 2. Was it easier or

more difficult to travel using an even or an uneven rhythm?

4. Create your own rhythmic pattern and practice moving one body part and then your whole body in this rhythm. Was this exploration easier when you created your own rhythmic pattern?

What Is Quality?

Quality refers to how you use energy to propel your movements. In dance, there are six basic movement qualities or ways of using energy. These qualities are sustained, percussive, vibratory, swinging, suspension, and collapse.

When you perform sustained movements, your actions are slow, smooth, continuous, and controlled. It is easy to stop sustained movement because it is so controlled. When I watch someone perform sustained movements, their actions remind me of characters in a slow-motion film.

In contrast, percussive movements appear to be explosive and strong. Percussive movements are also direct. This means a push performed in a percussive manner goes right to its end point without curving or meandering along the way. Karate actions are usually percussive, as is a punch.

Vibratory movements mimic their name, as they require a trembling or shaking of one body part or the whole body. Vibratory movements look as though the person performing them is nervous or scared.

If you have watched the movements of a pendulum on a grandfather clock, you were looking at a series of swinging actions. Swinging actions trace an arc in space and require that you relax on the downward part of the arc and apply energy during the upward portion of the arc to pull away from gravity. Simply moving a part of your body in an arc in space does not mean you are performing a swing because relaxing and applying energy are necessary aspects of swinging if it is done correctly.

To suspend an action is to hover in space. A dancer who is able to perform a leap well often looks as though he or she is suspended in space at the highest point of the leap. Suspending a movement produces a body feeling similar to the feeling that accompanies holding your breath for a second or two and then letting it go.

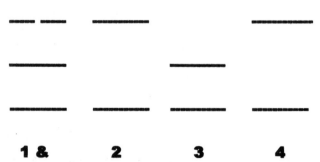

Figure 2.8. *The bottom row of dashes is an even rhythm, while the other two rows show uneven rhythms. The dashes indicate on which beats movements are performed.*

Finally, a collapse is again described by its name. To collapse means that one part of your body or your entire body moves toward the ground. A collapse can be done slowly by holding back or resisting the pull of gravity or quickly by giving in entirely and performing a rapid collapsing action. Care needs to be taken when performing collapsing actions.

Some dance theorists used different terms to describe energy. For instance, Rudolf Laban, who invented a notation system for dance called Labanotation, described use of energy with the motion factors flow and weight. Flow, he said, varies from being very free to very controlled, and weight varies from strong to light.[1] Free movements look like the movements of a rag doll that is being shaken, while controlled movements look a lot like sustained actions. Sustained actions and other controlled movements can be stopped easily and quickly. Strong actions, on the other hand, feel and look heavy, while light movements lack strength and effort. According to Laban, a typical pressing or pushing movement is strong, and a dabbing or flicking action is light in terms of energy quality.

Exploring Quality

1. Choose movements you can perform with your arms and upper body while you walk across space. Then, use at least two of the six movement qualities to perform these same arm and upper-body actions as you walk. Was one of the movement qualities easier for you to perform than the other one?

2. Laban described the movement component energy using somewhat different terms. He said that the use of flow or the quality of energy could be free or controlled, and the use of weight could be strong or light. Try performing the same arm and upper-body movements you used in the previous exploration in both a free and controlled way. Then, do these same actions using strong and light energy qualities. Did you find any other similarities between the six energy qualities and Laban's use of flow and weight?

3. Select another locomotor movement from the section titled "Exploring Speed and Timing." Then, see if you can perform this locomotor using at least two of the six movement qualities. Can you compare the body feelings you experienced when performing the locomotor in the two different ways. Compare the appearance of your movements that resulted from performing the locomotor in the two ways as well.

What Is Shape?

Your body can be stationary or moving while it assumes a number of different shapes. At their extreme limit, body shapes are wide or narrow, big or little, curved or straight, interesting or bland. The variations are endless. You can also perform any of these body shapes at high, middle, or low levels or with only one or two parts of your body. For example, you can make a semicircular shape with your whole body by bending your knees and reaching up and over with your arms and upper body. You can also make a semicircular shape by touching your thumb and forefinger or by touching your fingertips above your head and bending your elbows slightly (see Figure 2.9). In addition, when the shape of

Figure 2.9.   The dancers are making curved shapes with the whole body and with parts of the body. **Photo by Anna Newell.**

the right side of the body matches the one on the left side, the arrangement of body parts is balanced or symmetrical. Body shapes that do not match right side to left are unbalanced or asymmetrical (see Figure 2.10).

It is also possible to create group shapes that are symmetrical or asymmetrical. A symmetrical group shape is created when one side of the entire shape matches the other side. If a symmetrical group shape is drawn on paper and cut out, the two sides match when the paper is folded in half (see Figure 2.11). In asymmetrical group shapes, the two sides of the overall shape do not match. When creating group shapes, think of the shape as a building you put together one piece at a time. You can do this by having a single dancer make a body shape. Then, add other dancers' body shapes to the original one, making sure each body shape fits or complements the overall group shape. In terms of group shape composition, straight or angular individual body shapes go together, as do individual curved body shapes (see Figure 2.12). A group shape also needs a focal point.

Exploring Shape

1. Make your whole body into a wide shape and then into a narrow shape. Now, experiment with curved and straight shapes. Can you make sim-

Figure 2.11.   *This group shape is symmetrical and uses a lot of straight lines. The focal point is the face of the dancer at the middle of the group.* **Photo by Anna Newell.**

Figure 2.10.   *The body shape on the left is balanced or symmetrical, and the body shape on the right is unbalanced or asymmetrical.* **Photo by Anna Newell.**

Figure 2.12.   *This group shape is asymmetrical and uses a lot of curved lines. The focal point is the space between the two dancers who are standing.* **Photo by Anna Newell.**

ilar shapes with only one or two parts of your body?

2. Start with a wide body shape and gradually change this shape into one that is narrow. Next, begin with a curved body shape and gradually change this shape to one that is straight or angular. Which type of body shape seems more natural to you? How did each shape feel in your body?

3. Travel in as many directions and at as many levels as you like, but gradually change the shape of your body as you move across space. This means you will begin with one body shape and end with another.

4. Repeat the same exploration you did in number 3, but this time add some changes of speed or timing to your actions. Did the changes in speed change how your movements looked in the mirror?

5. Create two group shapes with another person so one shape is balanced and the other one is not. In a balanced shape, the right side visually matches the left side, and in an unbalanced shape, the two sides do not match. Then, see if you can move from the first group shape into the second one without stopping.

What Is Pathway?

A pathway is created by tracing a line in space with one part of your body. It is easy to see such a pathway if you hold a long ribbon in your hand and move your hand through space (see Figure 2.13). A pathway, also known as a floor pattern, is produced by tracing pathways on the floor with your steps as you travel across space. Pathways can be straight, curved, or a combination of the two.

If you trace a square with one part of your body, the pathway created is made up entirely of straight lines. In contrast, if you trace a circle with this same body part, the pathway is entirely curved. You can also trace a square and circle without stopping, producing a pathway that combines straight and curved elements. It is possible to travel across space using a floor pattern that is straight, curved, or a combination of the two types of pathways as well. Many ballroom dance manuals use diagrams of floor patterns to show the reader where dancers should move in space to perform steps from a fox trot or samba (see Figure 2.14). You also

Figure 2.13. The moving streamer traces a pathway in space. **Photo by Anna Newell.**

Figure 2.14. When a pathway is traced on the floor, it is called a floor pattern. Here the floor pattern is a semicircle.

need to remember that when tracing a pathway made up of straight lines, such as a square, you must change direction quickly and abruptly. Otherwise, you trace a square that is curved at the corners.

Exploring Pathway

1. Pick a simple geometric shape, such as a square or circle. Then, trace this pathway in space with

one part of your body. You may want to trace with your hand or foot, and then, see if you can trace this same pathway with a more unusual part of your body such as the top of your head or an elbow. How did it feel to trace this pathway with a more unusual part of your body?

2. Follow the exploration in number 1 by tracing this same pathway with your steps on the floor. As you trace this pathway with your steps, see if you can vary the quality of your movements. Did your pathway look smooth or sharp, or did it combine aspects of both of these movement qualities?

3. Draw a more complex linear design on a sheet of paper, and use this design as a map or pathway that you trace with walking steps on the floor. Can you trace this same pathway using other locomotors, such as running or hopping?

4. Finally, create a simple rhythmic pattern that is different from those you have used in other previous explorations. Next, see if you can trace the same pathway you used in exploration 3 while tapping out this rhythmic pattern on the floor with your feet.

What Is Position?

Position has to do with relationships in space. These relationships can be formed between two parts of your body, between the bodies of two or more people, or between one body and an inert object (see Figure 2.15). Positional relationships are described by using the words *over*, *under*, *around*, *through*, *between*, *in front*, *behind*, and *beside*. Positions can also be stationary or involve movement. For example, you can hold or move one hand above the other, hold or move your whole body above the body of another person, or hold or move your body above an object, such as a chair.

Position can also refer to the location of your movements within a defined space or where you place your body in the defined space. This means you can move or stand in the center of a room, and move toward or stand in one of the corners. In addition, you can be still or move while lying on the floor and be still or move while standing on a ladder. In any of these positions, your relationship to the space of the room is different (see Figure 2.16).

Figure 2.15.   The two dancers on the left are positioned above and below each other, while the dancers on the right are above the stool and perform a movement that reaches through the body parts of the other dancer. Photo by Anna Newell.

Exploring Position

1. Ask another person to assume a shape with their body that they can hold for a short period of time. Then, try moving your own body above, below, around, through, beside, in front, behind, and beside the shape made by the other person. Did you like some of these positions better than others? How did some of these positions feel in your body? For example, the various positions may feel expansive or cramped, tense or relaxed.

2. Move with another person so that you both are constantly changing the shapes of your bodies and defining new positions or relationships. This exploration may require some practice before

What Is Starting or Stopping Movement?

You can be either moving a part of your body or your whole body or not moving a body part or your whole body. When you travel across space, you are obviously moving. When you hold a shape or position, you have stopped moving. Although starting and stopping seem to be a very simple movement component, you will see later how this component can be used in the teaching process.

Exploring Starting and Stopping

1. Move one part of your body so that you stop at specific intervals. Stopping on counts 3 and 7 during an eight-count movement sequence is one way to perform this exploration. Does moving by starting and stopping create a rhythmic pattern? How does moving and stopping feel in your body?
2. Choose a locomotor movement that you have not used in previous explorations. Then, see how quickly you can stop and start this movement. Do you think it is easy to stop and start this locomotor movement?
3. Try the same exploration you used in number 2 using yet another locomotor. Compare the body feelings you experienced in this exploration to those you experienced in the immediately preceding exploration. Describe how your body looked when you were performing the locomotor and how it looked when you stopped.

Figure 2.16.   One dancer is near the center of the space, and the other two are located in the corners. Photo by Anna Newell.

SUMMARY AND CONCLUSIONS

It is important to become familiar with the components of movement in order to use them to transform academic concepts into actions. Transformations also involve knowing what the variations of the movement components look like and how they feel in your body. Eleven movement components were described in this chapter: direction, level, size, speed or timing, duration, rhythm, quality, shape, pathway, position, and starting or stopping movement. The fact that movement stops and starts was also included as one of the movement components.

An interesting or perhaps confusing aspect of the movement components is that they are interrelated.

you and the other individual can move and respond without talking or discussing how you each position your bodies. It may also help to begin this exploration by assuming body shapes that are related in some way. For instance, one person's body could be over or even surround the body of the other person.

3. Try traveling and changing your positional relationships with another person at the same time so that as you travel, your body is above or beside the body of another person. Describe how some of the traveling relationships looked in the mirror.

Take movement size and speed for instance. It is easier to perform a small movement at a fast speed than it is to perform a large, fast action. Second, some actions, such as sustained movements, are naturally slow because to perform a sustained movement quickly destroys its true quality. Other movements, such as vibratory actions, must be done quickly because vibrating slowly again changes its quality. Third, movements that trace a curved pathway have a softer quality than actions that follow straight or angular paths. Finally, to assume a narrow, low body shape facilitates fast movements, while a wide, high body shape causes one to travel more slowly.

At this point you have probably realized that understanding the movement components is a function of both the mind and body. Initially, the mind comes into play to help analyze various aspects of each component. The mind also helps one differentiate and make comparisons between one movement component and another. Ultimately, however, it is your body feeling or knowledge of each movement component that contributes to experiencing and understanding it holistically.

REVIEWING YOUR KNOWLEDGE AND UNDERSTANDING

Answer each of the following questions as completely as possible. Your answers should be given from the viewpoint of a teacher or future teacher.

1. There are eight basic directions in dance. How do these directions change when you face your body toward a different wall in the room? For instance, you might begin performing the different directions when your body is facing the front of the room, but how is your sense of direction altered if you turn and face the side of the room?
2. The three levels of movement are high, middle, and low. Do you think there are varying degrees of being high or low? Please explain your answer.
3. Do you think there is a customary or usual size for specific movements, so some are naturally performed in a large way and others are naturally performed using small actions?
4. If someone was watching you walk fast and as quickly as you can, what message do you think they would get from your actions? What message

would they get from watching you walk extremely slowly?
5. Duration is how long a specific movement is performed repeatedly. Is it possible to perform the same movement repeatedly at different speeds within a specific duration or period of time? Hint: Think about a particular movement first, and then decide if you can perform this action at varying speeds during a set time period, such as a minute.
6. What is the difference between an even rhythm and an uneven rhythm?
7. What is the relationship between the underlying pulse and a rhythmic pattern?
8. Select a simple gesture, such as waving, and explain how you would perform this action using two different movement qualities.
9. Rudolf Laban used different terms or words to describe the use of energy in the body. What were the terms used by Laban? Are there any similarities between the way Laban described the use of energy and the six movement qualities? For example, a slashing action is percussive, but it is also strong.
10. Many shapes exist in the environment that surrounds us. Look around your room and identify several shapes. Then, see if you can describe some of these shapes using the same terms used in the section on shape in this chapter.
11. What is the difference between tracing a pathway on the floor and in the air?
12. Compare the appearance of a curved pathway to that of a straight pathway.
13. The words *over*, *under*, *around*, *through*, *in front*, *behind*, and *beside* were used to describe the movement component position. Pick two of these positions, and describe how they feel in your body.
14. Starting and stopping was the final movement component discussed in this chapter. Do you think it is easier to stop a swinging action or one that is sustained? What about stopping a fast action compared to the ability to stop a slow action?

NOTE

1. Valerie Preston-Dunlop, *Rudolf Laban: An Extraordinary Life* (London: Dance Books, 1998).

CHAPTER 3

Transforming Concepts and Ideas Into Movement

One way to use movement-based lessons in your class-room is to attend workshops presented by someone who understands and uses the movement transformation process daily. Then, after taking notes on the movement activities and dances presented, you can reproduce the same action-oriented lessons in your own classes. An in-depth understanding of the movement transformation process, however, allows you to create new movement-based lessons tailored to meet the needs and interests of your students. Thus, you are able to go beyond copying movements and dances created by someone else because an unlimited number of creative possibilities are open to you. By focusing on the components presented in Chapter 2, you can transform many academic concepts not normally associated with movement into actions and body shapes.

You may also be surprised to find out there are two different methods that can be used to transform concepts and ideas into movement. These two methods include direct or literal transformations and those that are indirect or abstract. These two methods of transformation are not new to dance, as choreographers use them all the time. In the following pages, each type of transformation is defined, followed by a number of examples to demonstrate how the movement components are used in both literal and abstract transformations. Then, you have a chance to practice using both methods of transformation by creating some concept-based movements of your own.

BEING DIRECT: USING LITERAL TRANSFORMATIONS

The basic problem encountered when transforming concepts into movements is how to bridge the gap be-tween the two entities. Some have difficulty connecting concepts and movements because concepts are believed to be of the mind and movements are considered to be of the body. The gap between concepts and movements is easier to understand, however, when the two entities are considered in the light of the recent research mentioned earlier—a growing body of evidence in the neurosciences that demonstrates the brain–mind–body continuum. This research endorses the idea that what happens in the brain and body affects mind, while mind influences the body and brain.[1]

That said, the easiest way to transform concepts into movement is to use a literal transformation process. Literal transformations are very direct because you simply move like a concept or shape your body like it. In Chapter 2, you practiced thinking of words that described how different movements felt in your body or how your movements looked in a mirror. Knowledge gleaned from doing these explorations is key to creating successful movement transformations and to making active learning a reality in your classes.

Examples of Literal Transformation

The following is an example of how literal movement transformation is used to teach alternating current, a common concept studied in middle school science classes. The first step in this transformation is understanding that an alternating current moves in two directions. But what does this concept look like in movement? One answer is that you can literally move like the alternating current, reaching one part of your body in two directions, or by moving your whole body in two directions. This means you can move one arm right for four counts and then left for four counts. You

Figure 3.1.   Dancers make a shape that is like a mountain.
Photo by Anna Newell.

can also move your whole body right for four counts and left for four counts.

In a lesson dealing with earth science concepts, the children used the movement component shape by shaping their bodies like the concept. In this lesson, one of the concepts was the formation of mountains when the tectonic plates of the earth bump against one another resulting in an uplift. To give the students the feeling of the shape of a mountain, they partnered off, faced each other, lifted their inside arms high, and pressed the palms of their hands together (see Figure 3.1). To give the students the feeling of the cone shape and volume of the mountain, they continued to press the palms of their hands together while walking once around in a circle.

In a social studies lesson, students compared a cold climate to a hot climate. The questions here are: How does cold weather feel to the body in comparison to

the body's reaction to warm weather? and Which movement component can be used to create a literal transformation of these body feelings? The answers are: the movement component quality is a natural way to create this transformation; and vibratory movements represent one reaction to a cold climate, while soft, sustained, languid actions are the response to a hot climate.

Exploring Literal Transformations

The following explorations are a chance for you to practice doing literal movement transformations. More explorations are included later in this chapter so that you have additional practice with this same process. After you do the following explorations, try using these or similar explorations in your classes.

1. Some rivers flow in a meandering pathway on the way to lakes or oceans. This means that the river follows a series of *S*-shaped curves or a snakelike path rather than flowing in a straight path. How would you travel across space in order to transform the pathway of the river into movement? Remember you are using a literal method of transformation, so you would move like the meandering pathway of the river.
2. A triangle is a particular type of geometric shape, but there are many different types of triangles, such as right, equilateral, and isosceles. Remember, a right triangle has a right or 90-degree angle at one corner, an equilateral triangle has three equal sides, and an isosceles triangle has two equal sides. Can you make these different triangular shapes using different parts of your body? Can you shape your whole body like one of these triangles? How can you create one of these triangular shapes with a partner?

More Examples of Literal
Movement Transformations

Now, you are going to read a number of descriptions of how various academic concepts are transformed into movements and body shapes using the literal transformation method. The examples are arranged according to the individual movement components.

Direction

Remember, direction refers to moving a body part or the whole body or facing the body in any of eight directions. In a math lesson, the movement component direction was used to emphasize the result of simple math calculations. This lesson was presented in a 2nd-grade class. It began by having the students stand in a circle. Then, they reacted to a series of addition and subtraction problems by walking right if the result of the calculation was larger or to the left if the result of the next calculation was smaller than the one preceding it. The students also walked the number of steps to the right or left that equaled the result of each calculation. To represent the result of $4 + 4 = 8$, the students walked 8 steps to the right. The next calculation was $8 - 6 = 2$, so the students walked 2 steps to the left.

In a 1st-grade reading lesson, the movement component direction was used to help students understand letter blends, such as *bl* in *block*, *br* in *bread*, and *sm* in *smoke*. Creating this lesson was quite a challenge, but as I thought about how words like *block*, *bread*, and *smoke* are pronounced, I found that I had to shape my mouth differently when saying each different blend. When saying *block*, the lips move apart and to the side; for *bread*, the lips move together and narrow; and to say *smoke*, the speaker blows forward through the lips. The next step was to transform the movements of the mouth into directional actions in which the students moved their arms out to the side away from the center of their bodies when saying *block*; in toward the center of their bodies when saying *bread*; and forward when saying *smoke* (see Figure 3.2).

Level

Level can be high, low, middle, or somewhere between these three points in space. In a 7th-grade class, the teacher wanted his students to work with movement and fractions, and the level component was used to do this. Fractions consist of two numbers placed at two different levels divided by a horizontal line. These numbers, the numerator and denominator, can be demonstrated by having the correct number of students stand to represent the numerator, while the number students who sit or kneel equal the denominator (see Fig-

Figure 3.2.   *Movement of arms away, together, and forward complements the actions of the mouth when saying different letter blends.* Photo by Anna Newell.

ure 3.3). Students can even hold a ribbon at middle level to represent the bar of a fraction.

The movement component level was also the basis of an elementary school science lesson. At one school, the students were studying about the layers of the atmosphere that occur at a different altitude or level in relation to the earth. The atmospheric layers include the top layer, or exosphere; two middle layers, the mesosphere and stratosphere; and the lowest layer, or troposphere. To represent each layer, the students were arranged one behind the other as they held cards with the names of the atmospheric layers on them (see Figure 3.4). Each card was also held at the appropriate level—high, middle, or low. To make sure the students understood the concept of atmospheric layers, the order of the cards was shuffled, and a second group of students had to arrange themselves and hold their cards at the correct level.

Figure 3.3.   Grouped in this way, the dancers represent the fraction ½. Photo by Anna Newell.

Figure 3.4.   Each dancer represents a different layer of the atmosphere. Photo by Anna Newell.

Size

Size can be large, small, or somewhere in between these two extremes. It is easy to use the movement component size to transform concepts into actions in math lessons, particularly for elementary school students. In one lesson, two rows of numbers were written one above the other on a large sheet of paper. Then the students were divided into two groups and asked to compare the two rows of numbers. If the number in the bottom row was larger, the lower group of students made a larger movement and the top group made a smaller movement (see Figure 3.5). The relative size of the movements performed by each group was reversed when the number on the top was larger, and the one on the bottom was smaller.

The movement component size was also part of a social studies lesson presented at a middle school. The concept in this lesson was to compare the population of Canada to the population of the United States. Although the land mass of Canada is large, its population is about ¹⁄₁₀ of the population of the United States. To compare the populations of 2 countries, a group of 10 students stood together to represent the size of the population of the United States, while a single student stood next to them to represent the size of the population of Canada. (In Figure 3.6, the group standing represents a country with a population four times as great as the population of the country represented by the single seated student.) The populations of the two countries could also have been compared by having 1 group of students do a movement that was approximately 10 times as large as a movement performed by the single student.

Figure 3.5. *Larger movements below show the number represented is larger than the number represented by the movements at the top of the photo.* **Photo by Anna Newell.**

Speed or Timing

The speed or timing of movement can be fast, slow, or medium tempo. The movement component speed was used in a reading and writing lesson to help elementary school students understand word meanings. In this lesson, the students performed fast movements to show they understood adjectives that are synonyms for *fast*, such as *swift*, *quick*, and *rapid*. Fast movements can also be used to represent the adverbs *swiftly*, *quickly*, or *rapidly*. In a similar manner, nouns, such as *second* (of time), or names of animals, like *jaguar*, can be represented with fast movements because a second passes quickly and a jaguar is built for speed. In contrast, slow movements can represent adjectives, such as *delayed* or *sluggish*; adverbs, like *tediously* or *ponderously*; and nouns, like *millennium*, *sloth*, and *snail*.

The movement component speed or timing is also useful to teach mathematics, particularly multiplication. For instance, the number 4 is four times as great as the number 1 and two times as great as the number 2. If one student takes four counts to perform a simple

Figure 3.6. *The group in the background represents a country with a large population, while the single dancer stands for a country that has a smaller population.* **Photo by Anna Newell.**

action and another student performs the same action in one count, the first action takes four times as long as the second action. To compare the numbers 4 and 2, the first student performs the action in four counts, and the second performs this same action in two counts.

Duration

Duration is how long or for what length of time a particular movement is performed repeatedly. The movement component duration was used in a middle school lesson about ancient cultures in the Middle East. First, a long piece of tape was placed on the floor to represent the theoretical beginning of time. Next, cards marking points in time were placed in a vertical column off to one side and perpendicular to the tape. Thus, the card representing 3000 BCE was closer to the tape than the card representing 1500 BCE and so on. Then, different students representing each cultural group were lined up in a row along the tape. The student who walked for the longest duration of time represented the Middle Eastern cultural group that existed for the longest period of time (see Figure 3.7).

Rhythm

A rhythmic pattern is created when you move faster or slower than a steady beat or pulse. Silences or a lack

Figure 3.7.   *The dancer on the right represents a cultural group that existed for a short period of time, and two dancers on the left stand for cultural groups that had a longer history.* Photo by Anna Newell.

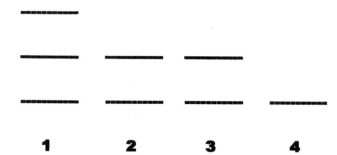

1   2   3   4

Figure 3.8.   *A simple rhythm can be created by moving on selected beats. The top two rows of dashes represent movements, and the bottom row of dashes is the pulse beat.*

of movement also help to create rhythms. Simple rhythms were used to represent fractions in a math class for older elementary school students. In this lesson, the students moved on one count out of four counts to represent ¼ and three counts out of eight counts to represent ⅜ (see Figure 3.8). Moving on one count out of four or three counts out of eight produces two simple rhythmic patterns.

In a reading and writing lesson at the primary level, rhythm was used to teach about the number of syllables in a word. Words such as *cat* and *dog* have only one syllable. Other words like *flower*, *blueberry*, and *automobile* have two, three, and four syllables, respectively. In this lesson, the children moved on one count out of four to represent the one syllable in *cat*; two counts out of four to represent the two syllables in *flower*; three counts out of four to represent the three syllables in *blueberry*; and on all four counts to represent the four syllables in *automobile* (see Figure 3.9).

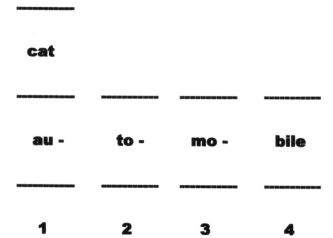

cat

au -   to -   mo -   bile

1   2   3   4

Figure 3.9.   *The top rhythmic pattern represents the word* cat, *while the bottom rhythm can be connected to the word* automobile.

1   2   3

Figure 3.10.   The simple drawing on the left is represented with the rhythmic pattern shown on the right in the top row of dashes.

The students also pronounced the syllables in each word as they performed the movements.

In a middle school visual arts lesson, the students looked at various paintings that included lines of different lengths. Some of these lines can be connected by continuously tracing from one line to the next with the fingertip. By tracing lines that were both long and short, and by doing this in a continuous way, a rhythmic pattern was formed to represent the series of connected lines. These small movements were exaggerated to create larger, full-body movements that copied the same rhythmic pattern. Figure 3.10 represents a simple rhythmic pattern of two longs and a short. It is typical of a linear pattern found in some paintings used in this lesson. See if you can transform this simple linear pattern into a rhythm in movement.

Quality

Quality refers to the way you use energy to propel movement. Remember, the movement qualities are sustained, percussive, vibratory, swinging, suspended, and collapse. Use of energy quality can also be free or controlled, strong or light. The movement component quality was useful in reading and writing lessons for both elementary and middle school students. I think you will agree that words like *bat*, *dish*, and *face* have different qualities. For me, *bat* is sharp, *dish* glides, and *face* has a dabbing quality. Say each of these words. Then, say the words and perform a movement in the appropriate quality at the same time.

Middle school students can work with longer words by focusing on the quality of each syllable in a word. The word *particularize* has five syllables. For me, the first syllable, *par*, glides upward or soars; the second syllable, *tic*, is sharp and staccato; and the third syllable, *u* swings back and forth. The two final syllables, *lar* and *ize*, again have a smooth, gliding quality. A sustained movement was used to represent the first sylla-ble, a small percussive action for the second syllable, and a small swinging movement for the third syllable. What movements would you use to represent the fourth and fifth syllables of this word?

In an elementary school science lesson, the movement component quality was used to represent varying amounts of air pressure. When air becomes warm, it expands. This makes the air thin, and its pressure falls. Cold air, on the other hand, contracts, which makes the pressure increase. To represent warm, light air, light, soft, floating movements were used, while heavy, pressing actions helped explain what happens when air gets cold.

Shape

Students can form shapes with one body part, two body parts, the whole body, or a partner. Shapes can be wide or narrow, curved or straight, symmetrical or asymmetrical, and so forth. The movement component shape was used to help elementary school children remember simple geometric shapes, such as circles, triangles, squares, and rectangles. Middle school students and their partners were even able to form more complex shapes, such as a parallelogram or trapezoid (see Figure 3.11).

The movement component shape can help young elementary school children recognize their letters, particularly the uppercase or capital letters. One way to teach about letters is to help children distinguish

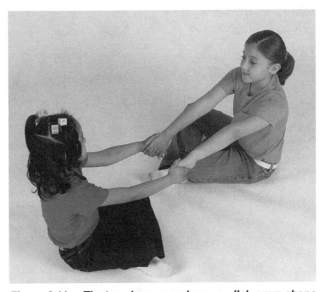

Figure 3.11.   The two dancers make a parallelogram shape with their arms. **Photo by Anna Newell.**

between letters that are made up entirely of straight lines; those that are formed solely from curved lines; and those that combine both straight and curved lines in one letter. The letter *A* is made up of straight lines, while the letter *C* contains no straight lines. A capital *P*, on the other hand, combines the straight and curved lines found in the other two types of letters (see Figure 3.12).

The movement component shape was used in elementary school science lessons, too. Think about the shapes of different types of clouds. Cumulus clouds, which we usually see during the summer, are puffy, rounded clouds that form at middle altitudes. Stratus clouds are rather wide and flat and form at lower altitudes. Shape, particularly the shape of the whole body, was used to represent these two different types of clouds. In addition, when the shapes were created at different levels, students connected these levels to the altitude at which each type of cloud forms (see Figure 3.13).

Pathway

A pathway is traced in space with one part of your body or on the floor with your steps. A pathway traced on the floor is also known as a floor pattern. You can trace a figure 8 with one hand, or you can trace a figure 8 with your steps on the floor (see Figure 3.14). Pathways in space or on the floor are made up of lines that are straight, curved, or a combination of the two. In two different lessons, young elementary school students reinforced their knowledge of numbers and letters by tracing the numbers and letters in the space in front of their bodies. They also followed a pathway on the floor that resembled a specific number or letter. In

Figure 3.12. *The three dancers form the capital letters, C, A, and a backward P, from left to right.* **Photo by Anna Newell.**

Figure 3.13. *The dancer on the bottom is a flat, stratus cloud, and the dancer on the top is a puffy, cumulus cloud.* **Photo by Anna Newell.**

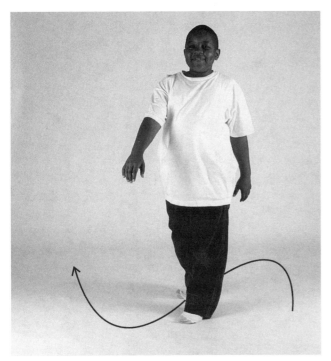

Figure 3.14.   The dancer is tracing the letter S *with his steps.* Photo by Anna Newell.

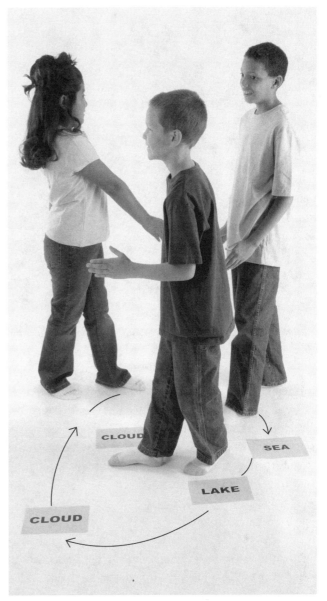

Figure 3.15.   The dancers are following a pathway that is like the water cycle. Photo by Anna Newell.

another class, kindergarten students also traced a floor pattern that resembled their initials.

Pathway is a particularly useful movement component for teaching concepts from science. From our place on earth, it appears that the wind blows in straight paths. In reality, the wind blows in a pathway that is a spiral. This pathway can be easily demonstrated by moving your hand in a spiraling pathway or by moving both hands around each other in a spiraling pathway.

The water cycle can also be demonstrated using the component pathway. In the water cycle, droplets of water evaporate from lakes and rivers. These droplets in turn come together high above the earth to form clouds. When enough droplets come together, they become heavy and fall back to earth, eventually entering our rivers and lakes and finally flowing out to the sea. To teach about the water cycle, a small group of students walked on a pathway connecting cards labeled *lake*, *cloud*, *river*, *lake*, and *sea* (see Figure 3.15). In other words, the students followed a pathway that described the water cycle.

In a middle school science class, pathway was used to teach how electrons move around the nucleus of an atom. In diagrams of an atom, electrons are pictured

moving in curved paths around the nucleus. Because there are multiple electrons in an atom, a small group of students simultaneously moved around the nucleus, ending back in their original spots in the circle. The nucleus was represented by placing a flat felt disk on the floor in the center of the circle of students, who had to avoid bumping into each other while following their individual paths (see Figure 3.16).

Streamers are an easy way to demonstrate the pathway movement component. As a streamer moves through space, it trails behind your moving hand, tracing a visible pathway in space. The pathway formed by

Figure 3.16.   The dancers represent electrons circling the nucleus of an atom. **Photo by Anna Newell.**

Figure 3.17.   The straight and curved pathways of the streamers represent the straight and curved lines in a painting. **Photo by Anna Newell.**

a streamer can be curved or straight, although it is more difficult to trace straight pathways because the streamer naturally rounds when you change its direction. Streamers were used in a middle school class to transform the straight and curved lines in a painting into movement (see Figure 3.17).

Position

Position describes a relationship between two or more entities. You can position your body over, under, beside, in front, behind, around, or through the body parts of another individual or object. Position was used to reinforce elementary school students' understanding of place value. To do this, a small group of students stood in a row while holding a numbered card to represent the digits in a number (see Figure 3.18). The other students then identified the number. Other numbers were produced by moving the students holding the cards to different positions in the row. The students representing each digit could also hold up a specific number of fingers or perform a specific number of movements to represent their respective place values.

Position was also used to teach middle school math concepts, such as bar graphs. To do this, I put a long piece of tape on the floor to form the abscissa of the graph and explained that the left end of the tape was

Figure 3.18.   What is the number represented? **Photo by Anna Newell.**

zero. Next, the students stood in vertical lines perpendicular to the abscissa to form bars on the graph (see Figure 3.19). In this lesson, the number of students in each bar represented the number of people living in their house. Other bar graphs can be formed in the same way when bars in the graph stand for the number of pets each student owns, the number of students who like a certain color, or a variety of other ideas. In the final part of this lesson, a long ribbon was held to connect the tops of the bars to create a kinesthetic understanding of a line graph.

Movement Starts or Stops

Remember, a body is either active or still. This movement component was used in a science lesson to demonstrate what happens to electrical current when you a flip a switch off. To demonstrate this concept,

the children stood in a circle, and four rectangular pieces of paper were placed on the floor outside the circle to represent switches. As the students walked around the circle, the music was stopped at intervals, and anyone who landed by a switch had to sit down on the floor (see Figure 3.20). When the music resumed, all the students stood and moved around the circle again. The point is that when a switch is in the off position, electricity no longer flows freely just as a student who is sitting on the floor is not free to move. A simple game can be made out of this exercise by keeping track of the number of times any one student ends up by a switch.

More Explorations Using Literal Transformations

Now, you can practice using all the movement components to create additional literal movement transformations. Each set of explorations relates to one of the

Figure 3.19.   *The columns of dancers form a bar graph by using a different number of dancers in each column.* Photo by Anna Newell.

Figure 3.20.   *The dancers freeze when the music stops to show that the electricity has been switched off.* Photo by Anna Newell.

movement components. Sometimes you are given a clue or hint to help with the transformation process. I encourage you to do the following explorations and try them out in your classes.

Direction

1. How would you use the movement component direction to help young children understand such words as *up*, *down*, *sideways*, or *diagonal*? How can direction be used to teach opposites—a concept appropriate for kindergarten classes?

2. Middle school math students study degrees of a circle. Forty-five, 90, and 180 degrees make up a segment of a full circle, while rotating 360 degrees means turning in a full circle. How can you use direction to transform each listed number of degrees into movement? Hint: Use the center of a circle as a pivot point for turning the body a particular number of degrees right or left.

3. How can you transform the compass directions north, south, east, or west into movements by using the component direction?

4. During an earthquake, the tectonic plates of the earth move in various directions, including toward and away from each other as well as sliding past one another. Can you use your hands to transform the actions of the tectonic plates into movements? How can you use the movements of two people traveling in space to transform these same actions of the earth's plates into movements?

Level

1. The level movement component can be used to compare nouns that are labels for different levels. How would you use movement to compare such nouns as *summit*, *peak*, and *acme* to other nouns like *base*, *foundation*, or *ground*?

2. Decimals can also be understood by using the movement component level. Keeping in mind that $^{10}/_{10}$ equal a whole, how would you use level to show $^{2}/_{10}$, $^{5}/_{10}$, or $^{8}/_{10}$? Hint: There are 10 students in a row, and each standing student equals $^{1}/_{10}$.

3. Middle school students frequently study the rainforest. Tropical rainforests grow in layers at different levels. The layers of the rainforest are known as the emergent, canopy, understory, and ground layers respectively. How can you transform the concept layers of a rainforest into movement? Hint: Some of the layers of the rainforest relate to the movement component shape or quality, too.

Size

1. There are many words that describe the relative size of people or objects (*huge*, *gigantic*, *immense*). These words can be compared to other words, such as *miniscule*, *petite*, or *diminutive*. How would you use the movement component size to compare such words?

2. The Aztec sun or calendar stone at 12½ feet in diameter is the largest sculpture discovered from this ancient culture. How can you direct two students to move in space to demonstrate the approximate size of this sculpture? Hint: Begin by placing the two students back to back at the center of a space.

3. How can you use the movement component size to compare the land mass of two countries?

Timing or Speed

1. A science lesson may involve studying such liquids as water and molasses, which have different viscosities and would move downward at different speeds when placed at the top of a flat, slanted board. How can you use the movement component speed or timing to demonstrate these differences?

2. Many animals have a typical speed at which they move. Using the movement component speed or timing, compare the relative speed of a sloth to a jaguar or a turtle to a shark.

3. We have eight planets in our solar system that rotate at different speeds. How can you use the speed of turning movements to compare the rotational speed of the various planets?

Duration

1. In a science lesson, the life span of different animals can be compared using the movement component duration. For example, for how long would

you repeat a movement to demonstrate the life span of a butterfly in comparison to the life span of a dog?

2. In another science lesson, the length of time it takes one planet to complete its orbit around the sun can be compared to the length of time it takes another planet to orbit the sun using the component duration. How long is a movement, such as walking, continued to represent the length of time it takes Mercury to complete its orbit in comparison to the length of time it takes Jupiter to orbit the sun? Hint: Have the students walk in circles of a different size.

Rhythm

1. Write a simple sentence such as *The flower is red.* Then, read the sentence aloud as you would read it normally. Now, read the same sentence again, but change the emphasis you put on specific words. For example, you can change the emphasis to the first or last words in the sentence. Next, draw a rhythmic pattern made up of different length dashes that represents each way of saying this sentence. Hint: Use longer dashes to represent the emphasized words. Can you perform movements that duplicate the two rhythmic patterns?

2. Poems are frequently based on different rhythms. The most popular poetic rhythm in English is a two-syllable form that stresses the second syllable. This type of poetry is called iambic verse. In trochaic verse, the emphasis is reversed, placing the stress on the first syllable or word. This produces a different rhythm.[2] In Figure 3.21, the top row of dashes represents iambic verse and the second row represents trochaic verse. How can you transform each of these poetic rhythms into

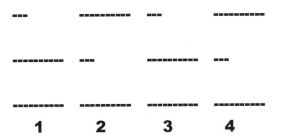

1   2   3   4

Figure 3.21. The top rhythm represents iambic verse, and the bottom rhythm stands for trochaic verse.

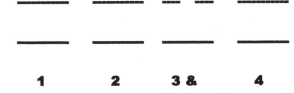

1   2   3 &   4

Figure 3.22. The cha-cha rhythm is at the top, and the merengue rhythm is represented in the bottom pattern.

movement? Hint: The movements representing the unstressed syllables take less time than those representing stressed syllables.

3. Rhythmic patterns are important when learning ballroom dance because different rhythms are basic to each dance form. Thus, the cha-cha is based on an uneven pattern, and the merengue is more regular.[3] The top row of dashes in Figure 3.22 represents a cha-cha rhythm, and the bottom row stands for the merengue. Can you transform each rhythmic pattern into movements performed with your arms?

Quality

1. Other electrical concepts lend themselves to movement transformations that involve the component quality. What movement quality can you use to transform the concept of static electricity into movement? What about the drifting of free electrons?

2. During an earthquake, the tectonic plates of the earth bump, vibrate, and slide. How can you use the movement component quality to transform these actions into movements?

3. Many students study the lives of George Washington and Abraham Lincoln in February in honor of President's Day. One important aspect of the careers of these two presidents was that they were connected to important wars in the history of our country—the Revolutionary War and the Civil War. What quality of movement can you use to show how the overworked, tired soldiers may have moved toward the end of these two long wars?

Shape

1. In middle school, students study angles (acute, obtuse, right, or straight). How can you shape

your hands to demonstrate each type of angle? Can you copy the shape of each type of angle using both arms or by working with a partner?

2. Humans live in dwellings that have a variety of shapes. An igloo is shaped much different than a thatched hut. Can you shape your hands like an igloo and also like a thatched hut? What about shaping your whole body like each of these types of dwellings? Can you work with a partner to duplicate these same shapes?

3. Valleys and mountains have many different shapes. Some valleys are shaped like the letter *U*, and others are shaped like the letter *V*. Mountains can be sharp and have the shape of an upside-down *V*, although many mountains are flat or rounded on top. Can you transform the shape of these valleys and mountains into body shapes?

4. The Underground Railroad is studied in a number of schools. One of the facts few people understand is that escaping slaves who followed the Underground Railroad were guided by symbols sewn into quilts. One of these symbols, the North Star, meant the slaves were supposed to travel north in order to escape to Canada.[4] What are some of the ways you can form a star to represent this important symbol? Hint: Think about how you can shape your body into a star or form a star with others.

Pathway

1. Locate several roads on a map. Transform these roads into movement by tracing their pathway in space with your hand or by moving across space by following a similar floor pattern. Can you trace these pathways by moving a different part of your body, such as an elbow or foot?

2. Pathway can be used to help students understand two types of electrical circuits: series and parallel. In a series circuit, electricity flows in succession from one part of the circuit to another. For example, all the Christmas tree lights in a series circuit go out if one light burns out. In a parallel circuit, electricity branches as it flows through the circuit, so when one light burns out, the others continue to burn. How can pathway be used to transform these two concepts into movement?

Hint: A series circuit is represented by walking around a circle in single file, while a parallel circuit is represented by a double circle in which students move shoulder to shoulder in the same direction. How can the outside person in the double circle move to represent the branching nature of a parallel circuit?

3. Lightning moves in a zigzag path. How can you show this path by moving one part of your body or by moving your whole body?

Position

1. In a geography lesson, maps become more real by using the movement component position. Look at a map of Japan. You should notice that the country is made up of four large islands plus a number of smaller islands and that the large islands form a crescent or curve.[5] How would you position four students to represent the relative position of the four large islands of Japan?

2. Look at the map of Canada. Canada is made up of provinces instead of states.[6] How can you position different students to represent the provinces that lie along the northern border of the United States? To help students remember the position of the provinces, go back through the group, and have each student say the name of the province he or she represents.

3. Fractions can be taught by using the position component. To do this, put a fairly long, straight piece of tape on the floor. If the left end of the tape equals zero, where can you position students along the tape to represent $\frac{1}{4}$, $\frac{1}{2}$, $\frac{3}{8}$, or $\frac{3}{4}$ of the entire length of the tape? Positioning students along a tape is also an excellent way to compare the size of different fractions.

BEING INDIRECT: USING ABSTRACTION

Concepts and ideas can also be transformed into movement using the process of abstraction. This means that instead of moving like the concept moves (e.g., changing direction like an alternating current) or shaping the body like the concept (e.g., creating a sharp, triangular shape like the shape of a volcano), transformations are accomplished by using more indirect methods.

One way to think about the indirect nature of abstraction is to consider the feeling response you have about different concepts. For example, being inside the lobby of a large building is a concept. This experience may give you a happy, expansive feeling, whereas you may feel sad or trapped in response to being inside a phone booth. Each of these feeling responses represents an abstraction that can be captured in movement. More literal movement transformations would be following a pathway that outlined the walls of the lobby or shaping your body like the space enclosed by the phone booth.

I think it is easier to think about the connection between abstraction and feeling by studying Figure 3.23. This diagram is a framework for creating abstract movement. On the top, abstraction begins with a concept. In the previous example, one concept was the lobby of a building. Next, feelings emerge in response to the concept. This response in turn can bring images to mind. These images can be memories of past experiences or images connected to your current feelings. Finally, the feeling response, in combination with the images and memories, is transformed into actions. If your feelings about the lobby are happy, your movements may be fast and large and performed at a middle or high level. In contrast, a sad reaction to the lobby may cause you to create small, slow movements performed at a lower level.

A final step in the movement transformation process is nonverbal communication. Nonverbal communication takes place when the movements you perform are viewed by others. These movements can result from literal or abstract transformations, but in both cases, when the movements are performed for an audience, nonverbal communication takes place. The questions remain, however, whether your movements communicate in the desired way and whether the nonverbal message is literal or abstract.

Modern painters have been using abstraction for many years because they have chosen to present their impression of what they see instead of painting reality as it is seen with the naked eye. When visual artists work abstractly, they attempt to capture the essence or core of their subject matter only. This mean the process of abstraction involves suggesting or hinting at the real.[7] Another way to describe abstraction is to say that the artist taps into the essence of his or her feelings, resulting in a concrete and tangible but abstract work of art.

Elliot Eisner, a well-known visual arts educator, stated that painters throughout history have used abstraction to some degree because they all wanted to create an illusion of reality on a two-dimensional surface. Eisner believed that saying abstract art began in the 1880s is somewhat of a misconception because all artists were engaged in capturing abstract shapes and forms on canvas to some degree. In the 4th quarter of the 19th century, however, painters began to free themselves from representing what was thought to be true or real and became more interested in abstracting or extracting basic shapes from a more detailed visual field.[8]

With this background in mind, let's look at an abstract visual design. Figure 3.24 is a cut-paper design I created as an abstraction of a tropical rainforest. In this design, I represented the colorful birds that inhabit the

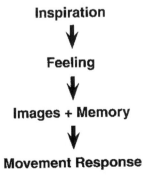

Inspiration

↓

Feeling

↓

Images + Memory

↓

Movement Response

Figure 3.23. Framework for creating movement. **Figure reproduced with permission of J. Michael Ryan Publishing, Inc.**

Figure 3.24. Abstraction of a rainforest. **Photo by Anna Newell. Cut paper design by author.**

upper or emergent layers of the rainforest with red, yellow, and blue wedge shapes because this is my impression of these birds in flight. The scallop shapes below the birds capture the umbrella-like quality of the canopy or second layer of the rainforest. I made the canopy green. In addition, the sharp, vertical, triangular shapes at the middle of the design are black and hint at the fear one may feel when exploring the unknown reaches of a rainforest. The circles beneath the canopy are also black and are a response to the depth and mystery that lurk within the lower layers of the rainforest.

We have been discussing the visual arts, but movement can also be abstract. You have already learned that the movement components can be used in different ways so that direction can be forward or backward, size large or small, timing fast or slow, and so on. In addition, when the movement components are used in different ways, these different uses can capture varied feeling responses. If you feel happy about a concept, the movements you use to capture this feeling are different than the actions you choose to capture a sad feeling. When you use the movement components in this way, you are using them to capture the essence of the concept, and abstraction comes into play. Thus, the abstract movement transformation process is similar to the abstraction in the visual arts.

Michael Michalko discussed levels of abstraction in his book by comparing these levels to having a changing viewpoint.[9] For example, when standing on a beach, you see many details, such as dunes, grass, and footprints. When you bend close to the sand, more details become apparent, including individual grains of sand, chips of shells, and remnants of seaweed. Now, imagine you are in an airplane flying over the beach. From this vantage point, individual details blend together, but other aspects of the beach are revealed because you can see the coastline and where the dunes end. You may even see buildings beyond the dunes. Michalko likens adopting different viewpoints to working at different levels of abstraction. To solve a problem, Michalko recommended choosing a viewpoint to guide data gathering.[10]

In terms of movement transformation, the various levels of abstraction also come into play. This means you can transform your feeling response to the dunes, grass, and footprints viewed at a midrange into movement, or you can use the shells or seaweed viewed at a very close

range as the motivation for your actions. It is possible to transform your feeling response to the beach when you view it from an airplane into movement as well.

Eisner's discussion of abstraction in art also relates to levels of abstraction. He said a work of art that reflects reality as seen by the naked eye exists at one level of abstraction. This is true because the artist has taken a viewpoint that requires including many real visual details in the work. A more abstract work that shows only basic shapes and forms exists at another level of abstraction and therefore reflects a different artistic viewpoint.[11]

You can discuss literal and abstract movements in terms of levels of abstraction. When you create literal movements, you choose actions or body shapes that are like the concept or idea. This means you take a more realistic viewpoint to create these movements. On the other hand, when creating abstract movements, you strive to capture the basic feeling about or essence of the concept or object in your actions. Capturing the essence of a concept requires using a much less realistic and more feeling-oriented viewpoint as the starting point for the creative movement process.

An additional key to understanding abstraction is to consider the human trait known as synesthesia. Synesthesia is a process in which one type of sensory stimulus produces a subjective sensation in another quite different sense. An example of synesthesia is an experience in which a particular color evokes a specific smell. In a similar manner, when you produce a movement abstraction, you use one or more of the movement components to represent something that is not moving or even alive.

The following is another example of abstraction as a synesthesia-like experience. Tempo and rhythm are important aspects of musical structure, and a movement abstraction of music can be produced by moving in specific directions, on particular pathways, or by shaping the body in certain ways. By transforming the music into directions, pathways, or body shapes, you have used your kinesthetic sense to react to an auditory stimulus, changing music into movement components normally not part of a piece of music.

Eisner also discussed synesthesia in his book. He stated that when a person looks at a painting, this experience can be transformed into other sensory forms. For example, the visual surface of a painting can elicit a tactile response, while the arrangement of lines and shapes is seen as rhythmic, producing muscular sensations. Eisner claims that much of our experience is multisensory, even though a particular experience is dominated by one sensory modality. According to Eisner, the process of transforming what we experience into speech and text is another example of a synesthesia-like phenomenon.[12] While Eisner discussed the process of experiencing the visual arts and using words to describe this experience, his statement can be applied to using words to discuss any form of experience.

Gardner and his fellow researchers have proposed that human intelligence takes many forms, one of which is bodily-kinesthetic intelligence. According to Gardner, having a high level of bodily-kinesthetic intelligence involves developing a keen mastery over the motions of the body. Gardner cites dancers and swimmers who move their bodies with great finesse as having high kinesthetic intelligence.[13] By learning to transform concepts into movement, you are also developing your bodily-kinesthetic sense. When Gardner studied human development, he noted that synesthesia is very common in children and may persevere into adulthood among artists. In his investigations, Gardner found that a number of children feel colors, see musical tones, and hear visual patterns. For example, young children often see yellow as happy and brown as sad.[14]

Examples of Abstract Transformations

Colors like blue or red can be transformed into movement using abstraction rather than using literal methods. It is difficult to move like blue or red, so a direct transformation is difficult, but you can concentrate on the feelings you associate with the colors and transform these feelings into movement. By concentrating on the feelings you associate with blue or red, you focus on the essence or personal meaning these colors have for you. For me, blue is calm, soft, relaxing, and somewhat sad. On the other hand, red is exciting, lively, bold, more upbeat, or even angry. The next step is to follow the framework in Figure 3.23 and use your imagination to transform your feelings into actions. This means that blue movements may be light in quality and rather slow and follow a meandering pathway in space, and red movements can be percussive or heavy and fast and follow straight pathways.

The connection between color and meaning is an integral part of life. In fact, you connect color and its meaning without thinking about it. If it is rainy and gray, you automatically wear bright, cheerful-colored clothing. Sometimes the connection between color and meaning is more conscious. During World War II, Britain's queen and her husband visited bombed sites throughout England to bolster the spirit of their people. Beforehand, the queen gave careful thought to the colors she would wear. After discussions with her advisors, the queen decided not to wear black because it is the color of mourning and communicates this message. Red dresses were also vetoed because red is festive. Instead, the queen settled on wearing dresses in dusty pink, blue, and lilac because these colors convey comfort, encouragement, and sympathy. The queen had these dresses designed especially for her visits and called them her combat frocks.[15]

Another way to view abstraction is to transform aspects of the life of a famous person into movement. Here, you need to focus on the overall impression you have of the life of the individual. The life of Abraham Lincoln was the focus of a series of lessons created for a 1st-grade class. After reading about Lincoln, my impression was that he was on a steady course throughout his life—one that led to the presidency. Lincoln's life journey began in childhood with his love of reading, followed by studying law, and finally running for president. For me, an abstract movement interpretation of Lincoln's life involves performing strong, defined movements that follow a straight pathway performed in a steady, even rhythm. In contrast, the life of an individual who experiences reversals and psychological problems can be transformed into movement using weak, erratic actions that trace a zigzag or less direct path.

Exploring Abstract Transformations

You can do these movement transformations by yourself and then try them with your students.

1. Hold an apple in one hand and note its color, scent, texture, and how its surface responds to your touch. After examining the apple in detail, focus on the feelings this experience brings to mind. Do you feel happy about the apple, or does

it make you feel sad? You can also ask yourself whether the qualities of the apple seem strong and steady or weak and irregular. You may want to think about your memories of apples and the meaning these memories have for you. Then, consider the way the various movement components, such as direction, quality, speed or timing, rhythm, and pathway, can be used to transform your overall impression of the apple into movement.

2. Find a photo of a person with an interesting face. You can use a photo of a clown, a very old person, or a young child. Look carefully at the photo, and focus on your overall impression. Next, note details in the photo, like the colors, textures, and shapes. Decide how you feel about the photo. Do you have one overall feeling about the photo, or does it bring a series of impressions to mind? How can you transform the feelings or impressions you have of this photo into movement?

More Explorations With Abstract Transformations

This is your chance to put your understanding of abstract transformation into action. Remember, when using abstraction, concentrate on your feeling response to the suggested concept. After you have tried these explorations yourself, present them or a variation of them to your students.

Direction, Level, and Size

1. The main character in a story is a strong, benevolent king. Would you move forward, backward, or sideways to portray the essence of this character? What size and level movements can be used to portray this same character?

2. The main character in a second story is a weak, corrupt king. What movement direction or directions can you use to portray the essence of this character? How can you use movement size and level?

Speed or Timing

1. For me, some colors are fast and others are slow. How do you feel about the two colors lavender and orange? Would you use fast or slow movements to represent these two colors?

2. One space is the lobby of a large hotel, and the other space is a small cubicle or the inside of a telephone booth. Would you use fast or slow movements to represent these two spaces?

Duration

1. Some colors endure, and others are delicate and probably last for only a short duration. Which of the two colors lavender and orange endures for a long time? How long would you repeat a movement to demonstrate the duration of each of these colors?

2. What about the lobby of the large hotel and a cubicle or telephone booth? How long would you repeat a movement to communicate your feelings about these two spaces?

Rhythm

1. A cube has six facets or faces, each of which is a square. Would you use movements that have an even, steady beat or rhythm or those that are uneven and interrupted to represent your response to a cube?

2. A conch shell has a cone shape at the top, a flared lip off to one side, and a series of pointed appendages that encircle its crown (see Figure 3.25). Can you use movements with an even or uneven rhythm to represent this conch shell?

Figure 3.25.   *Conch shell.* Photo by Anna Newell.

Quality

1. The leaves of an African violet are covered with short, fuzzy hairs. In addition, these plants have a profusion of leaves branching out from a single center and many small but attractive flowers in shades of pink or purple. The center of the flower is usually yellow (see Figure 3.26). Think about the feelings and memories you associate with African violets. Then, using the process of abstraction, transform your feelings into movements that have a specific quality or qualities.

2. The leaves of a jade plant are very smooth, waxy, and opposite the texture of the leaves of an African violet (see Figure 3.27). The jade's leaves also look shiny and branch in many directions rather than growing from one center. This structure makes a full-grown jade plant look like a small bush. What movement quality or qualities can you use to represent how you feel about a jade plant?

3. People who live in the United States speak English with a variety of accents. Those in the north usually talk more rapidly and have a clipped way of pronouncing words, while people living in the south talk in a softer, melodic manner. What movement quality or qualities can you use to represent these two ways of speaking?

4. The foods we eat have many different tastes. These tastes include spicy, sweet, and sour, among others. It is also possible to transform these different tastes into movement qualities. For me, spicy foods have a sharp quality. Think about your favorite food and find a movement quality or qualities that represent that food.

Figure 3.26.   *African violet.* Photo by author.

Figure 3.27.   *Jade plant.* Photo by author.

Shape and Pathway

1. For me, different types of music make me think about different shapes and pathways. These differences become evident when I listen to two very different pieces of music—a percussion ensemble in comparison to a new-age work composed for meditation. Listen to two very different pieces of music. Then, draw or scribble in a way that represents your feelings about each piece.[16] As you draw, pay careful attention to the type of shapes and lines you create. You should find that the shapes and lines you create in each drawing are different. These shapes and lines are your abstraction of each piece of music. Now, transform each of your drawings into movement by changing the shapes and lines into body shapes and pathways.

2. Think about the colors brown and yellow. What basic feeling do you have about each color? What body shapes and movement pathways can you use to represent each color?

Position

1. How can you position people to represent a crowded city environment? How would you

position them to communicate the feeling of a desert or open prairie?

2. How do you feel about music that has a steady beat or pulse, like a march, in comparison to the way you feel about more irregular or syncopated music, such as jazz? How would you place people in relation to each other to represent a march? How can you place these same people to represent an abstraction of jazz music?

Perfecting Your Movement Transformation Skills

You are going to read descriptions of two cultural groups. You should find that some of the following concepts lend themselves to literal transformations, and other ideas can be transformed into movement using abstraction. It is up to you to decide which method of transformation is more appropriate. Remember, literal transformations are direct, causing you to move like the concept, duplicate the size of the concept, or shape your body like the concept. Literal transformations can refer to the level or position of the object or concept as well. Abstraction, on the other hand, means capturing the essence of the concept in your movements. Abstraction is feeling oriented. It requires you to react to the concept emotionally before transforming your response into movement. Look again at the diagram in Figure 3.23 to refresh your understanding of abstraction.

The Navajo call themselves *Dineh* or "the people." It is thought they may have originally come from an area that is now northwest Canada and Alaska. The Navajo migration probably occurred in small groups over a long period of time. Originally, the Navajo settled in an area bounded by four sacred mountains, but today they occupy the Four Corners area of Utah, Colorado, Arizona, and New Mexico. Much Navajo psychology emphasizes motion because they were a nomadic tribe. Their involvement with motion also contributes to a belief that no state is fixed. The Navajo have a strong connection with nature and speak of Mother Earth and Father Sky. The Navajo also divide the natural world into male and female beings.[17]

Navajo legends are filled with many deities and heroes. One of these is the trickster Coyote. Tricksters occur in the legends of many diverse cultures, but they are usually an immature character who engages in mis-

chievous exploits. The Navajo are also known for their sand paintings, which are an important part of their ceremonies because symbols used in the paintings represent life forces. Usually a sand painting is begun at the center of the image, moving gradually to the outer edges of the painting. In 1886, the Navajo were forced off their land by the government and had to move east during the long walk—about 470 miles.[18]

The Irish have a long, colorful history. Ireland was originally settled by the Celts, an ancient people who came from central Europe by way of France. The Celts built huge stone forts on the coast of what is now Ireland. Today, remnants of this early culture remain in the stories of leprechauns and banshees. A leprechaun is a mischievous fairy who does anything to protect his pot of gold. Banshees are female spirits who wail outside houses to warn of a forthcoming death. St. Patrick is another more recent character found in Irish lore. As the story goes, St. Patrick traveled throughout Ireland teaching Christianity and baptizing people. He also likened the Christian Trinity to the shamrock because most shamrocks have three leaves. Since then, the shamrock has been Ireland's national flower.[19]

Some of the concepts or ideas in these two cultural descriptions can be transformed into movement using literal methods. Which movement components did you use in the literal transformations? What movement components did you use to perform abstract transformations? Which type of transformation was easier for you? Why do you think this was true?

If you decide to use a cultural group as an inspiration for creating movements and dances in your classes, be sure to select a group your students have read about and with which they are familiar. In other words, they should know something about the cultural group already and be interested in exploring it further. The information you choose to work with should also be age appropriate. Give some thought to a cultural group that can be developed into a movement-based lesson. Begin by discussing the important characteristics of this group. Next, work with your students to write a short description of the group. Begin the movement transformation process by suggesting how some of the concepts in your written description can be transformed into movement. Initiate the transformation process using literal methods because literal transformations are more objective and easier to work with. Because abstract transformations are feeling oriented, they are best left to a time when you and your students have gained confidence with the literal method of transformation. Finally, have your students create their own movements based on the cultural description. At this point, older students can work together in groups to create movements.

EVIDENCE FOR USING MOVEMENT AS A TEACHING TOOL

There is much evidence for using movement as a teaching tool. In his book, the *Arts With the Brain in Mind*, Eric Jensen makes a case for the educational value of the kinesthetic arts.[20] The kinesthetic arts are those that involve movement, such as dance or drama. Jensen writes that the kinesthetic arts can play a powerful role in education because they are a universal language and provide teachers with a huge potential for encouraging student learning along with a minimum of risk.[21]

Alain Berthoz is a French professor who is also concerned with the mind–body connection. He has studied this connection in his Laboratory of Physiology of Perception and Action. In his book, *The Brain's Sense of Movement*, Berthoz describes memory in a way that provides further evidence for using movement as a teaching strategy. Memory, Berthoz states, is of many different types that are implemented in different parts of the brain. Memory, in fact, functions at all cerebral levels. Even muscles have memory.[22]

Berthoz's discussion of spatial memory is of particular interest because this form of memory is essential when representing spatial aspects of human movement in the brain. Berthoz provides a practical example of this form of memory to make his point. He says that if you want to recall your route to work on a particular day, you remember it by recalling landmarks that you see along the way. Berthoz also asserts that you remember your route by recalling the movements you made as you drove or walked by the landmarks.[23] The landmarks you see and the associated movements you performed produce a spatial-visual map and a movement-based map in your brain.

Mark Reardon and Seth Derner discuss the use of movement in the classroom in their book *Strategies for Great Teaching*.[24] In this text, they use the term *Astaire movement* and encourage teachers to allow students to dance their way through content. Body movements like dancing, they explain, not only evoke and express emotion but are useful tools to improve memory. Muscle memory, the authors believe, is one of the strongest human memory systems. As an example, Reardon and Derner point out that we remember performing dances, such as the hokey pokey, in our childhood, and these memories seem to stay with us for a lifetime.[25]

SUMMARY AND CONCLUSIONS

As a result of reading this chapter and doing the explorations, it should be clear that literal movement transformations are much easier to create than abstract transformations. This is why you and your students should begin the transformation process using literal methods. Abstract transformations involve a feeling response, and students are reluctant to show their feelings early on. Later, after students gain a sense of satisfaction from creating literal movements, they are more likely to express personal feelings through their actions. Students may also feel insecure at the beginning of class because they are not sure what is in store for them. Once class routine is established, students know what is expected. Establishing a routine also leads to a classroom atmosphere that is safe, and feeling-based work can begin.

Another interesting aspect of the movement transformation process is that it is the same process used to create a dance in the fine arts sense. When I was teaching full time at a university, I created a three-part choreography based on the paintings of Wassily Kandinsky. Many of Kandinsky's paintings feature geometric shapes floating on an endless background. When I read about Kandinsky's life, however, I got a sense of the feelings he experienced while attempting to create his unique paintings. As a result, some of the movements I created were a literal transformation of the geometric shapes found in Kandinsky's paintings, while other movements were feeling oriented and drew on the abstract method of movement transformation.

It is remarkable that movement is not used today as a teaching strategy throughout all levels of education, considering the connections that exist between mind and body. While preschool, kindergarten, and 1st-grade teachers recognize the need to have students move and dance, those who teach grades 2 through high school use movement as a teaching strategy much more sparingly. Perhaps current emphasis on academic achievement does not allow sufficient time to introduce movement-based lessons, or teacher training programs may not include movement-based curricula throughout.

The fact that many students are tactile-kinesthetic learners and bodily-kinesthetic intelligence is one of the seven intelligences should foster interest in using movement as a teaching tool. In addition, movement is a universal language and can be helpful when working with students learning English as a second language. It also appears that we remember visible landmarks by associating them with the movements we performed in their physical presence. I am sure you remember dances and other activities you performed as a child along with the physical surroundings much better than you remember the academic exercises and problems that were part of your kindergarten through high school experiences. The fact that muscles do have memory should encourage the use of movement-based lessons as well.

REVIEWING YOUR KNOWLEDGE AND UNDERSTANDING

Now you have a chance to check your understanding of how to transform academic concepts into movement.

1. What is a direct or literal movement transformation? Give several examples in which concepts are changed into movements using the literal transformation process.
2. What is an indirect or abstract movement transformation? Give several examples in which concepts are transformed into movements using the abstraction process.
3. Can you draw a diagram of the abstraction process? Hint: This diagram is a framework for the abstracting process.
4. What is the basic difference between literal and abstract movement transformations, and in what classroom situations would you use each type of movement transformation?

5. What is synesthesia? How is synesthesia related to abstraction and the movement transformation process?
6. One of the authors mentioned in this chapter has written about levels of abstraction. What is a level of abstraction?
7. How can the idea of levels of abstraction be used in classroom lessons?
8. Why does using movement as a teaching strategy help memory?

NOTES

1. Renate N. Caine and Geoffrey Caine, *Education on the Edge of Possibility* (Alexandria, VA: Association for Supervision and Curriculum Development, 1997).

2. Stephen Minot, *Three Genres: The Writing of Poetry, Fiction, and Drama*, 6th ed. (Upper Saddle River, NJ: Prentice Hall, 1998).

3. Seymour Kleinman, *Social Dancing Fundamentals* (Columbus, OH: Charles Merrill, 1968).

4. Jacqueline L. Tobin and Raymond G. Dobard, *Hidden in Plain View: The Secret Story of Quilts and the Underground Railroad* (New York: Doubleday, 1999).

5. Bobbie Kalman, *Japan: The Land* (New York: Crabtree, 2001).

6. Bobbie Kalman, *Canada: The Land* (New York: Crabtree, 2002).

7. Pam Meecham and Julie Sheldon, *Modern Art: A Critical Introduction* (London: Routledge, 2000).

8. Elliot W. Eisner, *The Arts and the Creation of Mind* (New Haven, CT: Yale University Press, 2002).

9. Michael Michalko, *Cracking Creativity: The Secrets of Creative Genius* (Berkeley, CA: Ten Speed Press, 2001).

10. Michalko, *Cracking Creativity*.

11. Eisner, *Arts and the Creation of Mind*.

12. Eisner, *Arts and the Creation of Mind*.

13. Howard Gardner, *Frames of Mind: The Theory of Multiple Intelligences* (New York: Basic Books, 1983).

14. Howard Gardner, *The Arts and Human Development* (New York: Basic Books, 1994).

15. Kitty Kelley, *The Royals* (New York: Warner Books, 1997).

16. Sandra C. Minton, *Choreography: A Basic Approach Using Improvisation*, 3rd ed. (Champaign, IL: Human Kinetics, 2007).

17. Joseph Bruchac, *Navajo Long Walk: The Tragic Story of a Proud People's Forced March From Their Homeland* (Washington, DC: National Geographic Society, 2002);

Trudy Griffin-Pierce, *Earth Is My Mother, Sky Is My Father* (Albuquerque: University of New Mexico Press, 1992); Peter Iverson, *Indians of North America: The Navajos* (New York: Chelsea House, 1990); Virginia D. H. Sneve, *The Navajos: A First Americans Book* (New York: Holiday House, 1993).

18. Bruchac, *Navajo Long Walk*; Griffin-Pierce, *Earth Is My Mother*; Iverson, *Indians of North America*; Sneve, *Navajos*.

19. Brendan January, *A True Book: Ireland* (New York: Children's Press, 1997); Shannon Spencer, *Countries of the World: Ireland* (Milwaukee: Gareth Stevens, 2000).

20. Eric Jensen, *Arts With the Brain in Mind* (Alexandria, VA: Association for Supervision and Curriculum Development, 2001).

21. Jensen, *Arts With the Brain in Mind*.

22. Alain Berthoz, *The Brain's Sense of Movement* (Cambridge, MA: Harvard University Press, 2000).

23. Mark Reardon and Seth Derner, *Strategies for Great Teaching: Maximize Learning Moments* (Chicago: Zephyr Press, 2004).

24. Reardon and Derner, *Strategies for Great Teaching*.

25. Reardon and Derner, *Strategies for Great Teaching*.

CHAPTER 4

Teaching Through Dance Making

Until this point, you have been using single movements or short sequences of movements to transform academic concepts into actions. In other words, the movements you created were your teaching tools—a strategy that appeals to tactile-kinesthetic learners and makes bodily-kinesthetic intelligence a part of learning. Single movements or movement sequences are not dance, however. You now have a chance to combine single movements and movement sequences to create whole dances and make them part of your lessons.

When time is short, it may be necessary to simply teach students a dance you have choreographed—a dance made up of concept-based movements presented in a lesson. When class time allows, creative work in the form of movement discovery and dance making can be included to give students an opportunity to problem solve. Students gain a better understanding of concepts if they have a chance to transform those concepts into movement. In addition, by weaving the concept-based movements into a dance, students engage in another form of problem solving called dance making. Learning movements and dances created by a teacher involves kinesthetic learning but does not allow students to be engaged in the creative problem solving itself.

THE VALUE OF DOING CREATIVE WORK

E. Paul Torrance designed tests that measure a person's creative potential. In a recent book chapter, he summarized the work of M. K. Raina by describing Raina's insights into creativity. Creativity, Raina writes, is a diverse phenomenon that adds meaning and purpose to the lives of many. Engaging in creative work also gives one a sense of purpose in the larger scheme of things.

Creative thinking can provide international networks that cross national and cultural boundaries, leading to world peace and dealing with future threats.[1]

If the ability to think in a creative way is important to the future of the world, then teaching students how to think creatively should be part of education. In her book, Berenice Bleedorn asks, What shall we teach? In answer to this question, she says teaching basic skills is of paramount importance to enable students to go on to higher learning levels. One of these basic skills, Bleedorn continues, should be teaching students how to think, using the full range and potential of the brain. Using the full potential of the brain includes doing creative and critical thinking because such skills are necessary for those who live in a democracy; "no student should be left behind, but no student should be deprived of the right to move ahead and to develop to the highest possible individual level of intellectual capacity."[2]

Ruth Hubbard, who has researched creative development in children and adults, states that creativity should be thought of as a natural thinking strategy—one that is not a specific power but an aspect of general intelligence. Creativity, Hubbard says, encompasses the ability to explore, evaluate, and make associations. Creativity is important to learning in many subjects. Many other forms of learning, including language acquisition, are not limited to learning verbal skills but involve other reasoning and thinking abilities as well.[3]

Creative thinking is different than rote learning and memorizing facts because such forms of learning are reproductive, while creativity is productive. Individuals who can think creatively ask themselves how many different ways they can solve a problem instead of trying to solve a problem in a way they have been taught previously. Creative thinking can often generate solutions that are unconventional and at times unique. Another way to say this is that creative thinking provides alternate solutions to a problem.[4]

Creative thinking is different from rote learning because by solving a problem in their own way, children find personal meaning in what they learn. The brain's goal is to detect and create meaning by connecting bits of information. Information connected in this way forms patterns that have personal meaning for learners. The patterns formed can be a series of words upon a page or movements in a dance, but the more associations that are formed, the more firmly the information becomes embedded in the brain. When learners form associations with new subject matter, new patterns are formed based on existing schema or brain patterns.[5]

Elaine Johnson, an educational consultant, calls learning by making connections "contextual learning." This type of learning enables students to connect content in academic subjects with their own lives. Contextual learning gives meaning to what is being learned. It is a system that includes self-regulated learning and creative thinking.[6] One of the ways to connect academic content with one's own life is to do creative, artistic work based on that content. The creative process is an integral part of the teaching strategy described in this book because we are engaged in creating movements by using academic concepts as the inspiration. Now, we are creating dances by weaving concept-based movements together.

Elliot Eisner, long a proponent of arts in education, states that work in the arts can develop initiative, creativity, imagination, and planning skills. Often, student artwork may not look like it is relevant to what the student may be doing later in life. Nevertheless, skills developed through the arts are skills that are important in the workplace and enable students to become productive workers.[7] I would add that the skills developed by working creatively in the arts are especially important to success in one's profession because solving problems in a creative way is involved in many real-life situations.

Doing creative work also has a positive effect on self-esteem. Self-esteem is how we think of or feel about ourselves. It is the concept we have of the self. Self-esteem can be influenced by a number of factors:

how peers treat us, what we have accomplished in life, and our visual appearance. There is also a connection between self-esteem and doing creative work. I began to suspect this was true when students described the feelings of satisfaction they experienced after solving creative movement problems in dance classes.

Some of the research I have done explored the connection between creative work in dance and self-esteem. In a quantitative investigation, I looked at whether participation in dance had an effect on self-esteem. The 225 high school students in the study were divided into 2 groups—those enrolled in a dance class at their school and those who were not. A standardized paper and pencil test, the Culture-Free Self-Esteem Inventory, was given at the beginning and end of the semester to both groups.[8] This study showed a significant difference between the dancers' and nondancers' self-esteem at one school for social self-esteem, a form of self-esteem based on the quality of a student's relationships with his or her peers. The importance of this result, however, was that the dance teacher at this school used creative movement and dance making in her classes to a somewhat greater extent than the other dance teachers in the study.[9]

Carol Press, who has taught elementary school dance for many years, also values the use of creative and expressive movement. Creative movement, Press writes, challenges students to go beyond what comes naturally to them. It is a way to delineate and develop the self. By having a chance to perform their own movements and watch other students perform their movements, students have a chance to reflect on personal movement responses. The combined acts of being performer and then audience enables students to gain self-confidence and movement awareness.[10]

TEACHING BY USING DANCE MAKING

You have already read how concepts can be transformed into movement using literal or abstract methods. Here, many different ways to make dances based on diverse subjects are described. You may be familiar with many of these dance forms, but they are presented together in this chapter for easy reference. In each case, the dance form is described, and then you have a chance to create a dance in this form using different concept-based movements.

As you read through this chapter, keep some of the traits of a good dance in mind. Remember, single movements are combined to create a whole that has a beginning, middle, and end. Because a dance is a whole, it also has a feeling of unity and continuity yet sufficient variety to keep the audience interested and on their toes. On the other hand, some repetition helps viewers become comfortable with a dance because seeing a movement more than once creates a feeling of familiarity and recognition. Finally, transitions are created between separate movements, movement sequences, and sections of the dance.[11] Without transitions, energy flow and continuity are interrupted, and the audience loses focus and involvement. These interruptions are like dead air during the transmission of television or radio programming.

When dances are part your teaching strategy, I recommend talking about each academic concept first, followed by teaching or having students create movement based on the concept. Usually a dance that combines concept-based movements is taught at the end of a lesson. If time permits, have the students create their own movements and weave their movements together into a dance. This gives students a chance to hone their problem-solving skills. When I have a short period of time, however, I usually arrive in the classroom with prechoreographed movements and a prechoreographed dance. When possible, supply music so that movement is performed with accompaniment. Be sure to use music that motivates movement and that the children like.

Teaching Using a Text-Based Dance

One way dance can reinforce the meaning of reading that students must do in other disciplines is to create movements that follow the words in the text to create a text-based dance. The text you use to create such dances can be the words in a song, poem, or short story. The movements created can be a literal transformation of text or an abstraction of the words. The order of movements in a text-based dance follows the progression of words in the text.

An Example of a Text-Based Dance

One of the 2nd-grade teachers I worked with wanted me to create a dance based on the patriotic song "America the Beautiful." In this instance, the lines of the song were read with soft music playing in the background. After the reading of each line in the song, there was a pause, and the children performed a movement or movement sequence based on that line. Speed or timing was crucial, because if the pause was too long, the dancers stopped moving and waited to hear the next line. To make sure this did not happen, some transitional movements were created and inserted between those actions representing the lines of the song. The following paragraph describes the dance based on "America the Beautiful." Some of the movements resulted from literal transformations, and others are abstractions.

The dance began by reading the title of the song, "America the Beautiful." These words were the cue for the students to enter. Because the entire class performed the dance, they were arranged in three rows, with two rows entering from one side of the performance area and the third row entering from the other side. After entering, all students turned and faced the audience and swayed from side to side four times. The next cue was the line "O beautiful for spacious skies." When the students heard these words, they looked up slowly and then used both arms to reach out, tracing an arc through the space overhead. This action was performed slowly two times.

After the next line of the song, "for amber waves of grain," the students stayed in one spot and moved as though they were pushing grain to both sides away from the center of the body. This action was done four times. The line "for purple mountains majesties" was followed by having the second and third rows of students form mountains by pairing the students off. One student in each pair turned to face back, and the other student remained facing front. In addition, each student lifted their right arm high to touch the fingertips of the other student. Then, each pair walked around in a circle to form the cone shape of a mountain, while tracing its circular base with their steps. At the same time, the front row of students bent down near the floor, rising slowly as they copied the hand actions performed while climbing up a rope as if they were rappelling up a mountain.

To illustrate the line "above the fruited plain," the students performed actions that looked like they were picking fruit off a tree. This movement was done eight times. Following the refrain "America, America," the students again swayed from side to side as a group. The line "God shed His grace on thee" initiated a sequence of movements in which the students put one knee down on the floor, lifted both arms high, and then slowly lowered their arms as they returned to a standing position. These actions were performed by one line of students at a time.

Following these movements, the students in each line formed a circle, placed their right arm on the shoulder of the student in front of them, and walked once around the circle. These actions were performed in response to the words "and crown thy good with brotherhood." The dance ended with the line "from sea to shining sea." Here, the students exited the performance area with actions that looked as though they were paddling a boat. The three lines of students moved off with one line going in one direction and the other two lines exiting in the opposite direction.

This text-based dance reinforced student understanding of the meaning of the song "America the Beautiful" because performing the concept-based movements taps into the tactile-kinesthetic style of learning. Because the students had to work together to perform some of the actions in the dance, they were also experiencing cooperative learning.

Your Chance to Create a Text-Based Dance

The following text is an excerpt from a poem written by Emily Dickinson long ago, but it still relates to the natural world we see around us. Read through this poem several times. Then you or your students can transform some of the words into movement. Next, read the poem again as your students perform the dance. You may have to practice reading the poem and performing the movements several times until you and your students decide how long to pause between the reading of each line and how many times to perform each action.

XXXVII
The wind begun to rock the grass
With threatening tune and low,—
He flung a menace at the earth
A menace at the sky.

The leaves unhooked themselves from trees
And started all abroad;

The dust did scoop itself like hands
And throw away the road

The wagon quickened on the streets,
The thunder hurried slow;
The lightning showed a yellow beak,
And then a livid claw.

The birds put up the bars to nests,
The cattle fled to barns;
There came one drop of giant rain,
And then, as if the hands

That held the dams had parted hold,
The waters wrecked the sky,
But overlooked my father's house,
Just quartering a tree.[12]

Teaching Using a Series Dance

A series dance is created by linking movements together, one action after the other. The first step in making a series dance is to decide on the order in which you want to perform the movements. In other words, which movement comes first in the dance, which is second, and so on. Movement order should also make sense in terms of the relationships between the concepts being taught. For example, in the math dance that follows, the concept-based movements are arranged by introducing actions based on simple concepts first. The next step is to decide how many times each movement is performed. It may also be necessary to create transitional movements between the original actions so that the dance flows from one action to the next. Variety can be added by changing the use of some of the actions using the movement components.

An Example of a Series Dance

A math lesson was presented in middle school classes. The movements were selected for the dance based on specific criteria. First, movements needed to fit together to form a whole. Second, it had to be easy to go from one part to the next part of the dance. Third, variety was added by selecting movements that had different speeds. Thus, some of the movements were performed on each beat of the music, and other actions lasted for two or even four musical counts. For example, in the math dance, students performed a right angle shape four times on each beat of music. Then, in the next part of the dance, the students moved into the obtuse angle shape slowly, taking an entire four-count measure to arrive at this shape. As indicated earlier, movement order was determined by beginning with the simplest concepts.

The following math dance was performed while the students and I stood in a circle, but it could be done in a line or lines or with students scattered throughout the space. If the circle formation is used, front is the center of the circle. If the students are placed in lines or scattered throughout the space, they would all face the same direction. Each of the following statements explains a math concept. The concepts are followed by a description of movements used to transform the concept into an action. The number of counts or duration of an action is at the end of the statement. Lively, upbeat music in the techno style was used to accompany this dance.

Math Series Dance

Part 1 of this dance is based on the concept of fractions. Each measure is performed once. The actions are simple and short in duration. For example, a small, slashing action performed with one hand is a short, simple movement:

- For 1/4, move on one count of a measure of four beats (four counts).
- For 2/4, move on two counts of a measure of four beats (four counts).
- For 3/4, move on three counts of a measure of four beats (four counts).
- For 4/4, move on all four counts of the measure (four counts).

Part 2 is based on the concept of a different number of degrees in a circle:

- For 90 degrees, turn one quarter to face the right side, quickly turning back to front (2 counts). This action is repeated 4 times in right and left directions (total of 8 counts).
- For 180 degrees, turn to face back and quickly return to front (4 counts). This action is repeated 4 times to the right, left, right, and left (total of 16 counts).
- For 360 degrees, spin once all the way around (4 counts).

Part 3 is based on the concept of different angles:

- For a right angle, bring the fingers of the right hand to the left elbow (one count). For a second right angle, bring the fingers of the left hand to the right elbow (one count). These two actions are done alternately for a total of four repetitions to equal four counts (see Figure 4.1).
- For an obtuse angle, widen the last right-angle shape by opening the right arm gradually to the right side (four counts). This action is done slowly and takes all four counts (see Figure 4.2).

Figure 4.1.   *Two right angles.* Photo by Anna Newell.

Figure 4.2.   *Obtuse angle.* Photo by Anna Newell.

- For an acute angle bring the elbows together and make a *V* with the arms (one count). For a second acute angle, bring the fingers together to make an upside down *V* (one count). These two movements are performed alternately for a total of four repetitions to equal four counts (see Figure 4.3).
- For a straight angle, lift the right arm high while dropping the left arm low. This means that your right arm will be directly above your right shoulder, and your left arm will be hanging at your side (one count). For a second straight angle, lift the left arm high and lower the right arm (one count). These two actions are done alternately, switching the positions of your right and left arms for a total of four repetitions to equal four counts total (see Figure 4.4).

Part 4 is based on the concept of geometric shapes. To perform this part of the dance, remain in the circle, but face a partner. Your partner is the person who is on your right or left:

- Join hands with your partner so that your arms are extended and curved in front of your bodies to form a circle. Each partner's arms make up half of the circle (hold shape four counts; see Figure 4.5).
- For a rectangle, straighten your elbows, changing the circle to a rectangle (hold four counts; see Figure 4.6).

Figure 4.4.   Straight angle. Photo by Anna Newell.

Figure 4.5.   Circle. Photo by Anna Newell.

Figure 4.3.   Two acute angles. Photo by Anna Newell.

Figure 4.6.   Rectangle. Photo by Anna Newell.

- For a parallelogram, one partner shifts over to the side so that the sides of the rectangle become slanted (hold four counts; see Figure 4.7).
- For a triangle, one partner extends their arms straight out to the side, and the other partner places their arms on two front diagonals so that the fingertips of diagonal arms touch the partner's forearms (hold four counts; see Figure 4.8).

After making the triangular shape with your partner, face front or the center of the circle, and begin the dance again.

The structure of this dance is a series because one movement or shape is repeated or held for a number of counts before performing the next movement or shape. The development from beginning to end is based on movement complexity. The first action is relatively simple, but the second and third movements increase in difficulty. At the end of the dance, the students work with a partner, which adds another level of difficulty. Arranging the movements in this way gives students confidence because they are not threatened by learning difficult movements at the beginning of a dance. Remember, the brain-mind principles described in Chapter 1 state that the classroom atmosphere should be challenging but not threatening.

Your Chance to Create a Series Dance

Now, you have a chance to create a series dance. The following information includes concepts students learn when studying a rainforest. Your challenge is to transform some of these concepts into movements and form them into a dance using the series method.

Concepts for Rainforest Series Dance

- Tropical rainforests are located near the earth's equator.
- Rain falls nearly every day.
- Rainforests have a hot, humid climate.
- Today, rainforests cover approximately 2% of the earth's surface.
- Rainforests grow in layers.
- The top, or emergent, layer includes tall trees that extend above the rest of the forest.
- The next layer, the canopy, is formed from the crowns of lower trees that nearly touch. The canopy forms a lacy blanket above the ground, and many vines extend down toward the ground from the canopy.
- The understory is formed from smaller trees that have cone-shaped crowns and that can grow in the shade.
- The lower layer of the rainforest contains small trees, shrubs, and bushes.
- The ground layer includes ferns, herbs, and seedlings. This layer is very dark and moist. At this level, the trunks of the trees or buttresses are wide to help secure the trees in the thin rainforest soil.
- Many animals and insects live in the rainforest. These animals and insects include monkeys, eagles, butterflies, snakes, frogs, beetles, spiders, centipedes, worms, parrots, hummingbirds, hogs, jaguars, tigers, and many others.

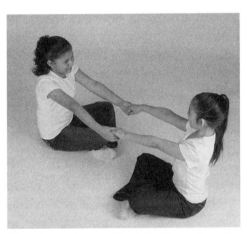

Figure 4.7.   Parallelogram. **Photo by Anna Newell.**

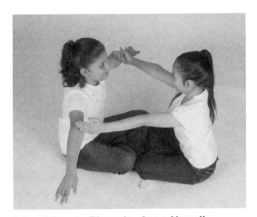

Figure 4.8.   Triangle. **Photo by Anna Newell.**

Select four or five of these concepts. When selecting concepts, make sure they are presented in an order that makes sense in terms of relationships. You need to preserve relationships as they are described in texts and curriculum matrixes. By structuring dances in this way, you reinforce academic content. It makes sense, for example, to present movements depicting the emergent layer of the rainforest first because it is the top layer; beginning your dance with movements based on the canopy would confuse students. In addition, specific animals live in different layers of the rainforest. The tapir lives in the ground layer of the forest, so performing movements mimicking a tapir before those representing animals living in the emergent layer is also confusing. Ordering movements to reflect relationships between concepts also follows the brain-mind principle based on relating one piece of information to another.

After considering relationships between the concepts, decide how to transform each concept into movement. As you create movements, concentrate on the movement components, and decide which component or components can be used to transform a concept into action. In the math lesson described earlier, body shapes were used to transform geometric shapes into actions, while rhythms were used to change fractions into movements. It would have been more difficult to transform geometric shapes into movement using the rhythmic component, and fractions do not lend themselves to movement transformations based on shape. You also need to consider whether it is best to use literal or abstract transformations.

Once you have created four or five actions, decide on movement order. As noted earlier, movement order should reflect the way in which one concept is related to another one. Make sure, as well, that you can move easily from one action to another. If parts of your dance seem disconnected, you may need to create a few transitional movements. Movement order is also related to the overall form of a dance, so your dance should have a beginning, middle, and end. Finally, decide how many times you want to perform each movement and the number of counts it will take to perform each action.

Teaching Using a Dance Tableau

The tableau is another dance form that can be part of your teaching strategies. A tableau is created when different movements are performed by different dancers at the same time in the same dance space. The effect created is one of a picture that has moving parts. A tableau dance also looks like the parts of a giant machine in action. In reality, a whole dance based on the tableau would probably include a number of separate tableaux linked together with transitional movements. This means the dance would consist of a series of moving snapshots connected by transitional actions that transport the dancers around the stage from one tableau to the next.

A tableau is useful in lessons in which the separate concepts have a simultaneous relationship. A painting is based on skillful use of unity of group shape, rhythmic relationship of line, and interesting use of texture. All of these elements are found in a painting in the same place at the same time, so it is helpful for student understanding to present movements representing these concepts as a tableau. In the same sense, a number of different animals live together in a single layer of the rainforest. Thus, movements representing animals living in one layer of the forest can logically be represented as a tableau. Care should be taken so the sections of the tableau differ in length. Otherwise, the dance becomes predictable and is no longer interesting for the audience.

An Example of a Dance Tableau

A tableau can be created around a central point within a circle. This arrangement of movements was used in the following example, but there are many other ways to arrange dancers in space while performing a tableau. For instance, the dancers can perform various movements while remaining together in a group and traveling throughout a space. In addition, separate groups of dancers can create a tableau by moving at different levels. The groups of dancers can also switch places in the circular arrangement so that the dancers in the center move to the outside of the circle and those on the outside move to the center.

In this tableau, the movements performed by one group of dancers are based on the different types of lines found in the cut paper design shown in Figure 4.9. These lines form the fishing poles; fishing lines; and outlines of the waves, fish, and bubbles. As you can see, these lines are both straight and curved. Stream-

Figure 4.9. **Abstract artwork based on aspects of the life of George Washington and the fact that he liked to fish in a lake on his farm. Photo by Anna Newell. Cut paper design by author.**

ers were used to trace the pathway of both types of lines. In one interpretation of this design, three or four students represented the lines by tracing straight and curved pathways with streamers. In another tableau, the students with the streamers circled around the outside of the tableau as seen in Figure 4.10. The actions with the streamers can continue for only a few counts or for a longer period of time.

A second movement in this tableau was based on rhythmic patterns created by connecting and tracing lines in the cut-paper design seen in Figure 4.9. For example, the lines forming the fishing poles are longer than those forming the lines and hooks, so the rhythmic pattern formed by the three lines together can be described as one long and two shorts. The dancers performed this rhythm by taking one long and two short steps in a repeated pattern. Because the dancers with the streamers circled on the outside of the tableau, those performing the rhythmic pattern moved on a second circular pathway inside the dancers with streamers.

The third element in this tableau was based on group unity or the relationship of shapes found in the design shown in Figure 4.9. For instance, the two fish and the larger bubble on the right side of the design form a triangular shape. To demonstrate unity in this group shape, these dancers formed a triangular arrangement at the center of the circling dancers. In other words, the third group of dancers remained in one spot in a triangular arrangement, moving only the upper body.

Figure 4.10. **Tableau with a group shape in the center and other dancers circling at the periphery. Photo by Anna Newell.**

By performing a movement tableau, the students worked in a cooperative way to show how all elements in a design come together to create a whole. The students also experience the separate elements that make up the design—line, rhythm, and group unity. Actively moving and getting a bodily-kinesthetic feeling for visual arts concepts brings multiple intelligences into play. Finally, the tableau gives students a feeling for spatial aspects of a design because the groups of dancers performed their movements in a restricted space, just as certain colors or shapes are placed in a particular space in a visual design.

Your Chance to Create a Movement Tableau

Following are a number of concepts students learn in the study of electricity. Your challenge is to transform some of these concepts into movements and mold these actions into a dance tableau.

Concepts for Use in Electricity Tableau

- The word *electricity* originated from a Greek word for amber because when you rub two pieces of amber together, static electricity is produced.
- Static electricity can be produced when two items of different composition are rubbed together, causing an exchange of charged particles (ions).
- Electricity flows toward its potential from negative to positive.
- Similar electrical charges repel, and opposite charges attract.
- Electricity flows in an unbroken pathway known as a circuit. A parallel or branching circuit is one electrical pathway.
- In order for electricity to flow through a circuit, there must be a force to propel the current. This force is called voltage.
- Some materials allow electricity to flow through them easily. Other materials impede the flow of current. The former type of material is called a conductor, and the latter type is a nonconductor.
- When electricity flows through a wire, it creates a magnetic field around the wire. This effect is increased by winding the wire around a metal core (usually soft iron). When electricity flows through the wire, the iron core temporarily becomes a magnet.

Select three or four of the described concepts that can occur in the same place at the same time. The last four concepts have to do with the flow of electricity through wires, giving them a simultaneous relationship. Next, decide how to transform each concept into movement. As you transform a concept into movement, think about the 11 movement components. Consider whether a literal or abstract transformation is most appropriate as well. Once you have created your movements, decide where in space you want place the dancers who perform each action. Remember that all the dancers move simultaneously in a tableau, so it is necessary to create a floor pattern or space for each dancer or group of dancers that does not interfere with movements of other dancers.

Teaching Using Chance Dance

Chance is another relatively simple way to make dance a part of your lessons. Chance can be used to demonstrate the occurrence of any number of chance events, such as a collision between an asteroid and the earth or the location of a violent storm. One way to create a chance dance is to make a map of your dance space and point to this map with your eyes closed to determine where in the dance space specific movements will be performed. Movement order can also be determined by chance. Simply write descriptions of each of your concept-based movements on separate cards. Then, close your eyes and draw each card, one at a time. The first card you draw is the first movement in your dance, the second card the second movement, and so on. Finally, you can roll dice to determine how many times a movement will be performed.

Example of a Chance Dance

I have used chance to help students fashion dances from locomotor movements and pedestrian actions. To do this, I prepare cards with names of movements on them. Next, the cards are placed face down on the floor, and each student selects four or five. The selection of the cards is the first chance element. The second chance element occurs when the cards are turned over one at a time to determine the order of the movements in the dance. Following this, each student decides how many times they perform a movement and create a floor pattern for the dance. I have also included a third chance element at times by arbitrarily selecting four or five students who simultaneously performed their dances in the same space so that chance determines how they relate to each other. You now have an opportunity to create a chance dance.

Your Opportunity to Create a Chance Dance

One of the concepts children are expected to understand is the many ways three objects can be arranged when the objects are each a different color. As a hint, think about the order in which the objects are arranged. Next, have your students create a different movement to represent each object. This means each child performs a different movement. Finally, use chance methods to determine the order in which the movements are performed. You may also need to provide some transitional actions to connect the concept-based movements. By using chance methods in this way, students experience a concrete example of the many ways the colored objects can be arranged and rearranged.

Teaching Using a Problem-Solving Dance

Dances created using problem-solving methods contribute to student learning in more than one way. When a dance is made up of concept-based movements, students experience these concepts using bodily-kinesthetic intelligence. Second, when the same dance involves problem solving, students learn to think in a critical and creative way.

In essence, you have been using problem solving to create text-based, series, tableau, and chance dances. There are, however, some specific techniques that can be used to create a problem-solving dance. One such technique is to select a number of movements or body shapes used to transform a group of related concepts into actions. Then, these movements or body shapes are placed at different points in the dance space. The problem to be solved is to create transitional movements that connect each of the other movements or shapes.

An important point must be considered when creating a problem-solving dance. This is to place the different parts of the dance in space in a way that makes sense in terms of the concepts. Say the concept is the order of the first four planets, Mercury, Venus, Earth, and Mars, moving outward from the sun. In terms of this concept, the movements representing these planets should bear the same spatial relationship as the one that exists between the planets. This means the dancers begin in the center of the space and perform the movements representing Mercury. Then they transition to a second location that is farther from the center of the space and perform the movements representing Venus and so on.

An Example of a Problem-Solving Dance

The following problem-solving idea has been used in teachers' workshops and with elementary school children. First, the class is divided into groups of an equal number (usually four to five people). Next, each group gets a map that is fictitious or real. A fictional map includes these landmarks: a curved bridge; sharp mountains; flat lake; tall, narrow building; and waving flag at the finish line (see Figure 4.11). If you use a real map, it is necessary to select specific landmarks to use as reference points.

After receiving the maps, the participants decide how to orient the map in the room. For instance, the starting point on the map can be positioned in any of

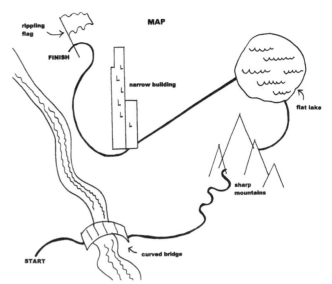

Figure 4.11.   Imaginary map.

the four corners of the room—a decision that changes the direction and facing of movements in the dance. Next, the students create group shapes that capture the shape or essence of each landmark and place each group shape in an appropriate spot in the room that corresponds to its position on the map. To create a dance, which is the problem to be solved, each group connects their group shapes with transitional movements. The transitional movements are like roads used to travel from one group shape to another. Each group also finds a beginning and ending for their dance and creates ways to move within some of the group shapes.

Your Chance to Create a Problem-Solving Dance

Choose a painting that includes a number of shapes and different colors. Then, select four or five of the shapes in the painting, and transform them into group body shapes. Next, decide where in the space each group shape is placed. Placement of the group shapes is determined by the position of the colored shapes in the painting. Decide as well how you can add movement to each group shape. One way to add movement is to think about how you feel about the different colors. Finally, create other movements to serve as transitions between the group shapes. A logical way to create transitional movements is discovering how your eyes travel around the painting as you view it or the way in which your eyes move from one colored shape to another. The transitional movements between group shapes follow the same pathways your eyes follow when you view the painting.

This problem-solving dance teaches students how the artist formed colored shapes in the painting into a composition. Through kinesthetic learning, students actively experience the composition in an artwork. When students create movements that are an abstraction of the colors in the painting, they also experience a relationship between the colors and their feelings. This means the painting becomes more than an example of good composition. It becomes a unique and personal experience for students.

Teaching Using the AB and ABA Dance Forms

There are many dance forms that choreographers have used repeatedly through the years, and these forms can also be part of your teaching strategy. Some of these forms such, as the AB and ABA, are based on musical forms.

The AB, a very simple dance form, consists of a beginning section called "A" and a second section known as "B." Each section is in turn made up of a series of movements or movement sequences. While the two sections of the AB dance must fit together in terms of intent, each contains elements that have a different tone.[13] For instance, an entire dance can be about the life of one person, but the A section shows the person during a happy time in their life, while the B section is about a sad time in the life of the same individual. The A and B sections of the dance explore a subject from different points of view. As another example, the A section of a dance can be based on the childhood of an individual, while the B section represents the person's adult life.

An ABA dance form has three parts, going a step further than the AB. There is an A section in which a series of movements is stated, followed by the B section that presents another series of movements with a contrasting theme or themes. In the third and final section, the ABA returns to the original theme or themes, but these movements are presented with a different twist. While contrasting elements exist in the A and B sections of the dance, the two sections are similar enough to fit together to form a unified whole. The use of skillful transitions between sections of an ABA dance help knit the piece together.[14]

Examples of AB and ABA Dances

Presidents Lincoln and Washington are studied in many elementary schools to honor President's Day. The life of Abraham Lincoln can be the subject of an AB dance in which the theme in section A is about Lincoln's early life, while thematic movements in section B relate to his later life. The complete dance is realized by varying the thematic movements and inserting transitions. Variations on thematic movements are created using the movement components described in Chapter 2. If one of the movements in this dance is planting crops, variations can be created by performing this action in different directions, at various levels, or by altering its timing. Repetition is also used to develop a dance.

Creating and performing a Lincoln dance gives students a chance to experience some of the activities that were a part of Lincoln's life in a personal way, using bodily-kinesthetic intelligence to interpret and perform these actions. Because the AB dance form is used here, students will also be able to compare and contrast the two parts of Lincoln's life by comparing and contrasting the kinesthetic feelings they experience when performing the two sections of the dance. Movements from Lincoln's early life, like planting crops or walking to school, feel decidedly different in the body than actions used to turn the pages of a law book or project the power of the presidency.

Lincoln AB Dance

These are concepts used to create the Lincoln dance. The movements used to transform the concepts into actions follow each description:

- Lincoln was born in a log cabin in 1809. When he was a young man, he and his sister helped on their parents' farm. The use of a literal transformation into movement is more appropriate here. The movements created include planting, hoeing, and picking crops.
- Lincoln and his sister walked two miles each day to school. This statement lends itself to either literal or abstract transformation. Literal movements are walking on a particular pathway to school. An abstract transformation is moving in a way that

captures the feeling of the long, tiring walk to school. Perhaps the movements can communicate Lincoln's determination or tiredness or a combination of these two qualities.

- Lincoln's mother died when he was nine years old. The movements created from this statement are based on abstraction in order to communicate Lincoln's feelings of sadness and loneliness.
- Lincoln's father remarried a year later. Lincoln's stepmother was very good to him, and he called her his angel mother. Movements created here can again be based on abstraction, communicating his stepmother's goodness or angelic qualities.
- In 1831, young Lincoln and two friends built a flatboat and floated down the Mississippi River to New Orleans. These movements can be literal and involve cutting wood, hammering nails, and paddling the boat.
- In New Orleans, Lincoln saw his first slave market. The chained slaves were being sold like cattle. Seeing the slave market made Lincoln miserable, and he never forgot this experience. Movements derived from this statement are literal, showing the crowded conditions and lack of freedom the slaves experienced. Other movements based on this same statement can be abstract, communicating Lincoln's personal feelings in response to seeing the slaves in the marketplace.

The movements resulting from the next set of concepts make up the B part of this dance because they deal with Lincoln's later or professional life.

- In 1834, Lincoln began his study of law and became an attorney two years later. Literal movements can be used here. For example, students can turn the pages of a book or gesture like a lawyer in the courtroom.
- In 1842, Lincoln fell in love with Mary Todd. Abstraction can be used to communicate feelings of love.
- Mary Todd was a lively, smart person. The movements here can be literal to demonstrate quick, lively actions.
- Lincoln ran for public office many times, serving in the Illinois legislature and in the U.S. House of Representatives. In 1860, he ran for president and

won. The movements created from the last statement can be an abstraction to communicate feelings of power and strength.

- Lincoln's dislike of slavery led to the Civil War. This was a long war, lasting four years, and many soldiers died. More literal movements of combat, fighting, shooting, and falling down to die can be used.
- Lincoln was shot in 1865 in retaliation for promoting the abolition of slavery. His body was taken back to Illinois on a train so that many citizens could say good-bye to him. This statement lends itself to both a literal and abstract transformation. Students can perform waving movements as a literal transformation and more abstract movements to communicate sadness and loss.[15]

This dance becomes an ABA by returning to variations of some of the movements used in the first section. This final section can be included as a flashback to Lincoln's early life.

Your Chance to Create an ABA Dance

You are going to create a dance in the ABA form. To do this, read the following statements and create a series of movements that transform the statements into movement. Remember, some concepts and ideas lend themselves to literal transformations, and other actions are produced more easily using abstraction. Next, decide which movements fit the A section and which movements fit the B section. In order to compose a complete dance, use variation, repetition, and transition as described earlier.

Concepts for an ABA Dance

The following concepts and ideas are from the book *Sweet Clara and the Freedom Quilt*.[16] This book was used in one of the elementary schools where I presented classes and is about Clara, a young slave girl who lived during the Civil War. It tells the story of how she constructed a quilt to serve as a map so that she and a friend could escape from a southern plantation. The book illustrates how quilts constructed during the Civil War era were used to guide escaping slaves on their journey to the north; the colors and shapes found in many of the quilts were symbols that served to guide escaping slaves on their journey:

- At the beginning of the book, Clara is sent from her home plantation to another plantation. It is the first time she has been away from her mother.
- In her new home, Clara is taken in by an older woman named Rachel.
- Rachel does not think Clara can endure working in the cotton fields on the plantation because this work makes Clara very tired.
- Rachel teaches Clara how to sew, and she becomes a seamstress for the plantation's mistress instead of working in the fields.
- One day, Clara hears about the Underground Railroad, which is not really a railroad but a route for escaping to the north.
- Like many others during this time, Clara decides to use her sewing ability to make a special quilt. She believes this quilt can serve as a map by marking a route to the north.
- Clara uses colored materials in her quilt. There are green patches for the fields, white strips for roads, and pink shapes for the buildings on the plantation.
- The quilt also includes a boat symbol so that the escaping slaves will know where a boat is hidden to carry them across the Ohio River.
- An old tree and a winding road are two other symbols on Clara's quilt map.
- A star is also sewn into the quilt. The star symbol is used to remind the slaves to use the North Star as their guide.
- Later in the story, Clara and one of her young friends follow the symbols on her quilt and escape from the plantation.
- In their travels, Clara and her friend hide during the day and travel at night.
- Eventually they find Clara's mother and sister.
- The story ends with Clara and her friend continuing on their journey to the north along with Clara's mother and sister.

An ABA dance based on this story can include separate sections paralleling the two parts of Clara's life—her life on the plantation (section A) and her escape to the north (section B). The final section of the dance can include some movements from the original A section with slight changes. Your challenge is to first create movements that relate to the thematic ideas found in Clara's story. Next, each of these movement themes can be varied, repeated, and finally woven together to make up the A and B sections of your dance.

By creating and performing movements related to the book *Clara and the Freedom Quilt*, students experience aspects of Clara's life kinesthetically. The movements and dance are also based on age-appropriate material because the book is written for elementary school children. Most important, however, is that by creating and performing a three-part dance, students draw relationships between Clara's life on the plantation and her life as a free person. Through the changing nature of the movements in the dance, they experience some of the same feelings experienced by Clara at different points in her life—experiences that add depth and meaning to their understanding of this story.

Teaching Using the Rondo Dance Form

The rondo is another common dance form. It is recognized by its many different sections following one after the other. The rondo can be described as ABA-CAD. This means that the A section is repeated throughout the dance separated by somewhat different B, C, and D sections. Each return to the A section includes either A in its entirety or just a portion of this section of the dance.[17]

An Example of a Rondo Dance

The story of Clara can have added meaning by using the rondo dance form. Here, specific movements depicting Clara's sweet character make up section A. Then, contrasting sections are based on different events in Clara's life, such as learning to sew, making the quilt, escaping with her friend, finding her mother, and traveling to the north. By structuring the dance as a rondo, students learn that Clara's sweet nature is a constant throughout this story, even though she is engaged in many different activities. Understanding Clara's sweet nature adds meaning to the story.

Your Chance to Create a Rondo

In one elementary school, I worked with a 2nd-grade class that was reading a story titled "Arthur's Pet Business." This story is about a young boy named Arthur, other members of his family, and his friends. As the story unfolds, we learn that Arthur wants a dog, but his parents doubt that he will be able to be responsible for a pet. Arthur's problem is to prove that he can be responsible. As a solution, Arthur's sister, D. W., tells him to get a job to prove he is responsible. As the story continues, Arthur and his friends discuss different ways he can earn money. One friend suggests working in a bank, and another mentions working in a junkyard. Finally, Arthur decides to take care of other people's pets because then his parents will know he can take care of his own dog.

One of Arthur's first customers is Mrs. Wood who wants him to take care of her dog, Perky. Arthur finds that taking care of Perky is a challenge and very tiring, but he perseveres. Soon, word gets around about Arthur's pet-sitting business, and before he knows what is happening, he is caring for many more pets: a canary, a few frogs, and a boa constrictor, among others. Arthur ends up taking care of quite a menagerie, and the pets are everywhere in his house. At this point, Arthur's mother puts her foot down and orders him to take all the pets to the basement. By bedtime, only Perky is allowed upstairs because she is not feeling well.

The next day, Mrs. Wood returns to pick up Perky, but her dog is nowhere to be found. Arthur searches the house but cannot find Perky. Mrs. Wood becomes upset, but fortunately, Arthur soon finds Perky under a bed with a new litter of puppies. Mrs. Wood pays Arthur for taking care of Perky, and because he has done such a good job, she gives him one of the puppies. Arthur's parents allow him to keep the puppy because he showed them he is responsible and can care for pets. At the end of the story, Arthur gives his sister most of the money he earned to repay money she had loaned him.[18]

One way to communicate this story through movement is to use actions representing Arthur's perseverance and determination as section A. Then, all the intervening events in the story—Arthur's challenge in caring for Perky, the arrival of the other pets, banishment of the pets to the basement, the search for Perky, the birth of the puppies, Arthur's payment from Mrs. Wood, and Arthur's payment to his sister—can be transformed into actions that serve as the basis for sections B, C, D, E, F, G, and H in the dance. You may think of other ways to communicate this story through movement using the rondo form. By using this dance form to interpret the story, students experience Arthur's determination and perseverance as a constant throughout this story. They not only learn that persistence pays off but that it can be applied in a variety of situations.

Teaching Using Theme and Variations Dance Form

Theme and variations is the final dance form to be discussed. It is also based on a form used in music. In theme and variations, a sequence of actions is created as the movement theme. This theme is changed and varied throughout the dance. Remember, movement components, such as direction, level, and timing, can be used to vary actions.[19] Let's say a movement theme consists of four forward-walking steps, two small jumps, and a slow collapse to the floor. A variation on this theme is four walking steps to the side, two large jumps, and a fast collapse. Again, the movements of your dance should fit together to form a whole with unity and continuity.

Example of a Theme and Variations Dance

Recently, I created an elementary-level lesson based on the Statue of Liberty. The dance that resulted was based on the following concepts:

- The Statue of Liberty is so large that people can move around inside of it.
- Liberty is also tall, and visitors must climb 168 steps to get to the observation deck in the Statue's crown.
- The Statue has a strong, steel skeleton.
- This skeleton is covered with a skin of gleaming copper.
- Liberty was a gift from France to the United States. To get the statue to the United States, the French government shipped it across the Atlantic Ocean in many boxes.

- Today, Liberty stands on a small island in New York harbor where she holds a raised torch in one hand.
- She has become a symbol of freedom and enlightenment for all who enter the United States from other lands.[20]

The theme for this dance is made up of four sequences of movement, beginning with actions that represent the inside of the statue and ending with those that stand for the flickering torch on the outside of the statue. The first sequence is a series of tired, marching steps to depict climbing the many steps inside the statue. The second sequence is more abstract, using strong, powerful actions to represent the steel skeleton inside Liberty. The third sequence relates to the gleaming, copper skin on the statue. This concept is transformed into movement by having one of a pair of students assume the shape of the statue, while a second student pretends to drape the copper skin over the first. A number of pairs of students can perform the third set of actions simultaneously so that all children are involved. A final sequence uses the arms to trace a wavy pathway. This action stands for the flickering flame in Liberty's torch. The four movement sequences making up the theme are varied, using some of the movement components. The variations of the theme form the entire dance.

By performing these concept-based movements as a single dance, students get a sense of how the different parts of the Statue of Liberty fit together from the inside to outside to form the whole structure. In addition, when the concept-based movements are abstract, such as those that represent Liberty's strong skeleton, students experience this strength in a personal way.

Your Chance to Create a Theme and Variations Dance

Your challenge is to create a sequence of movements or several sequences of movement that transform some of the following concepts into actions. These sequences of movement are the theme for your dance. This theme must be varied in a number of ways as described earlier to create a dance.

Concepts for an American Flag Dance

Remember that the concepts and concept-based movements must be connected in a way that makes sense in terms of the design and meaning of the American flag:

- A flag is a symbol that stands for the pride or loyalty individuals feel toward their country.
- In America, we recite the "Pledge of Allegiance" to our flag.
- Some people believe that a woman named Betsy Ross sewed the first American flag. Others think that the Betsy Ross story was made up by an early American patriot.
- The first American flag had 13 stars and 13 stripes, which stood for the original 13 colonies.
- There were many variations of our first flag because Congress was not specific about how the stars and stripes were supposed to be arranged. On some flags, the stars were in a circle and on others they were in rows. Sometimes the stars were even grouped to form a larger star.
- Today, there is only one form of the American flag, with alternating red and white stripes and a blue square in the upper left hand corner.
- Fifty stars are placed in rows, with the blue square as the background.
- Although all American flags have a uniform design today, they come in many sizes, ranging from very small to extremely large. One of largest American flags ever made was larger than a football field.[21]

More Practice With the Different Dance Forms

You are now going to transform an abstract work of art into movement, followed by weaving these movements together into a dance form of your choice. Single movements and short movement sequences are not dance, however. By learning to create dances made up of concept-based movements, you can also use dance as a teaching tool in your classes.

To begin this exercise, look at the abstract work of art in Figure 4.12. This work was created as an ab-

Figure 4.12.   Abstract artwork based on the book Clara and the Freedom Quilt. *Photo by Anna Newell. Cut paper design by author.*

straction of how Clara, the slave girl, may have felt as she escaped through the forest surrounding her plantation. The tall, thin rectangular shapes set at right angles to the bottom of the design are brown and represent the trees in the forests through which Clara and her friend traveled. The small triangular shapes set alongside the upper portion of the tree shapes are also brown. The thin, triangular shapes reaching diagonally upward from the bottom of the design stand for Clara's fear of leaving home and striking out into the unknown. These shapes are a dark red. The empty circles near the center are black and emphasize Clara's sense of a void in the unknown. The solid half circles alongside the trees are also black and communicate how alone Clara must have felt as she traveled to the north.

Begin by creating a number of different movements based on the story and on aspects of Figure 4.12. These movements will be the materials for your dance. Then, select one of the dance forms, and decide how you can shape the movements you have created into this form. Remember, the arrangement of movements you create for your dance should represent the relationships or patterns and overall composition you see in this design. The form of your dance should also be connected to the meaning or meanings you experience.

CONSIDERING YOUR ACCOMPANIMENT

While it is possible to create and perform dances without music, students usually prefer to move with some type of accompaniment. The problem is selecting appropriate music. For beginners, use music that has a steady beat and a recognizable meter such as 4/4 or 3/4 time. Such accompaniment helps performers stay together because they can easily count out each section of a dance. Also, choose a relatively short piece of music that complements the feelings or ideas communicated in a dance. Drum music was used for the rainforest dance, and a slow, lonely-sounding tune accompanied the dance about Clara. Whatever your music, it is important to understand its structure. This means knowing how many counts or measures are in each section of the music and being aware of points at which the music changes in feeling or tone. A list of music resources is included in the appendix.

SUMMARY AND CONCLUSIONS

Although single movements are used to help students understand academic concepts, single movements are not dance. Dance happens when movements are connected together so dancers can perform actions without disrupting the flow of the dance. There are many ways movement can be formed into dances, so it is important to select a form that fits the meaning(s) of lesson content. Thus, the series form is more appropriate for a dance about the alphabet because students perform the letter shapes in an order that is the same as the order of letters in the alphabet. A tableau fits a lesson on the visual arts because the lines and shapes are present in a painting at the same place and time. The AB form is an excellent form for comparing two different stages in the life of a person because the AB has two sections that fit together yet differ in tone.

When time permits, students should create their own concept-based movements and dances. Doing creative work provides students with feelings of satisfaction and accomplishment and teaches them to solve problems. Learning to think creatively should be included in the school day because it is much different than rote learning. Creative thinking is a higher-order thinking skill that can be applied to other endeavors. There are similarities between making a dance and writing a story. Even though one is composed of movements and the other is composed of words, both result from creative thought. Creative thinking can lead to new inventions, solve some of the world's problems, and is essential for those who live in a democracy. Although dances created by young students may not look like works of art, they are a proving ground for nurturing creativity and for practicing problem-solving skills.

Using movement and dance to teach academics is related to many educational theories. By learning concept-based movements, children actively participate in class—a goal achieved to a greater degree when students create movements and dances. Using movement as a teaching tool also involves tactile-kinesthetic, visual, and auditory learning styles. Dance making is multisensory and imaginative and appeals to human intelligences, such as bodily-kinesthetic, musical, logical-mathematical, and spatial. When teams of students make dances, interpersonal intelligence and cooperative learning come into the picture. Movement-based teaching can be used to teach both younger and older students as well. In addition, movement-based teaching, particularly dance making, fits the brain-mind principles outlined by the Caines because creating dances means arranging concept-based movements into patterns or relationships.

REVIEWING YOUR KNOWLEDGE AND UNDERSTANDING

Consider the information in this chapter and the first three chapters when answering these questions. Think about how each question relates to the other questions as well:

1. How do dance and movement used as a teaching tool relate to the zone of proximal development theory?
2. Do dance and movement used as a teaching tool connect with diverse learning styles and different forms of intelligence?
3. How can dance making involve students in cooperative learning?
4. Does dance making used as a teaching strategy connect with brain-based learning?
5. Describe several benefits of doing creative work in the classroom.
6. Are there any similarities between dance making and doing other types of creative work? Please explain your answer.
7. Explain how a text-based dance can help students learn in reading class.
8. The series dance was a dance form described in this chapter. What kinds of academic concepts might best be taught using a series dance?
9. What types of academic concepts can best be taught using the tableau dance form?
10. What types of academic concepts can best be taught using problem-solving dances?
11. How would you use the AB, rondo, or theme and variations dance forms to teach academic concepts? Describe the academic concepts you want to teach, and then explain how these concepts can be incorporated in the dance form you have selected.

NOTES

1. E. Paul Torrance, "Reflection on Emerging Insights on the Educational Psychology of Creativity," in *The Educational Psychology of Creativity*, ed. John C. Houtz (Cresskill, NJ: Hampton Press, 2003), 273–286.

2. Berenice Bleedorn, *An Education Track for Creativity and Other Quality Thinking Processes* (Lanham, MD: Scarecrow Press, 2003), 13.

3. Ruth S. Hubbard, *A Workshop of the Possible: Nurturing Children's Creative Development* (York, ME: Stenhouse, 1996).

4. Michael Michalko, *Cracking Creativity: The Secrets of Creative Genius* (Berkeley, CA: Ten Speed Press, 2001).

5. Mark Reardon and Seth Derner, *Strategies for Great Teaching: Maximize Learning Moments* (Chicago: Zephyr Press, 2004).

6. Elaine B. Johnson, *Contextual Teaching and Learning: What It Is and Why It's Here to Stay* (Thousand Oaks, CA: Corwin Press, 2002).

7. Elliot W. Eisner, *The Arts and the Creation of Mind* (New Haven, CT: Yale University Press, 2002).

8. James Battle, *Culture-Free Self-Esteem Inventories* (Austin, TX: Pro-Ed, 1992).

9. Sandra C. Minton, "Assessment of High School Dance Students' Self-Esteem," *Journal of Dance Education* 1, no. 2 (2001): 63–73.

10. Carol M. Press, *The Dancing Self: Creativity, Modern Dance, Self Psychology, and Transformative Education* (Cresskill, NJ: Hampton Press, 2002).

11. Sandra C. Minton, *Choreography: A Basic Approach Using Improvisation*, 3rd ed. (Champaign, IL: Human Kinetics, 2007).

12. Emily Dickinson, "XXXVII," in *The Selected Poems of Emily Dickinson*, ed. The Modern Library (New York: Random House, 1996), 108–109.

13. Minton, *Choreography*.

14. Minton, *Choreography*.

15. David A. Adler, *A Picture Book of Abraham Lincoln* (New York: Scholastic, 1989).

16. Deborah Hopkinson, *Sweet Clara and the Freedom Quilt* (New York: Alfred A. Knopf, 1993).

17. Minton, *Choreography*.

18. Marc Tolon Brown, *Arthur's Pet Business* (Boston: Little, Brown & Co., 1990).

19. Minton, *Choreography*.

20. Betsy Maestro and Giulio Maestro, *The Story of the Statue of Liberty* (New York: Lothrop, Lee, and Shepard Books, 1986).

21. Margaret Sedeen, *Star-Spangled Banner: Our Nation and Its Flag* (Washington, DC: National Geographic Society, 1993).

CHAPTER 5

Learning to Connect Dance Making and Thinking

You have been working with movement discovery and dance making for the purpose of transforming concepts into actions, followed by combining these movements together to create dances—a teaching strategy called active learning. The teaching strategies of movement transformation and dance making demonstrate how educational theories, such as multiple intelligences, can be used in the classroom. Movement transformation and dance making also help students learn to solve problems in a creative way. By having students transform concepts into movement and make these movements into dances, you are also encouraging students to think in many different ways.

Robert and Michele Root-Bernstein describe what they call thinking tools in their book *Sparks of Genius: The Thirteen Thinking Tools of the World's Most Creative People*. This book was written after many years of research on how creative people from many fields, including the arts, science, and industry, think when doing creative work. The thinking tools described by the Root-Bernsteins include observing, imaging, abstracting, recognizing patterns, forming patterns, analogizing, body thinking, empathizing, dimensional thinking, modeling, playing, transforming, and synthesizing.[1] When you work with movement transformation and dance making, you and your students also use the thinking tools.

Eleven of the thinking tools described by the Root-Bernsteins serve as the basis for a discussion that connects these tools to the creative process in dance. I have chosen, however, to discuss the thinking tools in a different order than the order used by the Root-Bernsteins. This new order fits the stages outlined in the creative movement framework more closely (see Figure 3.23). Each of the thinking tools is defined, followed by an example of the connection between the thinking tool, movement transformation, and dance making. You will also have a chance to practice movement transformation and dance making in conjunction with the thinking tools.

PARALLELS BETWEEN DANCE MAKING AND CREATIVE THINKING

The framework for dance making begins with an inspiration or input from the environment. In our case, the inspiration is an academic concept. Some writers who describe creative work in dance use the word *stimulus* for input that initiates creative work, but I have been using the word *inspiration* in recent years because it fits with language used in the arts and is more universal. An inspiration can come in many forms—visual, auditory, tactile, or kinesthetic—but it is your feeling response to the inspiration that initiates the transformation process. Keep in mind as well that the framework for transforming concepts into movement is tied to abstraction. When using a literal process to transform concepts into movement, you simply move, shape, or position your body like the concept. You have already used many concepts or inspirations as the starting point for creating movement.

Observing and Recognizing Patterns

Ruth Hubbard indicated that observation can be used in the classroom to help students remember information. She said that when observation is used along with writing and reflection, students are more likely to remember what they have observed. For example, students can observe the life cycle of a butterfly by watching the metamorphosis of a caterpillar into a live butterfly. In addition, by writing down their observations in a journal and then reflecting on them, students are able to describe this process with their own words. This makes the learning process more personal, reinforcing the ability to remember information. Hubbard believes that learning information by focusing on processes in a personal way leads to deeper memory.[2]

In *Sparks of Genius*, the Root-Bernsteins write that all knowledge begins with observation. Artists must learn to observe in a way that enables them to see what others do not. The two authors also point out that the way we think alters what we observe because we are more likely to observe in more detail what is more important to us. This means there is an intimate connection between how we think and how we observe. Truly talented observers continue to learn to observe in new and different ways throughout life.[3] The artist Georgia O'Keeffe is known for her huge paintings of flowers—paintings that were created only after a period of careful observation. Through her flower paintings, O'Keeffe makes us aware of the parts of a flower, patterns or relationships between these parts, areas of shade and light, and subtle variations in color—details that we may not notice on our own.

To begin movement transformation, an inspiration—in this case a concept or idea—is observed in detail and from many viewpoints. For example, when painters portray a body of water, they observe its colors, textures, movements, or the play of light and dark on its surface. The painter may also look at objects or animals that float on the water or those that disappear in its depths. Observing can lead to recognizing patterns, too. In the example of observing water, you usually see a series of waves that form a repetitive pattern of over and under curves. In fact, a series of over and under curves are a common symbol used to represent waves. You may also observe more than one bird floating on the water, and together, they form a relationship or pattern. In Figure 5.1, the series of waves are arranged in semicircular patterns, while the top and bottom flat boats mark the four corners of a parallelogram—another type of pattern.

One trait of keen observation is recognizing patterns. According to the Root-Bernsteins, when we recognize patterns, we identify general principles in what we perceive; later, we form expectations based on these pat-

Figure 5.1. *How many patterns do you see in this abstract work of art?* Photo by Anna Newell. Cut paper design by author.

terns and connect new observations to them.[4] Recognizing patterns provides us with a way to make sense out of nonsense or out of the multitude of sensations that bombard us. For instance, if I hear a siren and see smoke in the sky, experience tells me that the two events are connected and a pattern or relationship exists. I say to myself that the siren is from a fire engine racing to put out the fire that is making the smoke. Building facades are often designed with patterns in mind; music is composed based on auditory patterns; and movements are organized into patterns in dances. Information in textbooks is also grouped into related areas or patterns to make the information more meaningful.

Pattern recognition can be used to aid learning in many subjects. For example, in botany lessons, different plants are placed in groups based on their structure or on the climate in which they grow. For this reason, succulents have thick, rounded leaves; conifers have needles; and deciduous plants have flat leaves. In addition, cattails grow in swampy areas, cacti in deserts, and seaweed in large bodies of water. Once we learn the characteristics of each group of plants or the characteristics of the climate in which they grow, we come to understand why certain plants are in a particular group. In other words, we learn about the plants by recognizing relevant patterns that relate to and describe them.

Pattern recognition can be elusive, though. The Root-Bernsteins indicate it is sometimes possible to observe more than one pattern in a picture by focusing on different points in the visual field.[5] You can experience this phenomenon by looking at Figure 5.2 using two different viewpoints. First, focus on the upper left corner of this figure. When focusing here, you should see two heads atop a black draped body. Next, focus on the middle of this figure. Here you should see three heads, one of which seems to encompass the other two. The small bottom head also appears to be wearing a sailor's cap, while the hair on the top small head streams behind it in the wind. I think you will agree that you must change your point of view in order to see each of these heads clearly because simply staring at the entire picture makes it difficult to see any of the faces in detail. The Root-Bernsteins warn that observing patterns requires a certain amount of time or dawdling as the observer slowly explores how different aspects of the sensory field fit together.[6]

Betty Edwards, who was a visual arts professor for many years, developed a system of teaching drawing

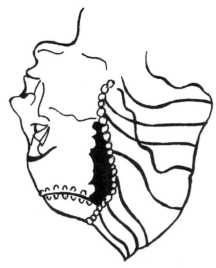

Figure 5.3. Can you see a number of relationships between the lines and shapes in this drawing?

based on identifying patterns or relationships. She has an exercise in her book *The New Drawing on the Right Side of Brain* in which she instructs the reader to copy an upside-down drawing of a seated man. At first, you might think this task is impossible, but Edwards suggests this picture can be copied by first observing certain details, such as whether the lines are straight or curved. She also encourages the reader to observe relationships between parts of the picture, the distance between parts of the picture and the edge of the paper, and directional relationships between various lines.[7] Look carefully at the drawing in Figure 5.3. How many different patterns or relationships can you see between the lines and shapes in this drawing?

At this point, you should begin to see that there are similarities between the movement components described earlier and observation and pattern recognition. When you observe a movement, you notice its direction, level, size, timing, duration, quality, shape, and pathway. Then, when you recognize relationships between these components, you are recognizing patterns as well. For instance, the rhythm component is based on temporal relationships. By noting the amount of time between various actions, you recognize a particular rhythmic pattern. The position component is also based on such relationships as over, under, around, and through. When we see one body shape is over another and the two shapes are also positioned next to a third shape, we recognize a triangular pattern (see Figure 5.4). Transforming concepts into movements requires

Figure 5.2. Can you look at this abstract work using one viewpoint and then another? Photo by Anna Newell. Figure 8.1 (p. 123) of *Dance, Mind, and Body*, by S. C. Minton. Champaign, IL: Human Kinetics, 2003, © 2003 Sandra Cerny Minton. Reprinted with permission from Human Kinetics.

Figure 5.4.   Can you see the triangular pattern made by the three dancers? Photo by Anna Newell.

Figure 5.5.   Front view of the shell. Photo by Anna Newell.

Figure 5.6.   Top view of the shell. Photo by Anna Newell.

Figure 5.7.   Back view of the shell. Photo by Anna Newell.

careful observation of the concept in terms of seeing details and recognizing patterns.

Teaching Using Observation and Pattern Recognition

Learning through movement and dance begins with detailed observation. This means you have to look carefully and analyze a concept before attempting to transform the concept into movement. The first following exploration is a sample of some of the details you will be expected to observe. After you have read through this sample exploration, go through the same process of observation and analysis in the other three explorations. Keep a notebook within easy reach so you can jot down what you have observed. These inspirations are from three subject matter areas of math, reading, and science:

1. Look closely at the three photos in Figures 5.5, 5.6, and 5.7. As you look at these photos, you should notice the shell is more than one shade of gray. It also has a rough or bumpy surface, and there are some dark splotches sprinkled over this surface. Some of the lines on the surface of the shell are wavy. The outline of the shell is punctuated with arms or spikes of different lengths that reach or curve out into space, while the opening looks like a gaping hole or open mouth.

2. Now, look at Figures 5.8, 5.9, 5.10, and 5.11, and observe each of these inspirations in detail. Do not forget to write down all your observations. Figure 5.8 is a set of overlapping geometric shapes;

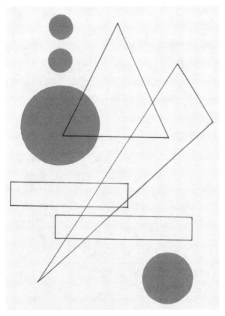

Figure 5.8.   Mathematics inspiration in the form of different geometric shapes. **Design by author.**

The

boat	**the**	**blue**
sailed	**land**	**red**
into	**pond** green	**waves**
yellow	**sunset**	**onto**

Figure 5.9.   Reading and writing inspiration.

Figure 5.10.   Science inspiration in the form of two different kinds of plants (cont.). **Photos by author.**

Figure 5.11.   (cont.) Science inspiration in the form of two different kinds of plants. **Photos by author.**

Figure 5.9 is an arrangement of words on a page; and Figures 5.10 and 5.11 are photos of two different types of plants.

3. Next, you are going to consider how to recognize patterns. In the shell photo, there are many different patterns. One of these is the almost perfect circle or mouth that can be seen in Figure 5.5. From this same view, we can see that the spines surrounding the mouth create a series of scallops when viewed together in a sequence one after the other. Let your eyes trace continuously from one spike to the next one without stopping, and you will see the series of scallops. The top of the shell, Figure 5.6, looks like a person's head; there appears to be a hat sitting on top of the head, and you can also see the top of the person's nose protruding forward. The two spikes or spines sticking out to the side resemble a girl's hair blowing in the wind. From the back of the shell, Figure 5.7, the wavy lines on the surface are somewhat parallel, while the outline of the entire shell forms a lopsided diamond.

4. Identify the patterns you see in Figures 5.8, 5.9, 5.10, and 5.11. Then, write a description of each of these patterns. The Root-Bernsteins point out that pattern recognition can be elusive depending

on your point of focus. Look at the same four photos again, but shift your point of focus. Did you notice different patterns when you shifted your viewpoint? Edwards talks about identifying patterns in what you see by observing relationships between visual details. Seeing in this way is a more global or holistic way of observing. The opposite way of observing is to ignore relationships and look at one detail at a time in a sequential or linear manner. Look at Figures 5.8, 5.9, 5.10, and 5.11 again by relating one part of each figure to another. Are you able to find more patterns by doing this?

Empathizing and Body Thinking

Let's return to the framework for transforming concepts or inspirations into movement. Observation of the concept leads to a response on the part of the individual doing the observing. In most cases, the response is based on personal feelings. The Root-Bernstein have used the term *empathizing* instead of the words *feeling response* to describe this occurrence. They state that practitioners of many of the arts, sciences, and humanistic professions use empathy because it enables them to understand in a way not attainable through any other means. Humans, the Root-Bernsteins believe, use empathy to connect with and understand both animate beings and inanimate objects. Empathizing goes beyond simply understanding because it is an integral part of the creative process.

The Root-Bernsteins provide many examples of the role that feeling or empathizing plays in creative work. They explain that Charles Kettering, who was director of research at General Motors, instructed his engineers to imagine what it feels like to be a piston in an engine they were designing. The authors also describe the creative process used by Alexander Graham Bell as he learned how to educate the deaf. To solve this instructional problem, Bell became a deaf mute in his mind so that he could experience how it felt to have this condition. At other times, Bell became part of the machine he was designing.[8]

Emotional intelligence has been identified as one of the keys to success in life.[9] In the book *Primal Leadership*, Daniel Goleman, Richard Boyatzis, and Annie McKee state that great leadership works through emotions because success depends on *how* a leader leads by driving and directing the emotions of those who follow. Many potential leaders talk about having a strategy, vision, and ideas, but emotion seems to be the governing force.[10] Certainly, our emotions are key to successful social interactions and healthy relationships. The ability to tune into one's emotions is also important to learning. According to Eric Jensen, we are inundated with information daily through television, radio, and the Internet, but it is human emotions that help us select what we need to learn from the vast array of input.[11] We willingly learn input that is important to us or about which we have positive feelings. Our emotions help us construct meaning from this information as well.

Feelings are also an important part of the educational process in a more specific way. James Byrnes writes that a class should be designed so that positive emotions are connected to achievement or learning. On the other hand, if emotions are too intense, they capture the students' attention and take attention away from materials to be learned. If learning is to occur, students must feel safe, positive, and as though what is being learned is connected to personal goals. When the classroom environment causes negative emotions, such as anxiety or fear, or lesson content seems irrelevant, these emotions intervene and disrupt learning. In fact, in the face of negative feelings, students will get more pleasure or have more positive feelings from behaving in a disruptive way rather than focusing on lesson content.[12]

But feelings are not simply of the mind because we feel with our bodies as well—something you have been doing in the exploration experiences. The Root-Bernsteins call this process "body thinking." Body thinking depends on our sense of muscle movement, posture, balance, and touch. Body thinking is used by actors to help create a character and by dancers to assist them in performing a role.[13] Body thinking is second nature to most people and occurs daily on a subconscious level. Think about the tension you feel in your muscles when you are angry or the relaxed sensation you experience in these same muscles following a day spent hiking in the mountains or strolling along a beach. Because body thinking occurs subconsciously, we tend to forget about body feelings and take them for granted. Body thinking, however, is a very important part of sensing and responding to our world.

Antonio Damasio, head of the Department of Neurology at the University of Iowa, connected mind and body when he said that feeling is a perception of a certain state of the body. According to Damasio, feelings do not simply appear in the mind but are the mental essence of a bodily reaction. If feelings were merely thoughts in the mind, Damasio continues, we would not be able to distinguish them from other types of thoughts. In fact, if the bodily essence of a feeling is removed, the feeling vanishes too.[14] For example, after a bad night's sleep, our body feels tired and sluggish. We may not think clearly, tend to be irritable, and experience negative feelings about a day's events. However, after a good night's sleep, our body feels better, and we are refreshed, positive, and energized to begin the day.

Ralph Adolphs and several colleagues investigated the underpinnings of empathy. In one of their studies, subjects had to describe their empathetic response to photographs of individuals with a particular emotion on their faces. To do this, the subjects had to put themselves in the other person's shoes. While most subjects could identify the emotions correctly, the subject who could not had brain damage affecting the amygdala (see Figure 5.12).[15] The amygdala is relevant to all hu-

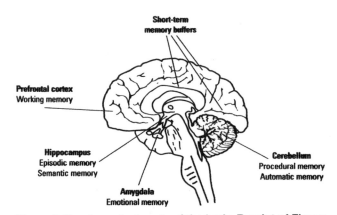

Figure 5.12.   Important parts of the brain. Reprint of Figure 4.1 (p. 55) from *Learning and Memory: The Brain in Action* by Marilee Sprenger, Alexandria, VA: Association for Supervision and Curriculum Development, 1999. Used with permission. The Association for Supervision and Curriculum Development (ASCD) is a worldwide community of educators advocating sound policies and sharing best practices to achieve the success of each learner. To learn more, visit ASCD at www.ascd.org.

man information transmission and screens input to determine its emotional importance to long-term memory.[16] Kinesthetic feedback is, of course, one form of incoming information. The amygdala also triggers alarm-related behaviors and the accompanying body changes of the flight-or-fight reaction. These body changes can refine our interpretation of an emotion and may influence our memories.[17]

In one of his books, Jensen said that the kinesthetic arts, which include dance, can play a powerful role in representing the world symbolically because they are a universal language. In fact, if used under the right conditions, dance and the other kinesthetic arts can become a teaching tool that enhances learning. One of the reasons dance can be used as a teaching tool is because movement affects the brain in many ways, and most of the brain in activated during physical activity.[18]

Jensen also states that there are two basic types of learning: labeled learning, which includes what we read, write, and talk about, and classroom activities that are hands-on and involve trial and error, role playing, problem solving, and life experiences. Many researchers now think active learning is more reliable than the old style of classroom teaching because it has been proven to be more robust and have greater effects that last for a longer period of time. Active learning is also age independent because it can be used at kindergarten through university level, provides for ease of learning, facilitates cross-cultural learning, and is independent of a student's IQ.[19] Although hands-on learning can be very effective, it can be messy when compared to a traditional classroom approach in which students remain seated at their desks. Increased activity can be a problem for students who lack self-control or who cannot work in groups.

The body thinking described by the Root-Bernsteins is dependent on the proprioceptors of the kinesthetic sense, which are described in more detail in Chapter 7. Jensen outlines how the proprioceptors provide a mind–body link when the brain creates movements by sending nerve impulses to the right muscles. Each movement in turn activates specific areas in the brain so that connections between brain and body are a two-way street. Simple movements, like chewing gum, are controlled by circuits nearest the spinal cord and influence a few systems. More complicated actions, like drumming, are controlled at other areas below the cerebral cortex, such as the basil ganglia and cerebellum, while highly complex actions involve most of the brain because such movements require making rapid decisions, maintaining attention, keeping track of feelings, remembering past experiences, and being alert to and solving problems on the run.[20]

The kinesthetic sense is also intimately connected to emotion and feeling because physical sensations, such as tension or relaxation, are the basis of different emotions. Dance instructors have long acknowledged the importance of the kinesthetic sense in developing their students' movement skills. To this end, when beginners learn a new movement, they must pay attention to feedback from their bodies that results from moving.[21] Such internal or proprioceptive feedback is one type of information that is used to become a skilled mover.[22] In their book *Teaching Dance Skills*, Marliese Kimmerle and Paulette Cote-Laurence point out that one way to learn dance skills is to pay attention to body information and describe how various actions feel when each is performed correctly.[23] The body awareness described by Kimmerle and Cote-Laurence is the same body awareness that is part of the feeling response in the creative movement framework. Increased body awareness helps students develop movement skills, and body awareness enables students to use movement as an expressive tool in creative work. In addition, when movement discovery and dance making are used to help teach academic concepts, body awareness becomes important in all learning.

But how does movement figure in the connection between learning, the kinesthetic sense, and our emotions? Jensen states that movement in and of itself can create positive feelings because it releases the chemicals noradrenaline and dopamine in the brain. Consequently, by moving, students usually feel better about themselves. The generation of positive feelings in turn gives students control over how they feel.[24] As indicated earlier, students who have positive feelings will also be more likely to pay attention in the classroom and be actively engaged in the learning. Movement used as a teaching tool, particularly when it is used in creative problem solving, also gives students feelings of control because they have a chance to solve problems in their own unique way.

Teaching Using Empathizing and Body Thinking

You can empathize with or explore your feelings about the shell in Figures 5.5, 5.6, and 5.7 as well. Remember, to empathize means to describe how the textures, lines, and shapes seen on the shell make you feel.

When I look at Figure 5.5, the spines on the shell appear to be stretching out into space. It is almost as if the shell has a multitude of grasping or reaching arms. The gaping mouth feels as if it is the doorway to some unknown place deep within the shell. It adds a feeling of mystery to the shell. The mollusk that lived in the shell must have felt protected when it retreated deep inside. From Figure 5.6, I get a feeling of endless spiraling, twisting, or turning. This makes me feel dizzy. Finally, in Figure 5.7, the face of the shell can be seen from the back, and it appears to be peering at me. The jagged outline of the shell seen in this view, however, has an exploding feeling to it.

What feelings do you have as you look at Figures 5.8, 5.9, 5.10, and 5.11? Be sure to write down a detailed description of each feeling you experience. Being able to connect emotions or feelings to body or kinesthetic sensations is an important part of being able to transform academic concepts into movement. If you can make this connection, you will be engaging in what the Root-Bernsteins describe as body thinking. In order to think with your body, you will need to decide how each emotion you experience feels in your muscles. Personally, if I am fearful, my muscles feel tense or may even vibrate, and if I feel calm, my muscles are loose and relaxed. In addition, it may help to choose only two or three of the feelings you experience rather than trying to work with all of the feelings you describe. The two or three feelings you work with should be those that are the strongest or clearest for you as well.

The reaching feeling seen in the spines on the shell in Figure 5.5 feels wide and relaxed in my body. The mysteriousness of the gaping mouth makes my body shrink and get smaller. The dizziness of the spiral on the top of the shell leads to a small, circular, nodding sensation in my head and neck, while the exploding feeling of the spines on the shell in Figure 5.7 makes my body feel huge and expansive.

How does your feeling response to Figures 5.8, 5.9, 5.10, and 5.11 make your muscles feel?

Imaging

Imaging is a skill used by many people to a varying degree. Most people use some form of imaging to help them process input from their surroundings. Writers observe life and daily events and then use their imagination to craft a story before putting pen to paper. Architects are keen observers of the shapes and forms found in nature, but they must have a vision in mind before beginning to draft plans for a building. Those who decorate cakes are sensitive to line and design and need to imagine colors and shapes before applying the frosting to a cake. Finally, photographers, who are also keen observers of the environment, must visualize what a scene will look like before snapping a photo.

In his book, Michael Michalko describes what takes place in the mind when people engage in creative thinking. Using Einstein as an example, Michalko says that the famous scientist thought in images rather than words. Michalko continues that by thinking in images, people are able to remember details more easily. According to Michalko, creative problem solving is also facilitated by using images because creative individuals can visualize and see parts of the solution beforehand.[25] In their book, the Root-Bernsteins describe how different inventors used imaging to visualize an invention in their minds before constructing it. Some of these inventors were even able to use visual imaging to change the structure of an invention, improve upon it, and try out the device before physically putting it together.[26]

Dance imagery is a tool used to help students develop movement skills because images enable them to get inside movement and find the right body feeling needed for correct execution. In his book *Dance Imagery for Technique and Performance*, Eric Franklin makes many connections between using appropriate imagery and achieving body awareness. Franklin explains that the more interesting dancers are the ones who really experience or are aware of their movements. Dance expression, Franklin notes comes from the physical experiencing of moving. Franklin continues that a skillful use of imagery is a primary method for increasing body awareness or the awareness of what movements feel like in the body.[27]

In this book, the interest is in how imaging facilitates the process of transforming academic concepts into movement. Remember, in the framework for transforming concepts into movement (Figure 3.23), there is a feeling response to the inspiration or concept first, followed by tapping into the imagination, memories, and past experiences. If you are interested in transforming the concept of rain into movement, you can focus on your current observations of rain and tune into your feelings about the observations. Then, you can see images of rain in your mind. Next, you can extend and elaborate on your feelings and memories by using your imagination again to produce movement. Imaging is also an integral part of the dance-making process because usually dance making is preceded by seeing or imagining the dance or parts of the dance in your mind before it takes shape.

The Root-Bernsteins point out that imaging can be multisensory or polysensual because it is possible to imagine sounds or music and kinesthetic sensations as well as seeing visual images in your mind.[28] To return to the example of rain, it is not only possible to see images of the rain in your mind, but you can imagine the sounds of falling rain and conjure up sensations of how rain feels as it touches your skin. In fact, dance itself is multisensual. Judith Lynne Hanna, who has taught, written about, and researched dance for many years, states that the multisensory nature of dance is evident from the sight of dancers moving; the sounds of their physical movements; the smell of their physical exertion; the tactile sensation of bodies touching bodies, objects, or the floor; and the kinesthetic sensation of movement.[29]

In dance, the multisensory nature of imaging usually includes visual and kinesthetic images, although auditory images are sometimes used. Visual imaging means having a picture in your mind, while kinesthetic imaging refers to the body feeling or feelings that accompany moving. Lynnette Overby, who has studied dance imagery for many years, states that images can also be direct or indirect. The visual and kinesthetic images described earlier are direct. Indirect images are like mental rehearsal.[30] When using indirect visual imagery, performers see themselves doing an action in the mind before actually performing a movement. Indirect kinesthetic imaging means previewing body feelings that accompany the actual performance of an action.[31]

Imaging is extremely important to movement-based learning strategies because visual and kinesthetic imagery are related to the movement components discussed in Chapter 1. Being able to see an image of directions, shapes, or pathways in your mind before transforming a concept into such actions helps you match concept and action. Quality and rhythm are more closely related to kinesthetic imaging because they are difficult to picture in your mind, but you can imagine how they would feel in your body. Consider the different body feelings that come to mind when you think about sustained movement in comparison to the body feelings you imagine while thinking about vibratory actions.

Teaching Using Imaging

Imagery can relate to the different senses—visual, auditory, tactile, or kinesthetic. In this set of explorations, you will describe various images that come to mind as you focus on each concept or inspiration. I recommend finding a quiet place in which you can sit or lie down with your eyes closed. Playing soft, meditative music may also help to increase your ability to concentrate on any images that come to mind.[32]

1. Let's begin by focusing on images that are based on the three views of the shell. First, the reaching and stretching feeling of the spines in Figure 5.5 makes me imagine a young child who is looking and searching for something. In association with the gaping mouth, I see the visual image of an endless pit, while I hear a high-pitched shrieking sound echoing off the sides of the inner recesses of the shell. The spiraling design on the top of the shell (Figure 5.6) brings the kinesthetic image of turning without stopping to mind. In Figure 5.7, the kinesthetic image is shrinking as the face from the back of the shell peers at me, and the many spines reaching outward brings the visual image of fireworks or other types of explosions to mind.
2. Review the feelings and body sensations you experienced when viewing Figures 5.8, 5.9, 5.10, and 5.11. Then, go to a quiet place and concentrate on the images that these feelings and body sensations create in your mind. Remember, images can be visual, auditory, kinesthetic, or tactile.

Transforming and Abstracting

Transformation, particularly abstract transformation, is important to learning because while some learning is concrete, other forms are abstract. Jensen tells us that working with your hands, such as learning to hammer nails in a shop class, is an exact, concrete skill. But learning in school also involves understanding less concrete, more abstract ideas in the form of mathematical formulas and written text. For some students, this abstract world is very difficult to understand because for them, abstract ideas have never been connected to the concrete reality in which they live. A connecting link here, Jensen writes, is the somatic, concrete, and real world of the body.[33] Neurologist Frank Wilson endorses this idea by saying that teachers need to learn how to apply what is now known about biology, the body, and learning physical skills to other types of teaching by uniting, not separating, mind and body.[34]

I remember having difficulty with advanced algebra in high school. Later, I had to study statistics as part of my doctoral work. Unfortunately for me, statistics is filled with formulas that must be manipulated algebraically. To combat my fear, I enrolled in a beginning algebra course at a nearby community college. The professor, who was an excellent teacher, helped me realize that I had been using the wrong method to master algebra. Instead of attempting to understand the abstract logic presented in each equation, I had been thinking in a concrete way by memorizing various equations. Once I understood the abstract nature of manipulating algebraic symbols, I become much more at ease and proficient in working with equations in statistics class. In fact, when I look back on this experience, I would describe the manipulation of algebraic symbols as being movement oriented.

The discussion of abstraction also brings the drawings of young children to mind. Recall the stick figures children use to represent humans or how they draw the sun as a yellow circle with lines extending out from its center. I would venture to say that children's drawings are a form of abstraction because they capture the basic aspects or essence of the subject matter. Elliot Eisner writes that by looking at the drawings of children in the same age group, we can see many similarities. First, children draw simple marks and shapes. Later, they attach figures to a baseline, followed by the use of overlap and location to indicate depth. Some older children are also able to use shading to create an illusion of volume.[35] Although Eisner does not say it, I would like to suggest that the development of children's drawings, and perhaps their perceptual processes as well, appear to progress from the abstract to the more literal or realistic.

It is interesting to note that some of my research has shown a possible connection between abstraction, the body, and movement. In this research, I compared the creative thinking abilities of 286 high school students using the Torrance Test of Creative Thinking.[36] I found that the dance students showed more ability to come up with abstract titles for their drawings than students who were not enrolled in dance classes.[37] In other words, the dance students could think of titles for their drawings that went beyond mere labeling by capturing the essence of their drawings.

The Root-Bernsteins provide many examples in their book of how creative people are able to transform stuff of the imagination into words, equations, inventions, or works of art. The authors also point out that multiple forms of imagery (visual, aural, and kinesthetic) are often used simultaneously by creative individuals as they struggle with the creative transformation process.[38] You have already used the transformation process in some of the explorations as you changed concepts and ideas into movements and body shapes. If you recall, movement transformations can be accomplished in two ways. These two modes of transformation were literal or abstract. When using a literal transformation, you moved like the concept or inspiration or assumed positions or shapes that were part of the concept. Examples of literal transformations are to move in two directions like an alternating current or to shape your body like a letter of the alphabet.

Abstract transformations are more complex and involve extracting the essence of the concept or inspiration and transforming this essence into movement. The essence of a concept can be captured by focusing on the feeling response you have in relation to it. Thus, a body of water can stimulate feelings of fear if your experiences with water included large, crashing waves or calm feelings if the body of water you remember was placid.

The Root-Bernsteins say that abstracting begins with reality but pares away the excess, revealing a critical and often surprising essence of the real. The Root-Bernsteins also state that the process of abstracting is relatively common in our society. We have all read summaries of books or worked with theories that represent a more detailed body of knowledge. The authors also point out that abstracting is rather mysterious and not very well understood. Here, the Root-Bernsteins use the example of an orange to make their point by instructing the reader to create an abstraction of an orange. Most people, they believe, would have some problems with this exercise. According to the two authors, experienced artists and writers often struggle with abstraction as well.[39] Many of my choreography students also struggled when asked to create a movement abstraction of an object, even when this object had personal meaning for them.

Teaching Using Transformation and Abstraction

Now is your chance to get up and move around by transforming imagery into actions through the abstract transformation process. One way to transform imagery into movement is to simply exaggerate the body feelings or kinesthetic images you experienced in the previous explorations. For example, if your body sensation or kinesthetic image is tension, you can exaggerate this sensation by performing pushing or pressing actions. If the body sensation is relaxation, an exaggerated action can be floating or soaring movements:

1. The following movements are based on the different forms of imagery described in Exercise 1 in the section titled "Teaching Using Imaging." The image of the young child searching was transformed into slow, stretching actions performed with both the arms and legs while in a seated position. These slow actions were punctuated by a few fast reaches. The image of the endless pit took the form of a slow, downward-spiraling action. The auditory image of shrieking was transformed into repeatedly opening the mouth and then separating the fingers while having the knees bent. The imagined whirling action evolved into actually turning, while the shrinking and exploding images were transformed into the

following movement sequence: standing, leaning backward slowly, going low to the ground, suddenly bursting outward, and then freezing in the resulting body shape.

2. Review the images that came to mind when you viewed Figures 5.8, 5.9, 5.10, and 5.11 in Exploration 2 in the section titled "Teaching Using Observation and Pattern Recognition." Next, find a space in which you can move. Concentrate on each image one at a time, and let your body begin to move. You should find that the different images cause you to move in different ways. In other words, your use of the movement components will change as you get involved in imaging and the movement discovery process.

Playing and Forming Patterns

The Root-Bernsteins discovered that scientists and artists alike engaged in creative play. They describe how engineer Elmer Sperry, who invented the gyrocompass, ignored information then available in favor of playing with children's toys. Musicians have also been known to perfect their compositions by playing with different arrangements of sounds. According to the Root-Bernsteins, Jean Piaget found that play can enhance thinking skills because it allows us to practice these skills in different ways. The authors also indicate that Piaget found play was a way to experiment with and learn about rules.[40] For instance, such liquids as molasses, water, and mercury have different viscosities. This difference can be demonstrated by playing around and letting each type of liquid run down an inclined plane. Jensen feels that play is the foundation for doing creative work because it is a link between an individual's inner and outer worlds.[41]

Michalko also discusses the connection between creative work and playing around. Creative work, he says, is the result of being able to fantasize possible solutions to problems. According to Michalko, the dynamic aspect of fantasizing is play. Creative geniuses take great delight in fantasizing and playing around with possible solutions to a problem. They are able to wed the childhood activity of play with knowledge and theories found in the adult world.[42]

Hanna indicates that teachers can use student play in a different way. She says that teachers can learn much from observing their students and how they like to dance during times of play. Aside from providing a baseline for dance instruction, such observations can lead to understanding students' personalities, creativeness, and their individual and group identity. Dance at play, Hanna says, is a window on a student's view of the world and a basis for future lesson planning. Teachers can use dance at play as a scaffold for designing movement-based lessons by matching the students' movement style to lesson content.[43]

The Root-Bernsteins also find that forming patterns or relationships is part of creative work in a variety of disciplines. For instance, forming patterns is an important aspect of composing music or creating a painting. Forming patterns is also relevant to understanding the behavior of electromagnetic or water waves in science and is key to discovering complex mathematical calculations. In fact, learning to form patterns is important to discovery and innovation in many fields. The Root-Bernsteins suggest that one way to learn about pattern formation is to select a limited number of words and figure out how many different ways you can put these words together while making sense. Playing with puzzles can also teach pattern-formation skills.[44]

Creative problem solving can involve working with abstract symbols rather than words. Such symbols are frequently combined to form patterns, and when the symbols are manipulated, the patterns change. Michalko says that symbols used in this way form a pattern language. He says that one of the first steps in using pattern language is to determine the major components of a problem, listing as many of these components as possible. Next, Michalko suggests describing each problem component by drawing an abstract symbol to represent it on the front of a card and writing words that describe each component on the back of the card. When the cards are placed on a table so all the symbols are visible, it is possible to create many patterns or arrangements of the symbols. Michalko says that when you see an interesting arrangement of symbols, turn the cards over and create a new sequence of ideas from the written components.[45]

Let's return to the framework for discovering movement pictured in Figure 3.23. Once you have discovered movements based on a concept or inspiration, it is important to experiment or play around with the movements you create. The process of playing around with movement involves arranging and rearranging movements. It also involves varying movements or making more out of less. You have already used such movement components as direction, level, and speed or timing to change or vary actions you created. These changes were made so that you can repeat the same movements in a dance without being redundant. A movement performed in a new direction or at a different level looks different and can be used to extend the movement materials in a dance.

Once you have created a number of movements for a dance, these movements are combined into patterns. Otherwise, the dance simply consists of a series of unrelated movements strung together without any reason or sense of organization. When working with concept-based movements, however, it is important to form the movements into a pattern that communicates the true meaning of a group of concepts. For example, the life cycle of a butterfly begins with an egg that changes into a larva. Next, the larva changes into the chrysalis, from which the adult butterfly emerges. The eggs, larva, chrysalis, and adult butterfly all represent concepts that make up the life cycle. Thus, the pattern created from movements that represent each of these concepts should copy the order that is the same as the order of events in the life cycle. To arrange the movements in another way would be confusing for students.

The idea of pattern language can also be used to create a dance based on a series of words. Simply write a description of the movement representing each word on one side of the cards. Then, draw symbols for the movements on the other side of the cards. Next, arrange and rearrange the symbols to discover how many patterns can be made. Which patterns make sense in terms of the English language?

Consider the concept of permutation. A permutation is an arrangement or the order in which objects are placed. The arrangement can be of books on a shelf, a box of different-colored eggs, or different-colored napkins placed on a table. Take the example of books on a shelf. If different movements are used to represent each book, the challenge is to discover how many ways these movements can be ordered or arranged. An easy way to do this is to use pattern language by writing a symbol for the color of each book on one side of the cards. Next, movements representing each book's color are written on the other side of the cards. Now,

the cards can be arranged and rearranged to discover the number of possible arrangements or patterns. Following this, the movements are performed by copying the order found in the first arrangement, the second one, and so on.

Teaching Using Playing Around and Forming Patterns

Movements can be formed into a variety of patterns by changing the way in which they are arranged, while playing around or experimenting with these arrangements helps you discover a number of different patterns. When movement is used as a teaching tool, however, it is important that the patterns created makes sense in terms of the patterns or relationships found in your inspiration. For example, if you are using different movements to communicate the essence of the planets Mercury, Venus, Earth, and Mars, it is important to have the representative movements arranged in an order that copies the order of the planets in relation to the sun. Playing around can also help you decide how to form your movements into a dance. This means that playing around and forming movements into patterns are the beginning of dance making.

The movements described in Exploration 1 in the section titled "Teaching Using Transformation and Abstraction" can be combined into a number of patterns. A pattern that makes sense in terms of Figure 5.5 would be to begin with the slow and fast stretching actions because these movements are my response to the spines and the spines are on the outside of the shell. Moving from the outside inward, perform the movements that represent the opening on the shell next. The last movement in this pattern would be the slow, downward spiral because this action represents the inside or depths of the shell. Taken together, the movement pattern can be described as four slow arm movements that reach away from the center of the body (eight counts); two quick arm reaches (two counts); open and close the mouth and fingers two times (two counts); and end with the slow downward spiral (four counts).

Now it is your turn to play around with the movements you discovered in Exploration 2 in the section titled "Teaching Using Transformation and Abstraction." The movements you use should be based only on Figure 5.8, 5.9, or 5.10 and 5.11. Do not mix movements in the same pattern that are based on different figures, and be sure to create patterns that make sense in terms of each inspiration. Have some fun playing around with the movements that you have selected by creating a number of different patterns. You may want to try Michalko's idea of pattern language to help you create movement patterns. To do this, write a description of each of your movements on one side of a card, and draw a symbol representing that movement on the opposite side. Then, arrange and rearrange the symbols to create a number of patterns. Finally, select the pattern that is the most meaningful in terms of teaching the targeted concepts.

Modeling and Synthesizing

The Root-Bernsteins write that a model can be created only after the creator becomes immersed in the real system or situation. Then and only then is it possible to abstract the critical features of the situation and rescale or reform these features into verbal, artistic, or mathematical models. In the case of science or mathematics, once the model is constructed, its accuracy can be determined by playing or experimenting with it.[46] In the case of a work of art, such as a dance, the creator evaluates his or her work and may rearrange or delete parts of it as a result.

The idea that a dance is a model of what one knows about an inspiration can be related to the larger sphere of knowledge and language acquisition. Noam Chomsky, who revolutionized the study of language development, created a model-oriented theory of knowledge acquisition. Chomsky writes that our perceptions are guided by notions that originate in the mind, and these notions provide a framework for interpreting sensory input. To create his model-oriented theory Chomsky returns to the work of Wilhelm von Humboldt, who states that mind is a system of rules that generates models and schemata when stimulated by our senses. It is this system of rules that determines how we perceive our world.[47] These rules shape our knowledge base, help us create patterns between parts of our knowledge base, and aid in constructing mental models.

The Root-Bernsteins state that synthesizing is the culminating result of transformational thinking because sensory impressions, feelings, knowledge, and memories come together in a unified way. Synthesiz-

ing also involves immersing oneself in an experience and connecting its many aspects to what we already know. The Root-Bernsteins use the word *synosia* to describe this combining of sensations, feelings, memories, and rational thoughts. They find that many creative people are synesthetic thinkers. The authors conclude this discussion by stating that synosia will be needed to solve many of the world's problems because these problems cannot be solved through the efforts of one person or even of one discipline alone. Instead, innovations that are interdisciplinary and multimodal will enable us to find solutions by integrating all ways of knowing.[48]

The final step in using movement to teach academic concepts is to bring your movements together in a way that meshes to create a whole or synthesis. While each separate movement in the dance is a model of an individual concept, a whole dance is a model of the relationships between a group of concepts. In other words, while a dance has a sense of development from beginning to end and while the movements fit together to make a whole, the arrangement of movements should form a model that represents relationships that exist in the subject matter being studied.

A final comment needs to be made about the framework for movement transformation in Figure 3.23. This framework involves an inspiration; the creator's feeling response to the inspiration; and involvement of the creator's imagination, memories, and experiences resulting in movements that are an abstraction of the inspiration. When these movements are combined, a whole dance is created. The progression through dance making is not linear, however, but circular because there is an interplay between the creator's inner and outer experiences during dance making.

Alma Hawkins, a 20th-century leader in dance education, describes this inner–outer experience as a forward–backward process.[49] When someone creates a dance, they discover many movements, which in turn are measured against the choreographer's inner or kinesthetic feeling of "rightness." The feeling of "rightness" mirrors the inspiration in some way. In addition, the person making the dance then focuses outward because each new movement can spark the discovery of additional actions.[50] In the case of movement and dance used to teach academic concepts, the person making the dance must focus inward to create movement, and then out-

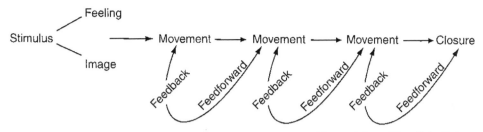

Figure 5.13. *The forward and backward process involved in dance making.* Figure 1 from "Parallels Between Alma Hawkins' Approach to the Creative Process and Contemporary Learning Theory," by Sandra Minton. *Journal of Dance Education* 3, no. 2 (2003): 74–78. Reproduced with permission of J. Michael Ryan Publishing, Inc.

ward focus is needed to make sure the movements are arranged in the dance to represent logical and meaningful relationships. Figure 5.13 illustrates the forward–backward process of creating a dance.

Teaching Using Modeling and Synthesizing

The culmination of my experience with the shell is to weave the movement patterns created together to form a dance. This dance is a whole or synthesis. It is also a movement model of my responses to the defining characteristics and structure of the shell. To a lesser extent, each movement pattern that makes up a dance is a movement model of individual characteristics of the shell. A description of a short dance based on the shell follows.

1. Begin with arms wrapped around the body, legs turned inward, and knees bent.

Pattern 1	Four slow arm movements reaching away from the center of the body (eight counts); two quick arm reaches (two counts); open and close the mouth and fingers two times (two counts); and end with a slow, downward spiral (four counts)
Pattern 2	Repeat the previous pattern (16 counts)
Pattern 3	Whirl, moving from low to high level (eight counts)
Pattern 4	Drop quickly to the ground (2 counts); begin to turn again while rising from ground but stop on Counts 6 and 10 (14 counts)
Pattern 5	Slow lean backward (six counts); explode arms outward (two counts)
Pattern 6	Repeat the previous pattern (eight counts); end in a high, reaching pose.

2. Now is your chance to combine some of the movement patterns you have created to form a dance. The movement patterns were based on Figures 5.8, 5.9, 5.10, and 5.11.

SUMMARY AND CONCLUSIONS

You have been reading about the thinking tools described by the Root-Bernsteins in their book *Sparks of Genius* and how these thinking tools can be part of your teaching strategies. According to these two authors, the thinking tools are used by creative people in a number of different fields as they process, integrate, build on, and reform ideas and information from the outside world. The thinking tools described in the preceding pages included observing, recognizing patterns, empathizing, body thinking, imaging, transforming, abstracting, playing, forming patterns, modeling, and synthesizing. The point here is the thinking tools can be used along with movement and dance to help students understand concepts and ideas because they are an integral part of the movement discovery and dance-making processes; they run in tandem with or parallel to the creative processes used in dance.

In order to transform concepts into movement, it is important to observe the concept in detail and note any patterns that exist. Transforming concepts into movement in a literal way means to move like or shape your body like the concept. When transformation involves abstracting, however, one has a feeling response to the concept. This is also where empathizing and imaging come in. Body thinking, though, is part of both forms of transformation. Body thinking is exaggerated to create movement, and the movements created are a model of the concept. When movements are put together in sequences, forming patterns comes into play. The patterns or relationships between movements must be similar to relationships as they exist in the subject matter being studied. Combining movement sequences together ultimately creates a dance that is both a model of a series of concepts and a synthesis of the concept-based movements.

REVIEWING YOUR KNOWLEDGE AND UNDERSTANDING

1. Describe some of the parallels or similarities that exist between dance making and creative thinking or problem solving. In other words, how can the thinking tools be connected with dance making?

2. What are some of the stages of the creative movement discovery process? Please use the framework for movement discovery in Figure 3.23 when you answer this question.

3. How can creative thinking as it is used in movement discovery and dance making help you teach academic concepts? Answer this question by using an example in which an academic concept is the inspiration or starting point that sets creative problem solving in motion.

4. How can the creative thinking tools of observation and pattern recognition be used to help students understand an academic concept?

5. What role do empathizing and body thinking play in the movement-based creative problem-solving process?

6. Give an example of how you can use imaging and creative problem solving to teach an academic concept.

7. What is the difference between using literal and abstract movement transformations to teach academic concepts?

8. Dance making is also part of the process in which movement is used as a teaching strategy. How can the thinking tools of playing around and forming patterns be used to teach academic concepts and make a dance at the same time?

9. What role do modeling and synthesizing have when dance making is used to help students understand academic concepts?

NOTES

1. Robert Root-Bernstein and Michele Root-Bernstein, *Sparks of Genius: The Thirteen Thinking Tools of the World's Most Creative People* (New York: Houghton Mifflin, 1999).

2. Ruth S. Hubbard, *A Workshop of the Possible: Nurturing Children's Creative Development* (York, ME: Stenhouse, 1996).

3. Root-Bernstein and Root-Bernstein, *Sparks of Genius.*

4. Root-Bernstein and Root-Bernstein, *Sparks of Genius.*

5. Root-Bernstein and Root-Bernstein, *Sparks of Genius.*

6. Root-Bernstein and Root-Bernstein, *Sparks of Genius.*

7. Betty Edwards, *The New Drawing on the Right Side of the Brain* (New York: Tarcher/Putnam, 1999).

8. Root-Bernstein and Root-Bernstein, *Sparks of Genius.*

9. Daniel Goleman, Richard Boyatzis, and Annie McKee, *Primal Leadership: Realizing the Power of Emotional Intelligence* (Boston: Harvard Business School Press, 2002).

10. Goleman, Boyatzis, and McKee, *Primal Leadership.*

11. Eric Jensen, *Arts With the Brain in Mind* (Alexandria, VA: Association for Supervision and Curriculum Development, 2001).

12. James P. Byrnes, *Minds, Brains, and Learning* (New York: Guilford Press, 2001).

13. Root-Bernstein and Root-Bernstein, *Sparks of Genius.*

14. Antonio Damasio, *Looking for Spinoza: Joy, Sorrow, and the Feeling Brain* (Orlando, FL: Harcourt, 2003).

15. Ralph Adolphs, Daniel Tranel, Hanna Damasio, and Antonio Damasio, "Impaired Recognition of Emotion in Facial Expressions Following Bilateral Damage to the Human Amygdala," *Nature* 372 (1994): 669–671.

16. Marilee Sprenger, *Learning and Memory: The Brain in Action* (Alexandria, VA: Association for Supervision and Curriculum Development, 1999).

17. Joseph LeDoux, *Synaptic Self: How Our Brains Become Who We Are* (New York: Viking, 2002).

18. Jensen, *Arts With the Brain in Mind.*

19. Jensen, *Arts With the Brain in Mind.*

20. Jensen, *Arts With the Brain in Mind.*

21. Richard A. Schmidt and Craig A. Wrisberg, *Motor Learning and Performance: A Problem-Based Learning Approach*, 2nd ed. (Champaign, IL: Human Kinetics, 2004).

22. Sprenger, *Learning and Memory*.

23. Marliese Kimmerle and Paulette Cote-Laurence, *Teaching Dance Skills: A Motor Learning and Development Approach* (Andover, NJ: J. Michael Ryan, 2003).

24. Jensen, *Arts With the Brain in Mind*.

25. Michael Michalko, *Cracking Creativity: The Secrets of Creative Genius* (Berkeley, CA: Ten Speed Press, 2001).

26. Root-Bernstein and Root-Bernstein, *Sparks of Genius*.

27. Eric Franklin, *Dance Imagery for Technique and Performance* (Champaign, IL: Human Kinetics, 1996).

28. Root-Bernstein and Root-Bernstein, *Sparks of Genius*.

29. Judith L. Hanna, *Partnering Dance and Education: Intelligent Moves for Changing Times* (Champaign, IL: Human Kinetics, 1999).

30. Lynnette Y. Overby, "The Use of Imagery by Dance Teachers—Development and Implementation of Two Research Instruments," *Journal of Physical Education, Recreation, and Dance* 61, no. 2 (1990): 24–27.

31. Kimmerle and Cote-Laurence, *Teaching Dance Skills*.

32. Sandra C. Minton, *Choreography: A Basic Approach Using Improvisation*, 3rd ed. (Champaign, IL: Human Kinetics, 2007).

33. Jensen, *Arts With the Brain in Mind*.

34. Frank R. Wilson, *Hand: How Its Use Shapes the Brain, Language, and Human Culture* (New York: Pantheon Books, 1998).

35. Elliot W. Eisner, *The Arts and the Creation of Mind* (New Haven, CT: Yale University Press, 2002).

36. E. Paul Torrance, *Torrance Tests of Creative Thinking: Directions Manual Figural Forms A and B* (Bensenville, IL: Scholastic Testing Service, 1990).

37. Sandra Minton, "Assessment of High School Students' Creative Thinking Skills: A Comparison of Dance and Nondance Classes," *Research in Dance Education* 4, no. 1 (2003): 31–49.

38. Root-Bernstein and Root-Bernstein, *Sparks of Genius*.

39. Root-Bernstein and Root-Bernstein, *Sparks of Genius*.

40. Root-Bernstein and Root-Bernstein, *Sparks of Genius*.

41. Jensen, *Arts With the Brain in Mind*.

42. Michalko, *Cracking Creativity*.

43. Hanna, *Partnering Dance and Education*.

44. Root-Bernstein and Root-Bernstein, *Sparks of Genius*.

45. Michalko, *Cracking Creativity*.

46. Root-Bernstein and Root-Bernstein, *Sparks of Genius*.

47. Noam Chomsky, "Language and the Mind," in *Language Development: A Reader for Teachers*, 2nd ed., ed. Brenda Miller Power and Ruth Shagoury Hubbard (Upper Saddle River, NJ: Merrill Prentice Hall, 2002), 36–42.

48. Root-Bernstein and Root-Bernstein, *Sparks of Genius*.

49. Alma M. Hawkins, *Moving From Within: A New Method for Dance Making* (Pennington, NJ: A Cappella Books, 1991).

50. Sandra Minton, "Parallels Between Alma Hawkins' Approach to the Creative Process and Contemporary Learning Theory," *Journal of Dance Education* 3, no. 2 (2003): 74–78.

CHAPTER 6

Creating Movement-Based Lessons

You have been working with movement transformation and dance making. Now, you are going to use your understanding of these processes into action by designing complete lessons. To do this, you are presented with a series of concepts relating to math, reading and writing, science, geography, and history. Then, a sample dance and movement lesson is described. Next, you will create movements and dances from other concepts in the same subject areas. Finally, you will design a complete lesson for each subject. Complete lessons include a description of each concept, movements that transform concepts into actions, and a dance incorporating some of the individual movements. Suggestions are provided to help you create lessons with a logical and meaningful sequence of activities and that integrate teaching aids, such as drawings, photographs, three-dimensional models, musical accompaniment, and videos.

AN EXAMPLE OF A MOVEMENT-BASED MATH LESSON

The Denver Public Schools Curriculum Matrix outlines math concepts that should be taught in elementary school. The concepts listed are drawn from standards written at the state and district level. Within each standard, concepts are arranged according to grade level.

Elementary School Math Concepts

Mathematics Standard 3 states that students should know how to interpret data displayed in various types of charts and graphs, while Mathematics Standard 5 describes measurement concepts.[1] Elementary school students are expected to understand these concepts in 3rd grade. The following concepts are arranged according to increasing complexity. In addition, similar concepts are grouped together. Ordering concepts in a lesson according to increased complexity is a good idea because the teaching of each succeeding concept is based on understanding those that precede it, while grouping concepts by similarity facilitates lesson flow and understanding relationships. In terms of mathematics, 3rd-grade elementary school students are expected to be able to:

- Compare and sequence objects according to measures of length or height;
- Use customary units of measure, such as feet on a ruler for length or degrees on a thermometer for temperature;
- Tell time according to the position of the hands on a clock;
- Understand the difference between yesterday, today, and tomorrow;
- Read and understand a pie graph;
- Read and understand a bar graph.[2]

Transforming Elementary-Level Math Concepts Into Movement

The first step in transforming these concepts into movement is to read or observe each one and understand its meaning. It is also important to recognize patterns or relationships that are an important part of a concept. Then, by using the process of responding or empathizing and body thinking, the concepts are transformed into movement. In most cases, math concepts can be transformed into movement using literal rather than abstract methods. The following movements were created as a result of the transforming process:

- Position can be used to compare and sequence objects according to length or height. To do this, have a group of students hold pictures of the objects to be compared. Then, ask the students to compare the objects by their length or height by moving into the appropriate position from left to right. This means the pictures of the objects will be arranged from the smallest or the shortest from left to right.

- Duration can be used to help students understand measures of length or height. This can be accomplished by having students walk for the number of steps that equals the number of feet in the length or height of a particular object.

- Shape can be used to help students learn to tell time. In this experience, the arms are positioned like the large and small hands on the clock so that the students face the clock and mirror the clock hands. Thus, for three o'clock, a student lifts the left arm directly above the shoulder, while the right arm is held out to the right side parallel to the floor; for quarter to twelve the left arm is held out to the side parallel to the floor and the right arm reaches straight up; and for twenty after ten the left arm is positioned on a high diagonal to the side, while the right arm is held on a low diagonal to the other side.

- Direction can be used to designate yesterday, today, and tomorrow. Here, students walk backwards to stand for yesterday, move in place to represent today, and walk forward to demonstrate the idea of tomorrow.

- Group shape can be used to help students interpret a pie graph. To do this, students put their right or left hand into the center of the circle so that their fingers touch the fingers of the other students. Arms are held at shoulder level, and the size of the space between adjacent students matches the size of each respective wedge in the pie chart (see Figure 6.1). The students need to get into the group shape of the pie graph quickly and then walk once around the circle while maintaining this group shape. This group shape is like the star right or left used in square dancing.

- A similar idea can be used to create a bar graph. In this experience, the students stand in vertical lines along a tape that represents the base line or abscissa of the graph. The length of each line correlates with the height of the respective bar on the graph.

Figure 6.1.   The dancers are creating a pie graph. **Photo by Anna Newell.**

Making an Elementary-Level Math Dance

Dance making follows movement transformation. Remember, movements do not become dance until they are combined together in some way. Some of the movements suggested earlier lend themselves to dance making while others do not. Thus, only some of the movements described are included in the following dance. The first step in dance making is to form the suggested actions into sequences or movement patterns. This process requires some playing around or experimentation before you may be satisfied with the patterns. You also need to play around with the order of the movement patterns or sequences to make sure that students can move easily from one pattern to the next while performing the dance. The final dance is a synthesis or whole created from all the selected movement patterns.

The math dance was created in a series form with the students standing in a circle. The parts of the dance are arranged in the sequence according to increased movement complexity. The first movement pattern is based on the concepts of yesterday, today, and tomorrow. To demonstrate the concept of yesterday, the students walk backward away from the center of the circle for a specific number of counts and say "yesterday." Then, they stand in one place, and move only their arms and upper body and say "today." This action is also performed for a specific number of counts. This section of the dance ends when the students walk forward toward the center of the circle while saying "tomorrow." The forward walk should be done for the same number of counts or use the same number of steps as the backward walk so that the students arrive at the same circular formation as the one used at the beginning of the dance.

The concept of telling time can be addressed next. Various time designations can be written on a large sheet of paper or on the board, and students read each designation out loud. At the same time the students move their arms so that the shape they create duplicates the shape made by the hands of a clock. The students change the shape made with their arms as they read each time designation. Each shape for each time designation is held for a certain number of counts.

To end the dance, the students put their right or left hand into the center of the circle to recreate the moving pie graph practiced earlier in the lesson. The time required to walk once around the circle may vary depending on the students' ages and the size of their steps. Once this part of the dance is completed, the dance is performed again from the beginning.

YOUR CHANCE TO CREATE A MOVEMENT-BASED MATH LESSON

The following math concepts are described in the Denver Public Schools Curriculum Matrix as those that should be learned by older elementary school students. These concepts are drawn from Math Standards 1, 3, 4, and 6. Standard 1 states that students should develop a sense of numbers and be able to use them to solve problems; Standard 3 is concerned with the collection of data; Standard 4 focuses on developing a sense of spatial geometric concepts; and Standard 6 has to do with computation.[3] A whole lesson can be created by introducing the math concepts one at a time. The introduction of each concept is followed by demonstrating and performing the movements connected to each concept. The lesson culminates by performing a dance made up of some of the math-based movements. You as a teacher can create this dance, or if time permits, students can create their own dances. You will now have a chance to create your own movement-based math lesson.

Math Concepts for Older Elementary School Students

The following concepts are grouped according to the standard to which they pertain. Concept 1 is found in Standard 6; Concept 2 in Standard 1; Concept 3 in Standard 3; and Concepts 4 through 6 in Standard 4. The concepts are also grouped with those involving mathematical computation first, while those related to geometry are presented second:

1. Fractions must be converted to those with like denominators so they can be added or subtracted (e.g., ¾ is the same as ½, ⅝ is the same as ¾).
2. Decimals are based on tenths.
3. Mean, mode, and median are all measures of centrality.
4. Symmetry and asymmetry are related to understanding geometric shapes.
5. Circumference, diameter, and radius all relate to a circle.
6. Two or more lines can have different relationships (e.g., lines can be parallel, perpendicular, or intersect).[4]

Transforming More Advanced Elementary Math Concepts Into Movement

The first step in transforming the math concepts into movement is to make sure you understand each concept. This means understanding details and patterns that are part of the concept. Then, use the following list of suggestions as you transform each concept into a movement, body shapes, or positions. In addition, you may be able to think of other ways to transform the concepts into movement:

- The position component can be used to convert fractions into movement. You can begin by having a set of basic fractions, such as ¼, ½, and ¾, written on cards and scattered across the floor inside a circle of students. Other less basic fractions, such as ⁵⁄₁₀, ⅝, and ⁶⁄₁₂, can be written on a sheet of paper positioned off to one side. How can you use position to demonstrate the conversion of such fractions as ⁵⁄₁₀ and ⅝ into the basic fractions?

- The level movement component can be used to demonstrate decimals, such as 0.2, 0.5, or 0.9. If you had 10 students standing or positioned in a line, how would you use level to demonstrate these and other decimals based on tenths?

- The mean is the sum of a set of measurements divided by the number of measurements in the set. It is sometimes called an average. The mode is a measure of central location. In a situation where one measure or number occurs more than once, the mode is the most frequently occurring value. In situations where all the numbers or values occur with equal frequency, no mode can be calculated. The median is the point on a scale at which half of the values fall above it and half fall below it. In the series 1, 5, 7, 10, 11, 14, and 19, the number 10 is the median. How can you use movement and body position to demonstrate these three concepts?

- Symmetry means to be balanced, and asymmetry indicates a lack of balance. How would you use the component body shape to help students understand these two concepts?

- The circumference is the outside or perimeter of a circle. The diameter is a line that cuts through its center. The radius is a line that extends from the center of a circle to its perimeter. How can you use the movement component pathway to demonstrate both circumference and diameter? How can you demonstrate radius?

- Intersecting lines trace pathways that cross in space, while parallel lines do not cross but are always equidistant from one another. Lines that are perpendicular meet at a right or 90-degree angle. How can you use pathway to help students understand these three concepts?

Making a More Advanced Elementary-Level Math Dance

The process of dance making often involves playing around with and varying some of the movements you have discovered. Dance making also results from creating patterns by arranging and rearranging movements. In the end, individual movements should fit together to create a whole dance that is a synthesis. How can you use some of your math-based movements to create a movement tableau? Remember, in a tableau, movements are performed in the same space at the same time. Thus, you need to select math concepts that have a similar or simultaneous relationship. Hint: Concepts 4, 5, and 6 can have a simultaneous relationship because it is possible to make a drawing on a paper that includes all of them. Write a description of the tableau you have created.

CREATING A MOVEMENT-BASED SCIENCE LESSON

Studying the atmosphere, weather, and climate is part of school curricula, particularly in the 3rd grade. These concepts are part of Standard 4 in the Denver Public Schools Curriculum Matrix. This standard deals with earth and space science.[5] The concept-based movements and the dance made of these movements comprise the whole lesson.

Elementary-Level Science Concepts

The following lists concepts that can be included in a lesson on the atmosphere, weather, and climate. The lesson begins by describing the makeup of the atmosphere, followed by introducing concepts that are more complex and have to do with weather:

- The atmosphere surrounds earth as a thick blanket of gas that stretches out into space for about 500 miles.
- Scientists describe the different parts of the earth's atmosphere by describing its layers. The exosphere is the outermost layer, followed by the thermosphere, mesosphere, stratosphere, and troposphere in descending order.

- Most of our air is in the troposphere, making air pressure greatest in the bottom layer of the atmosphere and least in the topmost layer.
- There is a close relationship between air temperature and its pressure. When air is warmer, its pressure becomes lower because it is less dense and rises. When air is colder, its pressure increases because it is denser and pressure falls.
- Weather changes are also dependent on air pressure, so that falling pressure comes before wet weather and rising pressure precedes good weather.
- Windy weather is created when colder, heavier air replaces warmer, lighter air.
- The wind does not blow in straight lines. Instead, the winds follow spiraling pathways because the earth is spinning. This phenomenon is known as the Coriolis effect.
- Climate is the pattern of weather that is found in a particular place on earth. In general, warm climates are found near the equator, wet climates near the sea, and variable climates near large mountain ranges.[6]

Transforming Elementary-Level Science Concepts Into Movement

The science concepts can be transformed into movement using the same process that was used to transform the math concepts into actions. Most of the transformations will again be literal rather than abstract:

- The movement component position can be used to show that the atmosphere surrounds the earth like a blanket. To demonstrate this idea, one student is the earth while two other students stand close to the first student, encircling him or her with their arms.
- The movement components level and position are used to demonstrate the layers of the atmosphere. Here, students hold cards with the names of the atmospheric layers written on them. Then, each student is positioned at a level that corresponds to the level of the correct atmospheric layer.
- Movement level and quality can be used to demonstrate how the layers of the atmosphere and air pressure are connected. Simply have one group of students perform strong, heavy movements at a low level, while another group performs light actions at a higher level.
- Movement quality can also be used to show the relationship between air temperature and air pressure. To do this, students pretend they are warm by basking in the sun, while a second group of students stands nearby performing actions that have a floating quality. To demonstrate the results of cold air, students shiver or vibrate, and a nearby group performs heavy, sinking, collapsing actions.
- The movement component quality can be used to demonstrate that low air pressure comes before wet weather just as increased air pressure precedes good weather. To demonstrate light air pressure, students perform floating movements, followed by lowering the hands and moving the fingers back and forth to show that it is raining. Increased air pressure is demonstrated by performing heavy, collapsing actions, followed by reaching movements that show the sun is shining.
- Direction and quality can be used to demonstrate how wind is created. To do this, students can use their right hand to represent heavier, colder air, while their left hand represents lighter, warmer air. Then, they push with their right hand against their left hand, moving their left hand off to their side.
- The pathway component can be used to show the spiraling of the wind by moving the whole body or one hand in a spiraling pathway. This same concept can be demonstrated by moving both hands around each other.
- Position can be used to show how location on the earth is related to climate. You can do this by placing cards labeled sea or mountains on the floor. In addition, tape can be put on the floor between the cards to mark the equator. Then, students can move around in the area where the tape and cards are placed. When they are near the tape (equator), they are in a warm climate. When they are near the sea, the climate is moist, and so on.

Making an Elementary-Level Science Dance

A simple way to form some of these movements into a dance is to use the series method of dance making. However, a rondo dance is more complex and has added educational benefits. The repetitive nature of the rondo, as indicated by ABACADA, can demonstrate important relationships between the science concepts. Because the A section of the rondo is repeated throughout the dance, the movements in the A section can be based on the most important concepts that you wish to reinforce with your students. It is also helpful if these movements are relatively simple and can be put together in a sequence that is easy to repeat. For example, if the difference between low and high air pressure is a key concept, the A section can be fashioned to highlight this principle.

To perform the A section, floating movements can be performed a specific number of times alternating with a certain number of collapsing actions. For example, the performers can do the floating movement four times and the collapsing action twice. Then, this movement sequence could be repeated two or even three times to make up the A section of the dance. While doing these two types of movement, the performers can also be positioned close together and remain in one spot.

During the B section, the students could walk in and out among each other while performing light movements at a high level and heavy movements at a low level. These actions would indicate that the air is heavier at a lower level of the atmosphere and lighter at a higher level. A repeat of the entire A section would follow with the students remaining in one spot.

The C section of the dance can use the actions of rain and sunshine to connect light air quality with rain and heavy air quality with sunshine. The students performing heavy actions and the reaching movements for high air pressure and sunshine can stay in one spot, while those who represent rain and low air pressure can circle around them. Again, the same A section is repeated.

The D section might involve combining the hand push to show how wind is produced with the spiraling actions that demonstrate the direction in which the winds blow. A likely pattern can be four hand pushes from side to side followed by one downward spiral performed with the whole body. The spiraling action can also be performed with one hand or by moving both hands around each other. It might even be possible to have this section of the dance build by dividing the dancers into several groups, bringing in each group in a sequential manner one at a time. The section can

end with everyone moving together. Closure is achieved by returning once more to the A section, with the dancers performing in one spot.

YOUR CHANCE TO CREATE A MOVEMENT-BASED SCIENCE LESSON

Now is your chance to create a science-based lesson. According to the Denver Public Schools Curriculum Matrix, earth science concepts are introduced at the middle school level.[7]

Middle School Science Concepts

In middle school, students learn about the structure of the earth and how this structure changes over short and long periods of time. The concepts are arranged in this lesson from simple to more complex. To create a movement-based science lesson, present each concept to your students followed by introducing the movement that is connected to the concept. Again, combine the movements together at the end of the lesson to create a dance:

* The earth is made up of layers like an onion.
* It has three basic layers.
* The outermost layer is a thin crust of hard, cold rock that is rather brittle. The crust is about three to four miles thick, but where there are mountains, it is thicker.
* The next layer of the earth is the mantle, which is hot and melted in some places.
* The inner part of the earth is the core. It is very hot and made up mainly of iron and nickel.
* There is some movement in the mantle, and it is possible that hot rocks rise and cold slabs sink.
* The surface of the earth is not continuous but made up of plates or huge, jagged pieces that are curved and fit the rounded surface of the planet.
* The plates move due to forces within the earth. This movement is usually extremely slow.
* Some authorities believe that the continents, which rest upon the plates, have moved as well and were originally much closer together.
* Movements of the plates vary and include colliding, separating, sliding past one another, and overlapping.

- A collision of the plates can produce mountains, while the sliding actions create no new land but do cause earthquakes.
- The colliding of the tectonic plates produces different types of mountains, such as those that are folded or shaped like a block or dome.
- A separation of the plates or a splitting of the earth usually produces a volcano.[8]

Transforming Middle School Science
Concepts Into Movement

Read the previous earth science concepts, and use the following list of suggestions as you transform each concept into a movement, body shape, or position. Feel free to use any of the movement components to transform these concepts into actions. The concepts are arranged to help students understand the overall structure of the earth, starting from the crust or outer layer:

- How can you use level or position to represent the layers of the earth?
- What type of energy or movement quality is suggested by the brittle nature of the earth's crust?
- What type of body shape might be used to represent the shape of the tectonic plates?
- How can you use quality, direction, and level to help students understand the colliding, separating, sliding, and overlapping actions of the earth's plates? Would you use the whole body or only part of the body to demonstrate these actions?
- What kind of body shapes may be used to help students understand the different types of mountains created from the movements of the earth's plates?
- What about the connection between the syruplike quality of the mantle and the quality of your movements?
- Can you use level or a change in level to suggest how the rocks and slabs move in the mantle?
- Can you use a specific movement quality to represent an earthquake?

Making a Middle School Science Dance

Now, you have an opportunity to create a dance based on chance methods. To do this, place a large, flat map of the earth's surface on the floor with the primary earthquake zones marked. Many of these zones are in the Ring of Fire that surrounds the Pacific Ocean. Next, toss a die on the map to indicate the location of the first earthquake. The students will perform movements of the tectonic plates in a spot corresponding to the earthquake zone in which the die landed. Tossing the die is repeated to find the location of the next earthquake and so on. The movements representing the tectonic plates can vary because the tectonic plates move in a number of ways. A die can also be tossed to determine how many times a movement is performed. Then, transitional actions are used to enable the students to travel from one spot to another.

CREATING A MOVEMENT-BASED SOCIAL STUDIES LESSON

In the 6th grade, many students study Canada—the physical characteristics of the land and the natural processes that shape the land throughout the country. They also look at the cultural patterns and the economic resources of Canada and a number of other countries.[9]

Middle School Social Studies Concepts

Some of the following concepts were part of a movement-based lesson presented for 6th-grade students. The concepts were arranged in the lesson so that geographical ideas were presented first, followed by concepts based on Canada's geology, industries, and people:

- In terms of land mass, Canada is the second largest country in the world and shares a long border with the United States.
- Much of Canada's land is largely undeveloped.
- Unlike the United States, Canada is divided into provinces. There are 10 provinces and the Yukon, Northwest, and Nunavut Territories. The provinces include Prince Edward Island, Nova Scotia, New Brunswick, Newfoundland, Quebec, Ontario, Manitoba, Saskatchewan, Alberta, and British Columbia.
- The capital of Canada is Ottawa. Other major cities include Montreal, Toronto, Winnipeg, Calgary, Vancouver, and Edmonton. Most of these

cities are located in a band of land that is about 200 miles wide along the U.S. border.

- The characteristics of Canada's land differ according to region. Along the Atlantic Ocean, the land is rocky, and there are some sandy beaches. There are also rich farms in this area. Farther inland, the land is also rocky, but there are many forests, too. The lowlands lie along Lake Erie, Lake Ontario, and the Saint Lawrence Seaway. Farther west, the Canadian landscape becomes grasslands, prairies, and rolling hills. The Rocky Mountains and forests make up the area along the Pacific Coast, while the northern part of Canada has a very short summer because for most of the year, the land is a frigid desert-tundra.
- Fishing is one of the primary industries along the east and west coasts of Canada, while the forests produce much wood for lumber and paper products. Grain is grown on the plains, and the area around Calgary is rich in oil.
- Because much of Canada is undeveloped, it has a low population in comparison to the United States. In fact, the total population of Canada is about 31 million, while the United States has a population of approximately 300 million people.
- Canada is culturally diverse like the United States. The Inuit are one of the groups of native or indigenous people. Other cultural groups include the French, British, and Asians.[10]

Transforming Middle School Social Studies Concepts Into Movement

Some suggestions follow as to how you can transform these concepts into actions:

- Pathway can be used to trace the lengthy border between the United States and Canada. What would this movement pathway look like?
- Position can be used to place students in the relative position of the different provinces and territories.
- In a similar manner, the students can stand in relative positions representing the respective location of Canada's major cities.
- The characteristics of Canada's land can be represented with a number of movement components.

The rocky land can be represented with a jagged pathway made with one hand in the air or with the students' steps on the floor. Sandy beaches can be understood by walking steps that look as though a person is wading through loose sand. The lowlands can be shown with low movement. Rolling hills can be demonstrated by rolling the hands around each other in a spiraling pathway. The western mountains can be sharp shapes made with the hands or by two students who connect their fingertips at a high level. Finally, the cold of the tundra can be demonstrated with shivering or vibratory movements.

- Canada's major industries and resources can be represented in a similar manner. To do this, the students trace a forward, wavy pathway with their hands to show how fish swim (see Figure 6.2). They can also shape their bodies like pine trees in

Figure 6.2.   *The dancers trace a pathway showing how fish swim.* Photo by Anna Newell.

a forest (see Figure 6.3). In addition, swaying movements can be used to represent fields of grain swaying in the wind (see Figure 6.4), while the students can move their arms upward with an explosive quality to show oil gushing from a well (see Figure 6.5).

Figure 6.3. *The dancers shape their bodies like pine trees.* **Photo by Anna Newell.**

Figure 6.4. *The dancers show the swaying quality of grain in the wind.* **Photo by Anna Newell.**

Figure 6.5. *The dancers show the gushing quality of oil coming from the earth.* **Photo by Anna Newell.**

- Group and individual shapes can be used to compare the population of the United States and Canada. For example, the population of the United States is about 10 times that of Canada, so a group of 10 students can be used to represent the U.S. population, while a single student stands for the population of Canada.

Making a Middle School Social Studies–Based Dance

The AB was selected as the form for this dance because the eastern and western parts of Canada have some similar characteristics of land and natural resources. These characteristics contrast with those of the central parts of the country. For example, the coastal areas are rocky or mountainous, and forestry and fishing are the primary industries. The center of the country, however, is relatively flat with rolling hills; farming and drilling for oil are the primary industries.

This dance can begin with movements representing the central part of the country. These movements include rolling the hands around each other (rolling hills), swaying (grain moving in the wind), exploding upward actions of the arms (oil gushing), and vibrating (the cold of the tundra). In addition, it is possible to vary and extend each of these movements. Thus, the rolling actions of the hands can become rolling or turning movements of the whole body; the upward exploding actions can evolve into jumps, leaps, or even lifts; and the vibrating movements can start with one performer and be transmitted to the entire group. Each of these movement themes would be developed and woven together with the other themes throughout the A section of the dance.

In the B section of this dance, the wavy pathways of the swimming fish can be performed first by one dancer and then by a group. The jagged rocks can be individual or group movements done in one spot or traveling, while the mountain and tree shapes can be represented by one performer or a group. As a contrast, another performer can move about and explore the mountains and forests. The vibratory movements representing the cold of the tundra can serve as a connecting link between the two sections of the dance because the tundra extends from the center of Canada to its western shores. Again, the individual movements would have to be varied and woven together to make up the B section of this piece.

YOUR CHANCE TO CREATE A MOVEMENT-BASED SOCIAL STUDIES LESSON

When I was teaching in the middle schools, I presented a movement lesson based on the geography and culture of Japan. According to the Denver Public Schools Curriculum Matrices, 7th-grade students study the countries and people of the eastern hemisphere.[11]

Middle School Social Studies Concepts About Japan

Japan is located on the eastern edge of Asia, facing the United States from across the Pacific. The country is geographically close to China and Korea, but its culture, which has developed over many hundreds of years, is unique. The following concepts are arranged beginning with those that are most concrete and describe the geography of Japan. Next, concepts having to do with the creation of the Japanese islands are introduced. The less concrete, culturally oriented concepts are presented at the end of the lesson:

- Japan is close to a number of other Asian countries. These countries include China and Russia to the northwest and Korea to the west.
- The landmass of Japan is approximately the same as the landmass of California. Overall the United States has a landmass that is almost 24 times as great as the landmass of Japan.

- Japan is made up of four large islands and a number of smaller islands that are really the tops of mountains poking up above the sea. From north to south, the four main islands are Hokkaido, Honshu, Shikoku, and Kyushu. These names are pronounced Ho-ki-e-do, Hon-shu, She-ko-coo, and Q-shu (*e, i, o,* and *u* are pronounced as long vowels except in the case of the *o* in *Honshu*).
- The four large islands of Japan are arranged in a half moon or crescent shape that looks like a backward letter *C*.
- Japan lies on the Pacific Ring of Fire. This ring is a grouping of volcanoes that encircle the Pacific Ocean.
- Japan sits at the meeting of four tectonic plates and was formed millions of years ago when these plates smashed together. This action caused the earth's crust to buckle and warp. As a result, Japan rose up out of the sea.
- At the same time, volcanoes erupted, spewing ash and molten rock and adding to the surface area of the country.
- Today, the tectonic plates off the coast of Japan continue to rub and smash together, causing periodic eruptions of volcanoes, earthquakes, and tidal waves.
- Many believe that the sea off the western coast of Japan was originally a large lake and that two land bridges connected the country to the mainland at Siberia and Korea. The land bridges submerged as the level of the sea rose.
- Sapporo, Nagano, Tokyo, Kyoto, Kobe, and Hiroshima are some of the largest cities in Japan. Sapporo has been the home of the winter Olympics; Tokyo is the capital and a world business center; Kyoto is a religious center; Kobe was the site of a huge earthquake in 1995; and Hiroshima was where an atomic bomb was dropped by the United States during World War II.
- A Japanese folktale says that earthquakes happen when catfish flap their tails.[12]

Transforming Middle School Social Studies Concepts Into Movement

Now, you will transform these geography concepts into movement using the literal or abstract methods. Again, some hints are provided to help you through the movement discovery process:

- You can use the movement component position to help understand the respective positions of Japan, Russia, and China. Are there any other ways you could show a relationship between the locations of the three countries?
- How can you use the size component to compare Japan to the United States?
- The position component can easily be used to understand the location of the four main islands of Japan and also the location of Japan's main cities. How would you use position to show these respective geographical locations?
- The fact that Japan sits on the Pacific Ring of Fire can be transformed into movement using both literal and abstract methods. What type of movements would result if you used abstract rather than literal methods to motivate your movement discovery process?
- Japan was created when the earth's tectonic plates smashed together and when volcanoes erupted. How can the direction and quality components be used to transform these natural phenomena into movement? What about using an abstract approach to transform these phenomena into movement?
- Many think that Japan was originally connected by land bridges to the mainland. There is also a folktale that says earthquakes are fish slapping their tails. How can these ideas be transformed into movement using literal methods? What about the movements that would result when abstract methods are used to transform these ideas into actions?
- You might also use abstract methods to convey the essence of the largest cities in Japan. What are some of the ideas that can serve as a focus for creating abstractions that symbolize these cities? In other words, what is your feeling response to the description of each of these cities?

Making a Middle School Social Studies Dance Based on Japan

Many dance forms can be used to shape the movements you have discovered into a dance. For me, however, the ABA form seems appropriate here. The A section can symbolize the forces of nature and the violent processes that created the Japanese islands. Then, the B section could include some of the movements that represent present-day Japan, such as the configuration of the islands or the location of the major cities. Finally, the second A section can include a recap of some of the cataclysmic events that created Japan. The actions included in each section of the dance can be represented in multiple forms by using movement variation. Movement variation is based on using the movement components to change movements you have already created.

CREATING A MOVEMENT-BASED HISTORY LESSON

In 7th grade, Denver Public School students learn about history by studying the people of other eras in terms of their society, religion, trade patterns, and economy. The focus is on the history of people and cultures found in the eastern hemisphere.[13]

Middle School History Concepts

The Middle Ages denote a period of time in European history that existed between Europe's domination by the Roman Empire and the emergence of an intellectual rebirth during the Renaissance. The Middle Ages lasted from approximately 400 to 1500 CE. Concepts pertaining to life during the Middle Ages are grouped with those from early times presented first. The concepts describing the later Middle Ages include a general description of this time period followed by details of daily life.

- The early part of the Middle Ages is sometimes known as the Dark Ages—a time of almost constant war and violence.
- Travel by boat was easiest because the roads were so bad.
- During the period from 1000 to 1300 CE, society become stronger and better organized through a system of government known as the feudal system. In this society, the nobility formed the upper classes while peasants made up the lower classes. Under the feudal system, strong men of the upper classes offered protection to a band of followers from the lower classes. In return, chieftains or lords expected their followers to support them in battles and supply them with food grown on their land.

- During the Middle Ages, women usually had little education.
- Lords lived in castles that had high, thick walls. Sometimes a deep moat surrounded the castle for greater protection.
- The Christian church was so powerful during the Middle Ages that the nobility often believed their power was granted to them by the church. Many people believed disasters were punishments sent by God. As a result, church buildings towered above the rest of the town as a symbol of their importance.
- The Crusades were an extremely important religious activity during the Middle Ages. The Crusades were pilgrimages resulting in holy wars fought to uphold Christianity and save Christian holy places.
- Technology and medical knowledge were very primitive during the Middle Ages. There were no printing presses, so all the books were produced by hand, usually by monks. Counting was done on an abacus, and medicine was a combination of prayer, folk remedies, and magic.
- Many people died from diseases for which there are cures today. The most feared disease was the plague known as the Black Death, which was carried by rats and fleas.[14]

Transforming Middle School Historical Concepts Into Movement

Some of the concepts from the Middle Ages lend themselves to literal transformations, while others fit the abstract movement transformation model:

- The term *Dark Ages* is nebulous rather than concrete. My response to this term is abstract and based on feelings of mystery and fear. Such movements as drifting, spiraling, sinking, withdrawing, and surrounding are some of those that can be used to communicate my feelings about the term *Dark Ages*. The movement components quality, direction, and position are the basis of this movement transformation.
- The fact that many people traveled by boat lends itself to a more literal transformation. Paddling movements and those performed with a gliding quality are appropriate here.

- Level is used to communicate the nature of feudal society. This can be done by having groups representing those of a different social status move at different levels. This is a more abstract transformation.
- The dominance of the church during this period of time can be represented literally with upward reaching movements, a processional, or bringing the hands together in prayer.
- Finally, the prevalence of disease and dying lends itself to more abstract transformations in order to communicate feelings of fear, sadness, mourning, and grieving.

Making a Middle School History Dance

You have read about the theme and variations dance form. It is made up of a sequence of movements of the theme that is varied throughout the remainder of the dance. One possible movement theme based on the Middle Ages could be four drifting actions performed with the arms and upper body (Dark Ages), followed by moving slowly in a group at different levels (feudal society), and ending with a short processional while praying (interest in religion). Possible variations on this theme would be to have two groups of dancers perform the key movement sequence in different directions or at different speeds. In addition, the theme can be performed by a soloist, while a larger group repeats only one or two of the thematic movements. The various movement components can be used to produce many variations on this theme.

Concepts From Middle School History

One middle school teacher asked me to develop a movement lesson based on the different historical cultures and people of the Middle East, the cradle of civilization. Some of these ancient people include Sumerians, Egyptians, Israelites, Assyrians, Babylonians, and Persians.

The following descriptions of the different cultures that lived in the Middle East are arranged in chronological order:

- The Sumerians lived from 3500 to 2159 BCE. They inhabited an area called Mesopotamia, which was located between two rivers, the Tigris and the Euphrates. The Sumerians farmed their land and built monumental structures called ziggurats, which were stepped towers.

- The ancient Egyptians prospered from 3100 to 1070 BCE. They were the first people to use writing in the form of hieroglyphics (picture writing). The Egyptians were ruled by a pharaoh who was believed to be a god. They buried pharaohs in triangular-shaped structures called pyramids.
- The Assyrians were a conquering people.
- Like the Sumerians, the Babylonians built ziggurats.
- The Hebrews or Israelites were another very significant group in the history of the Middle East. They built a large temple in what is now Jerusalem and believed in one god.
- The Persians created a large empire and had a system of roads, but they were later defeated by the Greeks.[15]

Transforming Middle School History Concepts Into Movement

As you create actions based on each of the cultural groups, think about the movement components and how each can be used in the movement transformation process:

- How can you use pathway and shape to transform your impression of the Sumerian ziggurats into movement? Is this a literal or abstract movement transformation?
- How can you use movement to demonstrate your impression of the Egyptian pyramids? Look at a photo of an Egyptian pyramid. What is your feeling response to this photo?
- The Assyrians were a conquering people. How can a literal movement transformation be used to represent this idea? How can abstraction be used to represent this same idea?
- The Israelite's concept of one god lends itself to a more abstract movement transformation. How would you use movement to demonstrate the concept of one god?
- The Persians built roads and were defeated by the Greeks. In this instance, you might use the literal

method of transformation to represent roads and abstraction to communicate your feelings about being defeated. How would you go about doing this?

Making a Middle School History Dance

There are many dance forms that can be used to represent the various aspects of these ancient civilizations. One possibility is to choreograph a series of tableaux because the ziggurats and pyramids were immoveable structures that had a particular shape. Then, the other concepts, such as roads and the idea of one god, can be transformed into movements that serve as transitions between the tableaux. The movement tableaux representing the different cultural groups should be performed in an order that matches the chronological order in which the civilizations existed.

CREATING A MIDDLE SCHOOL READING AND WRITING LESSON

In the Denver Public Schools Curriculum Matrix for reading and writing, Standard 6 states that students should read and recognize literature as a record of human experience.[16] Working with movement transformation and dance making is an ideal way to fulfill this standard. Some of the literature or myths of the Hawaiian people, particularly stories that concern their gods, give the reader a sense of the culture of these island people. You will read about some of the characters in these myths and learn how these characters can be transformed into movement and then into a dance.

Stories From Hawaiian Legends

Hawaiians attribute the powers of creation to Haumea, mother of Pele. One characteristic of Haumea is that she seemed to be both creative and destructive at the same time. The legends also tell of how Haumea used a stick to transform herself from an old woman into a young girl.[17]

Pele is the Hawaiian goddess of volcanic fires. She symbolizes woman at her most destructive. Pele was also a great traveler who came originally from Tahiti. Some say that Pele was driven out of Tahiti by her older sister, whose husband she stole. Others say that Pele was driven toward Hawaii by a flood. The legends also say that Pele went from one Hawaiian island to another, searching for a place to live. Every time Pele dug into the ground, though, the sea poured in and drove her out. At last, Pele burrowed into a great, wide volcano on the island of Hawaii and stayed there. Pele has become a very important local deity because the flow of lava is still present in Hawaii.[18]

Another Hawaiian story tells how Kamapau'a the hog man courted Pele. Kamapau'a had the power to change himself into a plant, fish, or pig. In his human form, he wore a cloak to hide the bristles on his back. When Kamapau'a courted Pele, she scorned him and almost overwhelmed him with fire. He fought Pele by dousing her fires with fog and rain and overrunning her with hogs. Finally, Pele yielded to Kamapau'a, and they divided Hawaii into districts. Pele took Puna, Knau, and Kona, where lava flows, while Kamapau'a took Hilo and other areas where it is rainy and moist.[19]

Hawaii makes up part of Polynesia, which stretches out to form a triangle from New Zealand to the Easter Islands. Despite the distances between the islands of Polynesia, similar stories can be found throughout the area, although the names for principal characters are usually different. One example of characters found in many of these legends has to do with the Polynesian perception of light. According to these legends, Atea (light) and Po (dark) are opposites. Po is also thought of as the emptiness that came before creation. Other important figures in Polynesian mythology are Hine, who rules the underworld, and Maui, the trickster hero who struggles with other gods to help humanity. According to one story, Maui once caught the sun in a noose and beat it so that it could only creep across the sky—an act that made the days longer at certain times of the year.[20]

Transforming Hawaiian Mythology Into Movement

The first step in structuring a movement lesson based on the Hawaiian myths is to read through this information several times. Reading and absorbing this information makes up the observation phase of the movement discovery process. In addition, it is important to recognize patterns or relationships in these stories, such as the idea that Pele is responsible for the flow of lava because she buried herself in volcanoes or that the islands of Polynesia are arranged in a triangle.

When these concepts are transformed into movement, students experience each concept in a concrete way. If the concept-based movements are created through the process of abstracting, students can connect their impression or feeling response with the concept. When students' feelings are engaged, they are also more likely to remember information.

In order to capture a feeling response in movement, decide how you and your students feel about the characters presented in the myths. One way to begin is to come up with a series of feeling-oriented words that describe each character. Describing the characters leads to body thinking or identifying how these feelings make your body feel. When reading about Haumea, I feel that she is changeable and represents both positive (creative) and negative (destructive) forces. In terms of my kinesthetic body feelings, "changeableness" translates into wavering or trembling; being creative feels larger and more relaxed; destruction is tense.

The next part of the movement discovery framework involves using your imagination to transform the characters and ideas in the myths into movement. Movement transformations also can be accomplished by exaggerating the body feelings connected with each character. For instance, I see Haumea as old and withered and Pele as a young but somewhat dangerous and flirtatious woman. Because Pele is the goddess of volcanoes, a literal movement transformation can be used to copy the movements of lava as it shoots upward and then flows down the slopes of the volcano. A more abstract transformation can capture your feelings about Pele in movement.

The following list describes the movements I created after reading and thinking about the Hawaiian myths. You may be able to think of other ways to translate these stories into actions:

- Perform slow, upward, or lifting movements of the arms with the palms facing the ceiling alternating with striking actions to represent the creative and destructive aspects of Haumea.
- Move with shaking and trembling actions that alternate with lively jumping and running to stand for Haumea's ability to change from an old woman into a young girl.
- Use the hands and arms to strike upward quickly, followed by downward actions performed in a

weaving pathway with the hands. These two movements copy the explosive quality of Pele, the goddess of volcanoes, and the subsequent flow of lava down her sides.

- Combine a sensuous walk with beckoning arm movements to represent the more abstract nature of Pele.
- Move the fingers back and forth while lowering the hands to stand for the moist, rainy parts of Hawaii.
- Make a triangular shape with the hands or body to present a literal transformation of the position of the islands that make up Polynesia.
- Perform wide, expansive actions that move from side to side. These movements are an abstract transformation of light (the entity Atea), while doing low, small, closed movements stand for darkness (Po).
- Finally, there is Maui, the trickster hero. A literal transformation of Maui's actions shows him catching or lassoing the sun in a noose.
- A more abstract representation of the trickster includes movements that quickly change focus and direction.

Making a Middle School Dance Based on Hawaiian Myths

The first step in forming movements into a dance is to play with the movements you have created by forming them into a number of patterns or sequences. Then, further play leads to discovering how the patterns can be put together to form a dance or synthesis of your creative efforts.

A problem-solving dance can be created from the movements culled from the Hawaiian myths. To begin, designate an area in which each mythological character can perform. Haumea, the creator, can then move about the whole area, addressing each of the other characters one at a time. Variations of Haumea's actions can be created by playing around with her movements and changing them. Once Haumea has traveled around the entire performance area, each of the other characters can perform a short solo. Next, an exchange between some of the characters can be choreographed by having them dance with each other. Such an exchange is ideal for representing the relationship between Pele and Kamapau'a. The dance concludes by having all the characters dance together in unison, ending in a triangular group shape to signify the geographical arrangement of the Polynesian islands.

YOUR CHANCE TO CREATE A MOVEMENT-BASED READING AND WRITING LESSON

You now have a chance to create your own movements and dance based on a Native American legend. As you read through the legend, determine how you feel about each of the characters. Then, list words that describe each character. Take special note of other important aspects of this story as you transform concepts and characters into movement.

The Legend of the Iroquois People

The following legend is called the Iroquois Hiawatha. It is the story of how the Iroquois League was founded. The story begins with Ta-ren-ya-wa-gon, who upheld the heavens and came down to save earthly people from monsters and giants. The first people Ta-ren-ya-wa-gon met he named the Mohawks, giving them squash, beans, and dogs for hunting. Continuing to the east, Ta-ren-ya-wa-gon also created the Oneida, Onondaga, Cayuga, and Seneca, giving these tribes the gifts of swiftness, canoes, and knowledge of eternal laws and how to make bows and arrows. Afterward, Ta-ren-ya-wa-gon decided to become a human by living among the Onondaga and by taking the name Hiawatha. He also married an Onondaga woman, and they had a daughter named Mnihaha. Time passed, and all the tribes grew, prospered, and were happy.

Sorrow followed happiness when wild tribes appeared from the north. The new tribes had no skills or knowledge and wanted to threaten and kill the others. The five tribes turned to Hiawatha for guidance. After four days, Hiawatha and his daughter appeared in a white canoe that floated above the people. Next, a huge bird descended. The people were afraid, but Hiawatha calmed them. Then, his daughter seated herself on the bird and they spiraled upward. After four more days, Hiawatha announced that his time with the people was ending, and they should focus on the future, not the past. He also said the tribes needed to reunite to defeat their enemies. To symbolize unity, Hiawatha gathered the feathers of the giant bird and gave them to each tribal leader. He stated that the five tribes would now be known as the Iroquois, and the feathers were a symbol of their unity. Finally, Hiawatha climbed into his white canoe and rose into the sky.[21]

Creating Your Own Middle School Reading and Writing Lesson

To begin, consider the characters and other aspects of the Iroquois legend that can be transformed into movement using literal or abstract movement methods:

- My first impression of the Ta-ren-ya-wa-gon character is that he was powerful and strong yet kindly and benevolent. What movement direction, size, level, quality, speed, and pathway can you use to suggest these traits?
- Ta-ren-ya-wa-gon gave each of the five tribes of the Iroquois Nation a special skill as a gift. Would you use literal or abstract methods of transformation to demonstrate each of these skills? Would you use one dancer or a group of dancers to represent each of the tribes?
- How would you show that Ta-ren-ya-wa-gon became a human and married?
- With the arrival of the tribes from the north, danger and other negative elements are introduced into the legend. Do you think the introduction of these elements would make up another section of the dance?
- The final part of the legend deals with unifying the Iroquois tribes into a single group. Mnihaha also leaves on the large bird, and Hiawatha leaves in a canoe. How would you show unity among a group of dancers yet demonstrate that Mnihaha and Hiawatha both leave the Iroquois?
- Hiawatha gives a feather to the leaders of each tribe. How can you show this activity in dance movement?
- What overall form would you use for this dance?

DESIGNING MOVEMENT-BASED LESSONS

There are several different methods you can use to design an entire movement-based lesson. One method is to introduce each concept and the accompanying movements one by one and then teach the students a dance you have choreographed. Of course, the concepts should be presented in the lesson in an order that makes sense. This means arranging concepts in chronological order, in terms of structural relationships, or by grouping like concepts together.

A second way to design a lesson is to introduce the concepts and let the students create their own movements and dance. In the beginning, you may need to guide the students as they discover movements and form the movements into a dance. You will also need to keep creative problem solving simple.

Finally, a third method for designing a movement-based lesson is most appropriate in classes where students are studying a story or legend. Here, you can read the legend to your students, followed by having the students analyze each character using descriptive feeling-oriented words. As the students suggest descriptive words to you, write them on the board or on a large sheet of paper. By taking time to write the words down, both you and the students will remember what you have discussed. Then, the students can create their own movements based on the words used to describe each character.

Using Supplemental Materials in Movement-Based Lessons

I have found that supplemental materials can help illustrate a lesson as well. These materials can include key words, photographs, drawings, objects, videos, or music that deals with the subject matter of a lesson. Let's begin with key words. Key words are important because they give meaning to a lesson by describing the main characters, events, or principles found in the subject matter being studied. Key words also explain relationships between one piece of information and another. As suggested previously, key words can be written on a board or large piece of paper. The sheets of paper can be taped to the wall or stapled to a bulletin board for ready reference during a lesson. It is also helpful if the key words lend themselves to movement transformation.

Photographs and drawings can also contribute a great deal to student understanding. Some students understand information through verbal explanations, but others are visual learners. These latter students appreciate seeing photographs, drawings, and diagrams. I have used many visual aids in movement-based lessons. For instance, in the lesson about electricity, students were presented with a diagram of series and parallel circuits; in the rainforest lesson, they viewed a drawing of the layers of a rainforest; and in the Canada lesson, they looked at some simple maps of Canada picturing the geology and products found in different parts of the country. In the rainforest lesson, students were also shown photographs of the indigenous people who make these forests their home. Whatever visual aids are used, they should be large and devoid of an excessive number of details. Colorful visual aids are more interesting for students.

Objects can also be visual aids and provide tactile stimulation at the same time. If an object makes a sound, auditory learning is integrated into a lesson as well. I was able to buy a large rain stick on a trip to Brazil that was used in rainforest lessons. Some of the other objects used in lessons included bubbles, shells, foreign coins, and a kaleidoscope. Bubbles were used with kindergarten and 1st-grade students to demonstrate personal space. To do this, the students imagined they were surrounded by a bubble. Then, they pretended to touch the bubble by moving their arms in different directions in order to imagine their own personal space.[22] The shell was used to communicate texture, while the coins were passed around during a middle school lesson about France. The kaleidoscope was a device used for demonstrating group shape, particularly unity of group shape in the visual arts.

A word of caution is in order concerning the use of objects as teaching aids. Any object brought into a class should be safe for students to handle. This means it should have no sharp edges, splinters, or protruding parts and no openings in which students might get their fingers stuck. These words of caution are especially important when you are working with very young children. For example, on the day I used bubbles in class, the students were instructed to remain in place so that they would not get soapy liquid on their bodies or in their eyes.

Any video used as a teaching aid must add to a class by clarifying lesson content. Sometimes the video was based on lesson content, such as rainforests, lightning, or volcanoes. If possible, however, I prefer to use dance videos because this strengthens connections between movement, dance, and what students are learning. Dance becomes less alien and more connected to students' lives. For example, in an elementary school math lesson, I wanted to show that counting is important to dancing. When the dance video was shown, I asked the students to count the number of times dancers performed a specific movement, such as turning. In another math class, the students counted the number of seconds it took for the dancers to perform a difficult feat. The alphabet and word recognition were topics in other elementary schools' classes. In these classes, students identified dancers' body shapes that resembled letters of the alphabet.

Sometimes I have been fortunate enough to find a dance video based on the subject of a lesson. This was the case for a lesson about the solar system and for another rainforest lesson. The first dance was titled *Planets*, and the second one was called *Rainforest*. Both dances were created by David Taylor, a local choreographer. Of course, it was possible to show only a small part of these dances, so I selected parts that were most interesting for the students. In a middle school history lesson, the video I showed was on historical dance forms. Whatever videos are used, it is important that the major focus of a lesson is moving and dancing. In addition, prescreen any video that you plan to use, making sure it does not contain objectionable words or content.

Using Music in Movement-Based Lessons

Finally, let's talk about the use of music as a supplement to your lessons. Any music you use should be closely connected with lesson content. For example, Inuit songs were used in the lessons on Canada, and French or Spanish music was included in lessons about France and Spain. Music is also useful in history lessons because students can compare the sounds and musical styles popular during different eras. If possible, point out specific sounds and musical motifs that are important to the music of a country or historical period. This helps students know how to listen to a piece. Again, remember to listen to all music before playing it in class. I usually label each of my tapes and CDs so that I can instantly know which tracks I·can play and which ones contain lyrics that can be objectionable. Of course, music without words is preferable.

Practice With Lesson Organization

The alphabet and the following simple words were the concepts presented in a 1st-grade lesson. Think about the order in which you can organize these concepts and where in the lesson you could use visual aids or other types of teaching aids to help explain content. The order in which you organize your lesson should also be meaningful and emphasize relationships between concepts.

- Some capital letters, such as *C* and *O*, are made up of curved lines only. Can you make the shapes of these letters with your body?
- All the letters of the alphabet are scattered on the floor. Three students hold cards with the letters *B*, *A*, and *T* on them to spell the word *bat*. The students standing in the circle must find other letters that can substituted for the *B* in bat to make rhyming words.
- Another way to make letters is to trace their shapes in the air or follow a specific pathway on the floor with your steps. Can you trace the initials of your first and last name on the floor?
- Which lowercase letters are made up of straight lines only? Which lowercase letters are made up of curved lines only? And which lowercase letters combine curved and straight lines? Try making these letters with your body.
- When you say the letter blends *bl*, *br*, or *sm* as part of a word, you blend the two letters together to make one uninterrupted sound. How do you shape your mouth when you say these letter blends? Can you say the words *block*, *bread*, and *smoke* while you move your hands in a way that copies the shape or use of your mouth as you say these words?
- Sometimes a video can be used to clarify concepts presented in a lesson. What sort of video can you use to complement a lesson based on the alphabet and words?
- Some capital letters, such as *B* and *D*, are made up of both straight and curved lines. Can you make the shapes of these letters with your own body or together with the body of another student?
- Different words have a different number of syllables in them. Pick four words, the first of which

has one syllable, the second two syllables, the third three syllables, and the fourth four syllables. How many times would you move throughout four counts of music to represent the number of syllables in each of these words?
- Some capital letters, such as *A* and *H*, are made up of straight lines only. Can you make the shapes of these letters with your body?
- Can you spell a simple word, such as *clock*, by shaping your body like each of the letters in this word? In this exercise, the order of your body shapes should duplicate the order of the letters in the word.
- Capital letters are printed on small cards and scattered across the floor. Students must find the same letter as the one you are pointing to on a chart. Once they find the target letter, they go over and stand around it.
- How can you make some of the shapes of capital letters with a partner?

More Practice With Lesson Organization

A middle school lesson on the Aztecs included the following concepts. How can you organize these concepts so they form a unified and well-organized lesson?

- Many other important events took place in other parts of the world at the same time the indigenous cultures of Mexico flourished. Thus, the high point of the Olmec culture preceded the birth and life of Christ. The Maya flourished somewhat after the life of Christ. The Toltecs lived at the same time that Christians and Muslims fought the Holy Wars, and the Aztec civilization coincided in time with the European Renaissance.
- The Aztec symbols used for counting were different than the numbers we use today. For example, dots were used for numbers from 1 to 19 by simply using one dot for the number 1, two dots for 2, three dots for 3, and so on. A flag represented 20, while a fir tree stood for 400.
- Several important groups make up the indigenous or native people of Mexico. These groups include the Olmecs (1200 to 300 BCE), the Maya (500 BC to 900 CE), the Toltecs (900 to 1200 CE), and the Aztecs (1200 to 1521 CE). How can you

arrange a class of students along a tape or time line to demonstrate the chronological relationship between these four groups?

- One of the things we have learned from the sun stone is how the Aztecs understood historical time—an important point because the Aztecs measured time in cycles instead of in the linear way we do. The Aztecs believed that each cycle was a creation, with each new creation beginning every 52 years.
- The volador or flyer dance was enacted to celebrate the end of a creation. In this ceremony, four men costumed as birds were attached to a tall pole with ropes. They jumped from a platform at the top of the pole, and each performer attempted to spin around the pole 13 times. If each performer was successful, the number of their combined revolutions around the pole equaled 52, the same number of years in an Aztec creation.
- The Aztec calendar was fairly accurate because they had a knowledge of astronomy.
- The end of a creation was believed to be a dangerous time in which people were advised to stay indoors and pray. The Aztecs also wore masks during these dangerous times.
- We have learned a lot about the Aztecs from their large sculpture called the sun stone or calendar stone. It is approximately 12½ feet in diameter.
- Aztec astronomers observed the position of stars and planets with an instrument similar to a cross-staff.
- The Aztecs had a name and picture symbol or glyph for each creation. The names for four of the creations were Jaguar, Wind, Water, and Rain.[23]

SUMMARY AND CONCLUSIONS

It is possible to design movement-based lessons for teaching many subjects. The beginning of this process is observing concepts you are teaching in detail. It is also important to recognize patterns or relationships that are part of a concept or that exist between one concept and another. Knowing details and recognizing patterns will help convey meaning. The process of transforming concepts into movement can be literal or abstract. When using literal methods, you move like the concept, duplicate body positions that are part of the concept, or shape your body like the concept. Abstract methods of transformation require a feeling response in which you empathize with the concept in some way. Having feelings about a concept also helps with the teaching process because being involved on a feeling level means students are more engaged. Transforming concepts into movement also requires the use of imaging and past experiences.

Discovering movements leads to fashioning movements into sequences or patterns and later into dances. To form movements into patterns, you must experiment or play around with arrangements of individual movements. You must also play around with movements in order to form them into dances. Most important, however, is the fact that the structure of movement patterns and an entire dance must make sense in terms of content. This means movement structure should reflect relationships of the content being taught. Another way to say this is that form follows function. Creating an entire dance is also a synthesizing activity that can give students feelings of satisfaction and an understanding of part–whole relationships.

Planning a movement-based lesson means introducing concepts in a logical way. This may mean beginning with simple concepts and working toward those that are more complex. Organizing a lesson may also require grouping like concepts together, organizing concepts based on structural relationships, or presenting concepts in chronological order. The order in which concepts are introduced in a lesson also implies that understanding a concept presented later is based on understanding concepts that were presented earlier. Teaching aids in the form of pictures, photos, diagrams, sounds, music, and videos should be included in a lesson when possible. Using such teaching aids clarifies lesson content and meaning. Using a variety of teaching aids also appeals to students with different learning styles.

REVIEWING YOUR KNOWLEDGE AND UNDERSTANDING

1. Provide an example of a concept that can best be transformed into movement using a literal method.

2. How does the literal method of movement transformation relate to body thinking?

3. What types of concepts might best be transformed into movement using abstract methods?

4. Empathizing is part of the creative process. What role does empathy play in student learning?

5. What connection exists between transforming concepts into movement using abstract methods and being able to think abstractly?

6. Why is it important to create a dance in a way that its structure reflects important patterns or relationships between concepts?

7. Creating a dance is a synthesizing activity. What can students learn from creating a whole dance?

8. A movement-based lesson can help students appreciate dance as well as help them learn academic content. What techniques can you use to encourage dance appreciation in movement-based lessons?

9. Why is it important to include visual and auditory teaching aids in a lesson?

NOTES

1. Denver Public Schools, *Curriculum Matrices for Geography, History, Mathematics, Reading and Writing, and Science* (Denver: Denver Public Schools Department of Educational Services, 2000).

2. Denver Public Schools, *Curriculum Matrices*.

3. Denver Public Schools, *Curriculum Matrices*.

4. Denver Public Schools, *Curriculum Matrices*.

5. Denver Public Schools, *Curriculum Matrices*.

6. Simon Adams, *The Best Book of Weather* (New York: Kingfisher, 2001); Chris Oxlade, *Science Projects: Weather* (Austin, Texas: Raintree, Steck-Vaughn, 1999).

7. Denver Public Schools, *Curriculum Matrices*.

8. Brian Knapp, *Plate Tectonics* (Danbury, CT: Grolier Educational, 2001); Steve Parker, *The Earth and How It Works* (London: Dorling Kindersley, 1989); Martin Redfern, *The Kingfisher Young People's Book of Planet Earth* (New York: Kingfisher, 1999).

9. Denver Public Schools, *Curriculum Matrices*.

10. Bobbie Kalman, *Canada: The Land* (New York: Crabtree, 2002); Bobbie Kalman, *Canada: The People* (New York: Crabtree, 2002); Barbara R. Rogers and Stillman D. Rogers, *Canada: Enchantment of the World* (New York: Children's Press, 2000).

11. Denver Public Schools, *Curriculum Matrices*.

12. Irene F. Galvin, *Japan: A Modern Land With Ancient Roots* (New York: Benchmark Books, 1996); Ann Henrichs, *Japan: Enchantment of the World* (New York: Children's Press, 1998).

13. Denver Public Schools, *Curriculum Matrices*.

14. Monica Dambrosio and Roberto Barbieri, *History of the World: The Early Middle Ages* (Austin, TX: Raintree Steck-Vaughn, 1990); Sarah Howarth, *The Middle Ages* (New York: Viking, 1993); Fiona Macdonald, *How Would You Survive the Middle Ages?* (New York: Franklin Watts, 1995).

15. Simon James, Anne Pearson, and Jonathan N. Tubb, *Ancient Civilizations* (Orlando, FL: Family Learning, 1998); Hazel M. Martell, *The Ancient World From the Ice Age to the Fall of Rome* (New York: Kingfisher, 1995); Margaret Oliphant, *The Earliest Civilizations* (New York: Facts on File, 1993).

16. Denver Public Schools, *Curriculum Matrices*.

17. Roslyn Poignant, *Oceanic Mythology: The Myths of Polynesia, Micronesia, Melanesia, Australia* (London: Hamlyn, 1967).

18. Poignant, *Oceanic Mythology*.

19. Poignant, *Oceanic Mythology*.

20. David Bellingham, *Goddesses, Heroes, and Shamans: The Young People's Guide to World Mythology* (New York: Kingfisher, 1994).

21. David Leeming and Jake Page, eds., *Myths, Legends, and Folktales of America: An Anthology* (New York: Oxford University Press, 1999).

22. Sandra C. Minton, *Dance, Mind, and Body* (Champaign, IL: Human Kinetics, 2003).

23. Elizabeth Baquedano, *Aztec, Inca, and Maya* (New York: Alfred A. Knopf, 1993); Imogen Dawson, *Clothes and Crafts in Aztec Times* (Milwaukee: Gareth Stevens, 2000); Fiona Macdonald, *How Would You Survive as an Aztec?* (New York: Franklin Watts, 1995); Fiona Macdonald, *Insights: Aztecs* (Hauppauge, NY: Barron's Educational Series, 1993).

CHAPTER 7

The Mind–Body Connection and Literacy

The goal throughout this book has been to demonstrate how movement and dance can be used to teach academic concepts. The successful use of movement- and dance-based lessons depends, however, on the fact that mind and body are not two separate entities but are intimately connected. This chapter explores this belief from various perspectives.

THE BODY'S ROLE IN THINKING

Harold Rugg, who taught at Columbia Teachers College for many years, discusses the mind–body connection in his book *Imagination*. He talks about the relationship between mind and body by presenting the reader with a biography of the creative act—an act that really begins in the body. According to Rugg, the creative act is similar across disciplines and includes four basic steps: a preparatory period of baffled struggle; an interlude of giving up; a sudden flash of insight; and a period of verification, critical testing, and reconstruction.[1]

The preparatory period usually goes on for a long time. Preparation can include many types of activities: reading, visiting museums, or interviewing individuals who have firsthand knowledge on an issue. Rugg found that preparation was marked by conscious effort and intense concentration. Then, the flash of insight occurs after a problem has been put aside during an interlude of giving up—a period in which the subconscious mind works on a problem while the individual continues daily activities. The flash of insight, which is very focused, is a sudden feeling of rightness experienced as the person zeros in on a solution. The last stage of the creative process, verification, involves critique and evaluation. Verification means testing and

making changes in science or altering or removing certain elements in a work of art.

What is most important to this discussion is Rugg's description of the flash of insight or third stage in the creative process. Rugg believes that the flash of insight is a key to the threshold between the conscious and subconscious mind—a threshold he calls the transliminal mind.[2] The transliminal mind, Rugg says, is accompanied by a flow of perceptual experiences; a continuing flux of imagery; motor adjustments in the body; and the tendency of the human mind to seek order by creating relationships, symbols, or concepts as an end product of creative work. Rugg calls these perceptual experiences, images, motor adjustments, and concepts the stuff of the mind.[3]

It is possible to discover other thinkers and writers who connected mind and body. One of these individuals was Spinoza (1632–1677), a Dutch philosopher. Without the aid of modern scientific methods, Spinoza maintained that mind and body were parallel attributes. He wrote that nothing could happen in the body that would not be perceived by the mind. In fact, Spinoza thought of the body as an extension of mind.[4] In his book, *Looking for Spinoza*, Antonio Damasio indicates that, considering the century in which he lived, Spinoza stood out as a lone voice in a sea of dissenting conformity in terms of the mind–body issue. Damasio adds that by believing mind and body were made up of the same components, Spinoza was compatible with the evolutionary thinking of Charles Darwin, who later proposed that components of mind and body could be combined in different patterns across species.[5]

In her book *Discovering the Body's Wisdom*, Mirka Knaster echoes the thoughts of Rugg and Spinoza, stating that people frequently have breakthrough ideas while moving their bodies. She explains that many innovative and creative thinkers have used their bodies as a sounding board. Thomas Edison, in fact, believed that great ideas begin in one's muscles, while Albert Einstein said that his primary process of thinking was muscular and visual. In addition, the composer Peter Tchaikovsky took daily walks that inspired many of his symphonies, as did Edwin Land when he came up with the idea for the Polaroid camera.[6]

The Body or Kinesthetic Sense

You have been exploring the movement components throughout this book to gain a personal and physical experience with them. Hopefully, these explorations also made you more aware of sensations that arise from your body as you move through each day. These bodily sensations result from the functioning of your kinesthetic sense. In dance, the ability to tune into kinesthetic sensations is an important part of developing a high level of technique or movement skill, although dancers do not usually talk about developing their kinesthetic sense. Instead, dancers believe they are honing or refining their technical abilities.

Unfortunately, the kinesthetic sense is probably the least understood of all the human senses. Like your eyes and ears, the kinesthetic sense is made up of a number of different receptors or proprioceptors located in your muscles, joints, tendons, and inner ears. These receptors include the muscle spindles, Golgi tendon organs, skin receptors, joint receptors, and the vestibular apparatus. The muscle spindles provide you with information about the absolute amount of stretch to which a muscle is subjected and the rate of change in a degree of stretch. Golgi tendon organs, located within tendons (the structures that connect muscle to bone), are sensitive to varying amounts of tension in a tendon. As a muscle contracts or shortens, the degree of tension on a tendon increases. The joint receptors appear to produce signals in response to extreme ranges of motion at a joint. The skin receptors give us information about pressure, touch, and even vibration. In addition, skin receptors, such as the Pacinian corpuscles, are located much deeper in the skin and respond to deep compression and high-frequency vibrations. The proprioceptors work in combination with the vestibular system located adjacent to the inner ear. From this location, these receptors respond to degrees

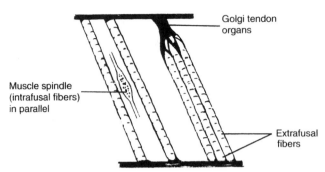

Figure 7.1.   Some of the proprioceptors. Figure 7.8 (p. 117) from *Dance, Mind, and Body,* by S. C. Minton. Champaign, IL: Human Kinetics, 2003. © 2003 by Sandra Cerny Minton. Reprinted by permission from Human Kinetics.

of acceleration or changes in movement speed and also contribute to our ability to balance.[7] Figure 7.1 is a diagram of some of the proprioceptors.

Dance kinesiologist Sally Fitt describes the kinesthetic sense as the forgotten sense. She says that the kinesthetic sense or sixth sense is traditionally not listed when discussing the other human senses of touch, taste, sight, hearing, and smell. Fitt describes the kinesthetic sense as perception of motion and position.[8]

The kinesthetic sense functions to provide feedback information to your brain. This feedback literally tells you about the direction, size, speed, and tension resulting from all your movements. In other words, your kinesthetic sense gives you information about how you are using the movement components. Because feedback is relayed automatically to your brain, you are usually not aware of the functioning of the kinesthetic receptors—a fact that makes it easy to take this sense for granted. *Proprioception* is the term used to refer to feedback from the kinesthetic sense.

Without the kinesthetic sense, it would be impossible to perform the most elementary movement tasks that are important in daily life. People who are paralyzed as the result of spinal cord injuries become acutely aware of the function of the kinesthetic sense and of the abilities they have lost. Such injuries require extensive rehabilitation in order to regain full or even partial functioning of the nervous system and the operation of the kinesthetic sense. In some cases, little or none of the nerve and kinesthetic functions can be regained, although medical science appears to be making some gains in this direction. Christopher Reeve, the former Superman, was a classic example of an individual who suffered severe injury of the spinal cord and a loss of his kinesthetic functions.

Exploring the Kinesthetic Sense

The following items are part of a Spatial Kinesthetic Awareness Test that a colleague and I developed for use with beginning dancers.[9] Read each item, and try to duplicate the shape or position with your body, but do so without looking in a mirror. Then, have a second person check the accuracy of your body shape or position. You can also look in a mirror to check your accuracy once you have tried to duplicate the body shape or position. After you try these exercises yourself, you can try them with your students to help their understanding of the kinesthetic sense and how it functions:

1. Stand with your toes pointed straight ahead, and move your entire left arm directly to the side of your body. Your arm should end up in a position parallel to the floor with your palm facing the front of the room. In addition, your arm should be bent slightly at the elbow to give it a curved appearance (see Figure 7.2).
2. Continue to stand with your toes pointed straight ahead, and place both hands at the side of your head so that your hands are directly opposite your ears. This means your hands are

Figure 7.3.   *Second body shape.* Photo by Anna Newell.

   equidistant from your head, your palms face your head, and your upper arms are parallel to the floor (see Figure 7.3).
3. Repeat the stance you used in Items 1 and 2. This time, however, lift both arms so that your fingertips are level with the tip of your nose. In addition, your fingertips touch lightly; your palms form a straight, flat shape; and your forearms are parallel to the floor (see Figure 7.4).
4. Now, stand with your feet under your shoulders and with your toes pointing along the two front diagonal directions. Your feet are on the same two diagonals and your knees are straight. In addition, your arms are held out to the side parallel to the floor (see Figure 7.5).
5. Continue to stand with your feet under your shoulders, but this time bend your entire body forward so that you are bending forward from your hips. This means that your body will be parallel to the floor and your back is straight or flat.

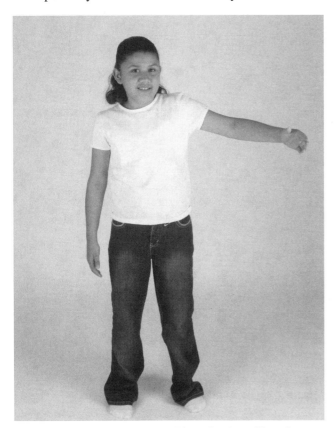

Figure 7.2.   *First body shape.* Photo by Anna Newell.

Figure 7.4.   Third body shape. Photo by Anna Newell.

Figure 7.5.   Fourth body shape. Photo by Anna Newell.

Your arms are also stretched outward from your shoulders directly to the side, and your head is in line with your back (see Figure 7.6).

6. Finally, lie down with your back in contact with the floor. Then, move your right leg to a position above your right hip and at a position of 90 degrees to the floor. Your knee and ankle should be straight in this position (see Figure 7.7).

Figure 7.6.   Fifth body shape. Photo by Anna Newell.

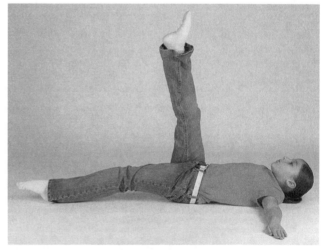

Figure 7.7.   Sixth body shape. Photo by Anna Newell.

Connecting Mind, Body, and the Kinesthetic Sense

In his book *The Brain's Sense of Movement*, Alain Berthoz explains that for champion skiers, it is not sufficient to simply process sensory cues to correct the trajectory down a mountain slope. Instead, skiers and many other types of athletes must go over their movements in their mind, anticipate the state of sensory receptors, foresee possible solutions to errors, and make decisions before performing strategic actions. Musicians and dancers also frequently go over movements in their minds before performing them. Stated in a more technical manner, the brain checks input from configurations of the body's kinesthetic receptors as it plans movement. Human thought and sensibility are dynamic processes, requiring change and adaptation in the relationships between the brain, mind, kinesthetic feedback, and the environment.[10]

Berthoz also connects mind and body in a more global way. First, Berthoz believes that the most refined forms of thinking are the product of our need to accomplish many tasks. For example, early humans survived by being able to capture prey. This means they had to anticipate the movements needed to accomplish this task beforehand. Early man also had to evaluate the size of the prey, its speed, and how it might attempt to dodge—all of which had to be completed very quickly. In other words, the hunter had to devise a construct of the mind or strategy that helped him have a successful hunt. As a result of this line of reasoning, Berthoz describes the brain as a biological simulator that predicts by drawing on memory and making assumptions.[11] Stated another way, the brain is an inventive simulator that forecasts solutions to future events based on past experiences. These solutions result in appropriate movements that accomplish specific tasks.

The Body Sense and Human Expression

There is an ongoing relationship between mind, body, and kinesthetic feedback. Rugg describes this relationship by coining a new term—*felt thought*. Rugg believes that specific types of body feelings come before an individual expresses a thought orally or before writing it down. In Rugg's estimation, there is a tensing, relaxing, or reorienting of the body that comes before one's thoughts can be revealed in speech or writing. In other words, the thought is felt in the body first before it can be expressed.[12] Rugg's concept of felt thought solidifies the connection between mind and body rather than endorsing the mind–body split found so often in Western literature. The point here is that any form of expression, whether it is through music, the visual arts, or dance, is probably anticipated with physical tensions or movements.

Rugg cites the work of Nina Bull as one reason for developing his concept felt thought and for using it as the basis of his theory of creativity. Bull, who was a researcher at the Psychiatric Clinic in New York, carried out a series of experiments over a period of years. During these experiments, a group of subjects were hypnotized and presented with stimulus words that described different feeling states. Some of the stimulus words included *fear*, *anger*, *joy*, and *triumph*. Although the students hallucinated or remembered situations connected to these words, almost all of their observed responses were accompanied by body attitudes. In fact, postural adjustments in response to the feeling-oriented words were particularly evident, and the subjects could not block their physical responses to the words when instructed to do so.[13]

Evidence of the connection between mind and body is also woven throughout the writings of Edmund Jacobson. In his book *Biology of Emotions*, Jacobson states that the experience of an emotion is accompanied by a neuromuscular response. Jacobson uses the feeling of anxiety as an example, pointing out that body tensions are identified while an individual mentally experiences this emotion. In response to this finding, Jacobson developed a system of releasing body tensions accompanying anxiety. This system, known as progressive relaxation, can reduce feelings of anxiety and accompanying body tensions by relaxing muscles.[14] Jacobson also found that his research on brain and muscle activity challenged the idea that the brain controls the muscles exclusively. Instead, Jacobson discovered a connection between the brain and muscles, indicating that activity passes back and forth in both directions in a reciprocal way. Jacobson jokingly compared the notion of the brain as the ultimate controller of what man does and knows to the medieval notion that the earth was flat.[15]

Exploring the Body and Feeling in Academic Settings

To do the following exploration, return to the section in Chapter 4 titled "Concepts for an ABA Dance." Next, read the bulleted list, which summarizes the story described in the book *Sweet Clara and the Freedom Quilt*. Now, find a quiet place where you can sit in a comfortable chair or lie on the floor. If you choose to lie on the floor, make sure it is fairly warm and covered with a carpet. Then, close your eyes, and take several deep breaths, breathing in as fully as possible as you inhale and emptying your lungs as much as you can as you exhale. In these explorations, you are going to identify the body feelings you experience as you focus on different parts of the story about Clara. Be sure to keep a written record of your body feelings because you will return to them in later explorations. After doing the explorations yourself, try these or similar explorations with your students:

1. Begin by thinking about the beginning of the story. Here the reader learns that Clara is taken from her mother's home and sent to live on another plantation. If you were Clara, how would you feel at this point in the story? Once you have decided how you would feel, continue to focus on this feeling and mentally scan your body. How does your body feel? For example, are your muscles tensed or relaxed, and are particular parts of your body more tense than others? Try to use words to describe the body feelings you experience.
2. Now, think about the second part of the story, in which Clara sews a quilt and uses it as a map to escape from the plantation. Put yourself in Clara's shoes, and imagine how she must feel as she and her friend set out on their long journey through unknown territory. What feelings would you experience in your body if you were in this situation?
3. At this point, focus on the end of the story, in which Clara and her friend find her mother and sister. How do you think Clara feels now? How would this emotion feel in your muscles? Can you use words to describe these body feelings?

Mind, Body, and Imaging

Imaging is also important in education. In his text on learning theory, Dale Schunk promotes the use of imagery in the classroom because it is central to long-term memory. Schunk uses spatial imagery to explain how imagery can be used in teaching geology. For example, students can be shown two-dimensional pictures of ridges, plateaus, or mountains and imagine a three-dimensional representation of these formations in their minds because it is possible to mentally rotate the two-dimensional pictures. Schunk also recommends using imagery to teach language arts and history. In a language arts class, students can read a set of instructions for completing a task and imagine performing each of the steps in the task. As part of a history lesson, students can visit a Civil War battlefield and imagine what it was like to fight the actual battle at that site.[16]

Imagery is also useful for developing the ability to remember and grasp meaning. In a text on educational psychology, Stephen Elliott, Thomas Kratochwill, Joan Cook, and John Travers recommend using imagery to help students remember information. This can be done by encouraging students to form a mental picture that links items they are supposed to remember.[17] Thus, if students are supposed to remember that Lincoln was the 16th president of the United States, they can imagine a picture of Lincoln giving a speech with the number 16 printed on a card that is hanging around his neck.

In another text, Harvey Silver, Richard Strong, and Matthew Perini describe a teaching strategy called "mind's eye." When this strategy is used in reading classes, the teacher selects keywords from a story the students are reading, and lists these words on the board. The students then listen to the teacher read each of the words aloud and with exaggerated emotion. As the students listen, they are expected to construct mental images of what they think will happen in the story. This activity is followed by having students draw a picture of what they have seen in their mind or describe the emotions that they think are connected with the story. Finally, the students share their predictions about the story with the class.[18]

My interest in imagery, both as a dance student and teacher, led me to do a study in which I looked at the types of imagery used by seven university dance teachers in their classes. I found these dance teachers preferred visual over kinesthetic imagery—a result that is interesting and a bit curious because they were teaching a kinesthetically oriented subject.[19] But this result is not that strange when one remembers that the kinesthetic sense is very poorly understood in comparison to the other human senses. Even though dancers work in a kinesthetic realm, their thinking seems to mirror the thinking of society in general. This study also showed that there was more imagery used in intermediate dance classes and in modern dance classes than in beginning dance classes or jazz dance classes.[20]

Although many dance and physical education teachers know that imagery helps students learn movements and sports skills, researchers have struggled with an explanation of how imagery actually works in these situations. That is, we do not know exactly how imagery affects learning to do a movement correctly. An article by James Afremoiv, Lynnette Overby, and Eva Vadocz suggests some answers to this question can be found in symbolic learning theory and psychoneuromuscular theory. According to symbolic learning theory, imagery gives the learner a chance to rehearse a sequence of movements in a symbolic way and perfect movements in the mind before performing them with the body.[21] Stated in another way, symbolic learning theory is like the mental rehearsal or indirect imagery described earlier in this book. Psychoneuromuscular theory states that muscles become innervated while the learner imagines movements. Of course, this innervation is less than but similar to the innervation that produces visible movement. This theory also explains that such innervation improves an individual's motor program connected with learning a task or movement skill because imagining movement provides kinesthetic feedback to the learner's brain.[22] Such innervation may reinforce the motor program.

Imaging is also an important part of the movement transformation process or being able to transform academic concepts into actions. Movement transformation begins with observing a concept and recognizing relevant patterns that are part of the concept. Then, your work with observation and pattern recognition are combined with imagery and memories of past experiences to produce movement. The movements in turn are woven together into a dance; it is also helpful to be able to imagine a dance or parts of a dance in your mind before setting it.

Exploring Imagery in Academic Settings

You will need to return to the section in Chapter 6 titled "More Practice With Lesson Organization." This section describes concepts from a lesson on the Aztecs. You are going to explore imagery as it relates to the Aztec concepts. Be sure to keep a written record of the images you experience because you are going to return to them in later explorations. After you have tried these explorations yourself, you can try these or similar explorations with your students:

1. One of the concepts in this lesson is a description of the symbols the Aztecs used for counting. What are the symbols the Aztecs used for the numbers 12, 20, and 400? Can you see a picture of each of these number symbols in your mind?
2. The volador or flyer dance was performed to celebrate the end of each creation in the Aztec calendar. Four dancers participated in the volador dance. What was each dancer expected to do during each part of this dance? Think about what it might feel like to perform this dance from beginning to end. Then, see if you can come up with body feelings or kinesthetic images that you would experience during each part of this dance.
3. The Aztecs used pictures or glyphs to represent both animate and inanimate entities. Which glyphs were used to represent the four creations in the Aztec calendar? Can you imagine the sounds that go with each of the glyphs? For example, if the glyph is a picture of a wolf, you would imagine the sound of a wolf howling.

MOVEMENT, LITERACY, LANGUAGE, AND THE BODY

According to a standard dictionary definition, *literacy* is the ability to read and write.[23] Words are mental or cognitive constructs. They are symbols that represent something else, whether this something else is an object, person, or feeling. Words make up the many languages humans use to communicate with each other mind to mind. Words also form the body of knowledge in many fields, such as psychology, linguistics, meteorology, math, and even dance. Of course, the letters of the alphabet, formulas, equations, and diagrams are also symbols, but we can use words to describe these symbols, too.

Understanding Movement Literacy

In many of the previous explorations, you were asked to tune into your body or kinesthetic sensations and use words to describe them. To be able to use movement and dance as a teaching tool, you will need to learn to tune into your kinesthetic sensations with sensitivity and clarity. Being able to describe your body feelings with words helps refine and develop kinesthetic sensitivity. Having such sensitivity to kinesthetic sensations also enables you to select the right movement components when creating movement-based teaching experiences.

Movement literacy is a term that describes the condition of being highly aware of and sensitive to the many nuances of movement. It also refers to a refined ability when using movement for both technical and expressive purposes. The technical aspect of movement involves developing skill in athletics or dance, while the expressive aspect of movement pertains to performance or choreography. Movement literacy includes being able to use words to describe body sensations accurately as well. To say this another way, movement literacy is the process of tuning into your kinesthetic sensations and connecting these sensations with appropriate descriptive language. This process is a way to make your kinesthetic sensations more concrete. You could even say that movement literacy is a new and different way to talk and think about literacy or what humans know.

Exploring Movement Literacy

You can develop some insights into movement literacy by doing the following explorations. The action-oriented words and movement suggestions are drawn from the book *Primer for Choreographers*.[24] Try these explorations yourself, and present them to your students to help them refine their movement literacy skills:

1. *Ooze* and *melt* are two movement-oriented words. How can you move if you are oozing or melting? What other words can you think of that accurately describe these same movements?
2. What about movements that are like the words *wiggle*, *jiggle*, and *pitter-pat*. Do these three words cause you to move in similar or different ways than the words *ooze* and *melt*?
3. How can you translate the words *soar* and *slink* into movement? Think of other words that describe these same actions.
4. Move as though you are walking across a tightrope. Then, describe how this action feels in your body and looks in a mirror. Think of a single word that describes your movements.
5. Can you move like chewing gum? What words can you use to describe the quality of such actions?
6. It is easy to bounce a ball. How would you move if you are moving like a bouncing ball? Come up with words that appropriately describe your bouncing actions.

Understanding Nonverbal Communication

We have established that literacy is the ability to read and write, but I have broadened this definition to include various nonverbal forms of communication, such as visual images, sounds, and, of course, human movement.[25] For example, a painting that is made up of sharp shapes and bright colors sends a different message to viewers than a painting that includes rounded shapes and muted tones. We usually find that the first painting communicates excitement, activity, or even fear, depending on the exact use of color. The second painting, on the other hand, sends a message of calm or even blandness. Sounds can also be used to communicate different messages; loud sounds may scare or excite, while soft sounds can calm and sooth. The messages that we receive from a painting or a piece of music take place without the use of words and are known as nonverbal communication.

In a similar way, movement can send a message, too. Think about the message you get from watching a dancer perform fast, energetic movements, including jumps and leaps, in contrast to a dancer who is using slow, sustained actions done at a low level. For me, the first dancer communicates excitement, while the second dancer projects a feeling of calm or even sadness. Movement can communicate nonverbally in many ways. When a person moves toward someone, their advance makes them appear increasingly larger and more powerful. When the same person moves backward, he or she retreats and becomes smaller and less powerful. As a result, moving forward communicates a feeling of strength, and moving backward communicates weakness.

Let's look at one more example of how words can be used to describe the nonverbal aspects of movement. When your body shape is wide or large, it probably feels like you are really stretching or reaching away from the center of your body. In contrast, your body feels cramped or compressed when its shape is narrow or small. Someone watching you shape your body in these two ways would probably think that your wide body shape looks imposing, while your narrow body shape appears timid or as if you were trying to hide.

Exploring Nonverbal Communication and Movement

Now, you will practice choosing words that accurately describe the message you receive from viewing different types of movements. In doing these explorations, you are exploring the communicative or nonverbal aspects of movement. The first set of explorations focuses on the nonverbal aspects of the movement components direction, level, and size:

1. Begin by standing in front of a mirror. Then, travel through space so that your body moves from one side of the room to the other side. While performing these actions, make sure you keep your shoulders and hips facing the mirror. When I move from one side of a space to the other, my body feels as though I am slicing through the space with the side of my body. Perform the side-to-side movement several times, and then describe how you think this movement communicates to an observer. Now, change the direction of your body's movements. Did changing the direction of your actions send a different message?

2. Walk around in front of a mirror so that you travel at each of three levels: high, middle, and low. When I move at a low level, it looks to me as though I am trying to hide. See if you can think of other words that describe how moving at each level communicates to an observer.

3. Walk around your movement space using large steps, and decide what walking in this way communicates. Now, walk in a manner that is opposite in size. What is the message you send by walking in this second way?

The next three explorations are designed to help you focus on the message sent by your use of the movement components time, duration, and rhythm:

4. For me, performing small, very fast actions, such as quickly waving your hand, communicates nervousness. Try performing a wave or other small action very slowly. What is the message sent by this slow action?

5. Select another small movement that can be repeated many times, but perform this action with a different part of your body. For example, I can tap my foot on the floor repeatedly. Then, extend the duration of the action by repeating it over and over. What do you think repeated performance of this movement communicates to an observer?

6. Select several simple actions that can be performed in sequence one after the other without stopping. Then, do these movements so that part of the sequence is done slowly and part is done fast. You can also stop at one or two places while performing the movement sequence. By performing these actions in this way, you have created a rhythmic pattern. What message does performing the actions in this way send?

The final set of explorations deal with the movement components quality, shape, pathway, and position:

7. Walk around your space using the following movement qualities: sustained, percussive, vibratory, and collapsing. What do you think each way of walking communicates? Can you think of other movement-oriented words to describe each way of walking? For instance, walking in a sustained manner can be described as creeping, especially if you move at a low level.

8. Stand in one spot, and make three shapes with your body, but make sure each shape is different from the other two and that you can move easily from one body shape to the next. Then, watch yourself in a mirror as you move. What message does each shape send?

9. Walk around your space so that your movement pathway is made up entirely of straight lines, such as the pathway of a square. What message does walking along this pathway send? Contrast this

message with the message sent by walking along a curved pathway, such as a circle or figure 8.

10. Put a large, sturdy chair in the middle of your movement space. Travel around the chair so that you move in at least four different positions in relation to the chair. Remember, movements can be above, below, beside, in front of, behind, at the side of, through, or around an object. What message does each of these positions send? In my mind, hovering over the chair may look predatory, while hiding beneath it can show that you are fearful.

Multiple Forms of Literacy

You have already read about how the shapes, lines, and colors in a painting communicate or send a message. The ability to interpret what is being communicated is visual literacy. In a similar manner, the sounds in a piece of music communicate, as do the movements in a dance. These multiple forms of literacy are related to different senses.

Visually literate people are aware of details in what they see and appreciate works of art, such as sculpture. Auditory literacy refers to those who can distinguish nuances when hearing a variety of sounds and who appreciate the structure and complexity of different forms of music. Finally, those who have acquired movement literacy are able to differentiate between the body feelings experienced when performing actions that use the movement components in diverse ways. For instance, when experienced kinesthetically, sustained, fast, or large actions feel different in the body. Those who are literate in terms of movement also appreciate the subtleties of a more sophisticated choreographic work. The problem here is that unless people are made aware of the other forms of literacy, they will never learn to appreciate the finer aspects of the visual arts, music, or dance. Alternative forms of literacy are alternative forms of nonverbal communication.

It is interesting to note that a lack of visual literacy is why we listen to people like Martha Stewart. Most people have not been trained to create an appealing design on a cake or to arrange a pleasing holiday dinner table. Stewart, however, has given considerable thought to these and other aspects of visual literacy. Lack of training in auditory and movement literacy also encourages many adults to enroll in courses in music and dance appreciation. Cutting the arts from school curricula creates future generations who will be illiterate in terms of nonverbal forms of communication.

The road signs we see on a daily basis are good examples of visual literacy, but they are also connected to movement because these signs tell us to stop, yield, or how to traverse a traffic circle (see Figures 7.8, 7.9, and 7.10). When we see these signs, our eyes receive the light, which is converted into electrical impulses

Figure 7.8.   Stop sign. Photo by author.

Figure 7.9.   Yield sign. Photo by author.

Figure 7.10.   Traffic circle sign. Photo by author.

by our retinas. Then, the optic nerve transmits these signals to our brain, and almost instantaneously, we process this visual information with our minds. Processing this visual input has implications for actions we need to take, like stopping the car, yielding to other cars, merging into traffic, and moving in an orderly fashion around a traffic circle.

When you think about it, there is an intimate connection between the mental meaning of road signs and our movement responses. A stop sign can be interpreted by stopping your car or your body or by holding your hand up with the wrist bent at a 90-degree angle and the palm facing forward. The yield sign is a triangle, and when we yield, we usually stop moving and then merge into the traffic by moving along a diagonal pathway so that our merging pathway forms a triangle or the top of a triangle with the pathway of ongoing traffic. Finally, the traffic circle sign is a circle, and when we move around a traffic circle, we move in a circular pathway.

It is interesting to note that dance educator Loren Bucek connects movement meaning and the meaning of other types of symbols known as motif notation. In an article, Bucek uses the term *dance literacy* to describe the process of integrating motif symbols into children's theme-based dance classes. In these classes, the symbols are viewed as a general outline or blueprint of a dancer's movements in space.[26]

Connecting Movement and Language

It is possible to draw many parallels between movement and language using the figures of speech simile and metaphor. A simile compares one person or object to another dissimilar person or object. It is a way of conferring the attributes of one thing on another to highlight their similarity. When you use a simile, you are saying that the first entity is like the second one in some way, although the two are really quite different.[27] The most common way to identify a simile is that it includes the words *like* or *as*. Examples of similes are "The child's tears flowed *like* a river" and "The man's generosity was large *like* the ocean." In the same sense, movements or body shapes can be described as being like a dissimilar person or thing. For instance, the shape you are making with your body is like a triangle or you are moving like a lumbering bear.

A metaphor is a literary device in which one thing is spoken of as if it is actually another quite different thing.[28] In a metaphor, one thing *is* the other. Examples of metaphors are "Love *is* a blooming rose" and "He *is* a machine." Note that each of these phrases becomes a simile simply by adding the word *like*, as in "Love is like a blooming rose" and "He is like a machine."

Simile and metaphor force the reader or listener to draw comparisons between two things and are often used to describe or assign a deeper or novel meaning. When using a simile or metaphor, a writer is trying to clarify what he or she means because simile and metaphor paint meaningful pictures in the mind of the reader. Movement can also create a specific feeling in your body and look a certain way in the mirror, but the meaning of movement is communicated nonverbally. Each aspect of movement—the kinesthetic sensation, the appearance of an action, and the nonverbal message—contribute to movement meaning. Kinesthetic feelings also provide feedback to the mover that is intimately connected to the meaning of an action, as does observing one's own movements in a mirror.

Exploring Simile, Metaphor, Movement, and Meaning

Your next challenge is to create verbal similes or metaphors, and then interpret these similes and metaphors with movement:

1. Return to the section of this chapter titled "Exploring the Body and Feeling in Academic Settings," and review your description of each feeling you experienced in this exploration. Then, select one of the descriptions, and construct a simile that expresses the meaning of your feeling. An example of a simile based on a feeling is "Her fear is like the sharp edge of a knife." After you have created an appropriate simile, transform it into movement. The simile "Her fear is like the sharp edge of a knife" can be transformed into a quick, slashing action.

2. Select a second description of a feeling from the same exploration, but this time, create a metaphor based on this feeling. My metaphor is "Her fear is a sharp knife." Now, transform your metaphor into meaningful movement. For me the metaphor "Her fear is a sharp knife" becomes an action in

which I use my arm to slash back and forth through space.

Comparisons Between Linguistics and Movement

According to those who study language, there are five ways humans use language to communicate. As a child develops, he or she gradually learns to use the different aspects of language: phonology, morphology, syntactics, semantics, and pragmatics.[29] Many of the aspects of language parallel aspects of movement because they play similar roles in terms of verbal and nonverbal communication.

Phonology refers to small units of sound that make up a language and that humans produce with their vocal apparatus. For example, in order to pronounce the letters *b*, *ph*, and *g*, one must make different sounds. Taken together, these sounds make it possible to orally reproduce the words of a particular language. The human ability to distinguish vocal sounds actually begins in the last two months of prenatal development.[30]

Movements do not produce sounds, but sounds can be produced in response to various movements. In terms of direction, moving forward communicates greater power, and it can be accompanied with a vocal sound that increases in volume, while a backward movement goes with a sound that gradually becomes soft. In the same sense, high movements go with high sounds and low movements with low sounds; fast movements with high, quick sounds and slow movements with low, long sounds; movements performed in an even rhythm with evenly paced sounds and movements performed in an uneven rhythm with sounds vocalized at irregular intervals; sustained movements with long, enduring sounds in a middle register and percussive movements with sporadic, loud sounds; straight movement pathways with harsh sounds and curved or weaving paths with wavering sounds.

Morphemes are the smallest unit of meaning in a language. Words are one type of morpheme. Children begin learning the meaning of simple words early. By their first birthdays, most infants learn that *mama* means a different person than *dada*. Other types of morphemes are the endings we add to words to differentiate meanings. This type of morpheme changes the meaning of a word by being bound to the word, so *cat* and *go* mean something different than *cats* and *going*.

Compound words like *baseball* are also a type of morpheme because *baseball* has a different meaning than its respective parts *base* and *ball*.[31]

Single movements can also have meaning. Think about moving your right hand through a continuous, curved pathway that begins near your right hip, travels in a curved path in front of your body, and ends by touching your right fingers to your left shoulder. Some would call this a beckoning action that means "let's get going" or "come over here." Traffic police use another common movement that means "stop." They simply lift one arm up with the wrist bent and the palm facing oncoming traffic.

Syntactics refers to the rules of grammar that govern a language. It is the characteristic pattern or patterns used in a language. Children must learn the basics of syntactics if they hope to make sense in both oral and written communication in a particular language. One rule of grammar is to use words in the proper order. Children learn early on that the sentence "The bus hits the boy" does not mean the same thing as "The boy hits the bus." Syntax differs from language to language, however.[32] A good example of difference in syntax is the position of adjectives in different languages. For example, adjectives such as *red* or *new* come before the noun in English and after the same noun in Spanish and French. Based on these grammatical rules, *red hat* is the correct usage in English, while Spanish speakers say *sombrero rojo* and those who speak French say *chapeau rouge*.

The syntactic aspects of language have many parallels in movement, particularly to the movements used in mime and dance. In terms of syntactics, imagine a mime who performs the following sequence of actions. First, he pulls a drawer open, picks up an object, places it in the drawer, removes his hand from inside the drawer, and closes the drawer. Now, imagine the same mime performing the next sequence of actions. He pulls a drawer open, picks up an object, places it in the drawer, leaves his hand in the drawer, and closes the drawer. The order of actions in these two sequences of movement ensures that the first sequence communicates quite a different result or meaning from the second.

The subtle shades of meaning that can be conveyed by a language are known as semantics. Thus, in cooking we can combine cream and a bowl of berries by stirring them together or by pureeing them. Stirring would leave the berries largely intact, while pureeing would reduce the cream and berries to a soupy mixture—two quite different results. Semantics also refers to the meaning found in phrases and in whole sentences. Throughout life, we build up semantic word networks that are remembered as cognitive structures and that contribute to the meanings found in a body of knowledge.[33]

In terms of semantics, visualize the movements that might be choreographed for a romantic ballet versus the actions created for a sword fight. In the romantic ballet, many of the movements are soft, graceful, relatively sustained actions performed slowly or at a medium speed. In a romantic ballet, the performers also travel primarily in curved pathways across the stage, executing most of their movements at a middle level. The sword fight, on the other hand, requires movements that advance and retreat along straight pathways. Most of the actions in the sword fight are also strong, percussive, and faster than the movements created for the romantic ballet. In addition, the combination of movements found in a romantic ballet differs in meaning from those found in a sword fight.

Finally, pragmatics is the aspect of language embedded in a society or culture. By learning to take turns in conversation, we learn about one facet of pragmatics. Another aspect of pragmatics is connected to social class.[34] Consequently, individuals who are part of the working class usually speak differently than professionals with a college education, while different cultures use different sayings or idioms to mean the same thing. This use of language can lead to confusion if the listener knows only the standard or grammatically correct form of a language. For example, a saying in English like "Don't put the cart before the horse" can be confusing when translated literally by someone from another country or culture.

Many movements or gestures have meaning only for a certain cultural group, while other gestures are universal. For instance, raising one's hand in school indicates a desire to speak or ask a question, while shaking hands is a greeting that can lead to conversation or friendship. Both motions are fairly universal and have a similar meaning across cultures. In contrast, southern Italian men may shake their tie to show that they are not fooled by the actions of another person.[35] This gesture is not common throughout the world but has meaning for a relatively small group of people.

In their book *Mosaic of Thought*, Ellin Keene and Susan Zimmermann talk about understanding meaning in the concrete and practical context of teaching reading to elementary school students. They explain how meaning is constructed from written text by relating the text to memories of one's own sensory experiences. To connect text and memories, the authors use visual, tactile, and olfactory experiences from the past to help students interpret what they read. For example, the memory of a grandfather gives visual substance to a character in a poem, while experiences with different textures and smells add depth to the textures and smells described in the same piece of literature.[36] It is my contention that memories of kinesthetic experiences can also provide an avenue for understanding word meaning and interpreting text.

Several years ago, I was coaching 1st- and 2nd-grade students as they were learning to read. When they stumbled over a word, I frequently helped them sound out the word by giving them the sound of the first letter or first several letters. At other times, however, I used movement cues to help students identify words. To help students identify directional words, I pointed up, down, or sideways. I even got up and galloped when a student stumbled over the word *horse*. I was pleased to see that usually students could pronounce the problem word by connecting my movements with the letters written on the page in front of them.

THE MIND–BODY CONNECTION AND CREATIVE PROBLEM SOLVING

Creativity refers to the ability to generate new and unique solutions to a problem. The problem to be solved can be the creation of a new work of art or a new invention. Creative problem solving involves using your mind in two different ways, however, because two different mental processes are involved. Sometimes these two mental processes are called right and left brain modes of thought. Creative problem solving can also have a positive effect on the mental construct self-esteem or how a person feels about himself or herself.

Creativity and Mode of Thought

The explorations throughout this book are miniature creative problem-solving experiences. Creating an entire dance was a larger and more challenging opportunity to solve a problem. As you engaged in exploring and dance making, you actually used your brain in two different ways.

Betty Edwards's use of pattern recognition to teach drawing was described in Chapter 5, but she is also interested in the two modes of thought and how each helps students learn to draw. Edwards states there are two parallel ways of knowing.[37] The first involves thinking, analyzing, and evaluating, and the second includes feeling, intuiting, and having insights. Edwards says the first way of thinking uses the left brain, while the second uses the right brain. To explain the two modes of thought, Edwards uses the example of a researcher working on a problem for a long time without finding a solution. After a period of struggle, the solution appears to the researcher in a dream metaphor and is intuitively recognized as the answer to the problem.[38] Later, of course, the researcher tests the solution to his problem by evaluating each part of the solution step by step.

I read detective novels for fun and to help me fall asleep at night. I have found that the stories in these novels include examples of the two modes of thought. Frequently, the lead detective in these stories interviews a suspect by listening closely to the suspect's words and analyzing their content and meaning. Later, the detective reviews the suspect's statements and suddenly and intuitively decides that the suspect's words when taken together do not feel right. The detective's use of analysis and evaluation represents the left brain mode of thought, while the use of intuition represents a right brain way of thinking.

Edwards attributes the two modes of thought to the different ways the hemispheres of the brain may process information. In most people, the two sides of the brain are connected internally, and there is little awareness that the brain functions in two different ways. Most people automatically switch from one mode of thought to the other without being conscious of making this switch. To describe this idea in another way, one hemisphere probably dominates, while the other one is inhibited. Then, the switch is made unconsciously when the other form of thought is needed. Edwards clarifies the difference between the two modes of thought by stating that the left hemisphere thinks in words and by using analysis. It counts, reasons in a step-by-step linear way, uses logic, and is objective. The right brain is more global. It imagines, visualizes, sees how parts make up the whole, how objects exist in space, and thinks in metaphors.[39]

Fredric Schiffer does research on the functioning of the two sides of the brain. In fact, much of his work has been done with split-brain patients, in which the corpus callosum—a large nerve bundle that connects the two hemispheres of the brain—has been surgically severed to relieve seizures. In most people, an image in the right visual field seen by the right eye is transmitted by the optic nerve to the right side of the brain. An average individual also sees an image that is in the left visual field with the same eye, but this image crosses over through the corpus callosum and is transmitted to the left side of the brain. The images travel to different hemispheres of the brain because the two halves of the retina are connected to different sides of the brain. With the left eye, images seen in the left visual field travel to the left side of the brain, and those seen in the right visual field cross over and are transmitted to the right side of the brain.[40]

Schiffer describes an experiment with a split-brain patient to make his point about the different functions performed by the two sides of the brain. In this experiment, pictures were transmitted only to the right side of the subject's brain. This was accomplished by having the patient wear a special contact lens that permitted transmission of images only to her right brain. After several seconds, it was clear that the patient could recognize photographs but was not able to use words to describe the content of the pictures.[41] Remember, the right brain thinks in images, while the left brain thinks in words.

Another experiment described by Schiffer is related to a split-brain subject's ability to match an object held in the right hand with a picture of the object. When this object was held in the right hand so that the image was transmitted to the left brain, there was some difficulty in identifying the correct picture. It was easier, however, for the subject to match objects and pictures that could be described with words. Such objects usually had regular shapes, such as a cube or sphere. In this same experiment, more irregular or amorphous objects held in the right hand and transmitted to the left brain were extremely difficult to match with the correct picture.[42]

Schiffer writes that other experiments proved ordinary people think in two different ways as well. For example, an ordinary person will respond more quickly to verbal instructions when these instructions, such as the ability to tell whether a dot is inside a circle, are transmitted to the right brain. Ordinary people are also better at noticing details when these details are flashed to the left brain, and they can recognize a whole picture more easily when it is flashed to the right brain.[43]

Both modes of thought function during creative problem solving. Rugg describes four steps in creative work: preparation, giving up, a flash of insight, and verification and reconstruction. The preparatory period usually involves research on a subject and learning elements of the craft. This means that if you want to create a dance based on electricity, you need to learn important electrical concepts. You also need to learn about dance making. Learning about electrical concepts and dance making involves conscious, left-brain thought. During the interlude of giving up, subconscious processes are at work, engaging the right-brain mode. The interlude of giving up is frequently interrupted by a flash of insight—also a product of the right brain. By using the right-brain mode, you can also see parts of your dance in your mind's eye. The final stage of the creative process, verification and reconstruction, is a return to the linear, analytical left brain.

*Exploring Right and Left Brain Thinking
in Academic Contexts*

According to Edwards, you can trigger right- or left-brain thinking by presenting students with an inspiration or stimulus preferred by one brain hemisphere or the other. Keep in mind that the left brain is dominant and faster than the right brain. Thus, triggering right-brain thinking means using an inspiration or stimulus that the left brain will reject. The right-brain mode thinks in relationships, spatial images, and comparisons.[44] It is attracted to images, pictures, and other stimuli in which content is presented as a whole rather than one bit at a time. The left brain thinks or absorbs information in a linear or sequential manner. Once you have tried the following explorations yourself, try these or similar explorations with your students:

1. Begin by reviewing the body feelings you experienced in the explorations in this chapter in the section titled "Exploring the Body and Feeling in Academic Settings." Then, select the body feelings you experienced in the first, second, or third exploration, and come up with one image that stands for all of Clara's experiences in each part of the story. Can you create a single movement that represents this image? For example, if I am planting flowers in a garden, my overall image of this task is of being dirty—an image that is unpleasant. This single image represents a right-brain way of thinking that can be transformed into one movement.

2. Return to the same part of Clara's story, but this time, create a series of movements that represents an actual sequence of events in the story. To return to my example of planting flowers, I dig the hole in the soil, place the young plant in the hole, fill the hole around the plant with dirt, and press the dirt firmly into place. This series of movements represents a left-brain way of thinking.

3. Review the images you discovered in relation to the Aztec concepts. These concepts were described in the section of this chapter titled "Exploring Imagery in Academic Settings." Select one of the concepts, and focus on the images you discovered. Then, select one image, and create a single movement that captures the essence of this image.

4. Return to the same Aztec concept, and create a series of movements that represent the actual sequence of events described in this concept.

SUMMARY AND CONCLUSIONS

The mind–body connection has been a subject of conjecture for hundreds of years. There does, however, appear to be a growing number of individuals from a variety of fields that endorse the idea that mind and body interpenetrate each other. This means that the mind can affect the body, and conversely, the body can affect the mind. If the body can affect the mind, logic says teachers should be able to use the body and movement to help students learn, but this is not how most lessons are delivered in our schools. The use of movement as a teaching strategy seems to be largely ignored, particularly when instructing students above the kindergarten level.

One step in discovering how movement can be used as a teaching strategy is to understand the functioning of the kinesthetic sense and how this sense delivers messages to the brain. The proprioceptors—of which there are many different types—are responsible for monitoring the body in terms of muscular tension, speed of movement, and a number of other bodily actions and responses. When the proprioceptors send a message to the brain, decisions are made determining further actions. The skier decides to slow down, or the hunter decides to move in for the kill.

While the kinesthetic sense helps determine our actions for practical reasons, as in the preceding two situations, it is also an important part of human communication. Rugg's felt thought is a primary example of the bodily reaction that precedes the human desire to express oneself. This desire to communicate is in turn tied to our feelings and emotions, bringing us back to the body. It is impossible to experience a feeling without reacting in some way with the body. The bodily reaction may not be visible to the naked eye, but it is there nonetheless. When movement communicates in a visible way, we say that it communicates nonverbally.

The Caines acknowledge that true learning takes place when students are engaged on a feeling level. Movement used as a teaching strategy has the capacity to tap into the connection between the body and emotion. When the discovery of a concept-based movement is motivated by a student's feelings about the concept, particularly when these feelings are positive, a personal connection is created. It is this connection between content and feeling that helps students remember. Concept-based movements can also be combined to create patterns or sequences, and these patterns can help students recognize important relationships in the subject being studied. Furthermore, concept-based movements can evolve from various forms of imagery and help students crystallize and understand the essence of a story or other types of text.

Being sensitive to input from the kinesthetic sense is the beginning of the ability to use movement as a teaching strategy. Kinesthetic input is the basis of the movement transformation process used to create concept-based actions. This sense tells us whether a movement is fast or slow, high or low, large or small. The kinesthetic sense also enables us to combine movements together into patterns and patterns into dances.

Sensitivity to the nuances of movement and to the ways in which the subtleties of movement can be used in teaching is a nonverbal form of communication I have termed *movement literacy*.

The connection between communication, the body, and movement is also evident in many figures of speech and aspects of language. You explored how the figures of speech simile and metaphor can be transformed into actions. It was also possible to connect movement with aspects of language, such as syntactics or the structure of a language, because the order of words in a sentence determines the meaning of the sentence and the order of movements in a pattern determines the meaning of the pattern. It is in the areas of semantics or meaning and pragmatics or the way in which culture and language are entwined that language and movement parallel most closely. Nevertheless, single words have a meaning, as do single movements. Certain combinations of words are understood by the native speakers only, as are some of the gestures common to a cultural group.

Transforming concepts into movements and making dances is a creative process in action. While teachers can create concept-based movements and weave these movements together into dances, it is beneficial to encourage students to create their own movements and dances. Creative work involves thinking in two different ways, involving both right- and left-brain modes of thought. When students create movements and make dances, they experience these two modes of thought firsthand. Literal movement transformations are a conscious, precise method for discovering movement and are of the left brain, while abstract transformations capture the essence of a concept that involves the right brain. Dance making can also engage both sides of the brain. When movements are arranged one by one, the left-brain mode of thought is engaged, but imagining a part of a dance moves one into the domain of the right brain.

REVIEWING YOUR KNOWLEDGE AND UNDERSTANDING

1. What is felt thought, and what role does it play in the human ability to communicate?
2. What is the kinesthetic sense, and how is it related to the movement components and to movement literacy?

3. What is the connection between having a feeling and the muscles of the body? How can the connection between feelings and the body be used as part of your teaching strategy?

4. What types of images have you read about in this chapter? How can imagery be used in the classroom?

5. There are multiple forms of literacy. What does this statement mean? How can you combine multiple forms of literacy in a single lesson?

6. Describe two figures or aspects of language. Then, draw a parallel between the figures or aspects of language and movement.

7. Describe how you can use this comparison between language and movement in a classroom setting.

8. Students should have a chance to do creative work or problem solving in their classes. What benefits do students accrue from doing creative work?

9. How can the use of creative work in movement and dance develop thinking skills?

10. Does creative work with movement and dance encourage learning to think in more than one way? Please give some examples to explain your answer.

NOTES

1. Harold Rugg, *Imagination* (New York: Harper and Row, 1963).

2. Rugg, *Imagination*.

3. Rugg, *Imagination*.

4. Errol E. Harris, *The Substance of Spinoza* (Atlantic Highlands, NJ: Humanities Press, 1995).

5. Antonio Damasio, *Looking for Spinoza: Joy, Sorrow, and the Feeling Brain* (Orlando, FL: Harcourt, 2003).

6. Mirka Knaster, *Discovering the Body's Wisdom* (New York: Bantam Books, 1996).

7. Bruce Abernethy, Vaughn Kippers, Laurel Mackinnon, Robert J. Neal, and Stephanie Hanrahan, *The Biophysical Foundations of Human Movement* (Champaign, IL: Human Kinetics, 1997).

8. Sally S. Fitt, *Dance Kinesiology*, 2nd ed. (New York: Schirmer, 1996).

9. Sandra Minton and Karen McGill, "A Study of the Relationships Between Teacher Behaviors and Student Performance on a Spatial Kinesthetic Awareness Test," *Dance Research Journal* 30, no. 2 (1998): 39–52; Sandra Minton and

Jeffrey Steffen, "The Development of a Spatial Kinesthetic Awareness Measuring Instrument for Use With Beginning Dance Students," *Dance: Current Selected Research* 3 (1992): 73–80.

10. Alain Berthoz, *The Brain's Sense of Movement* (Cambridge, MA: Harvard University Press, 2000).

11. Berthoz, *Brain's Sense of Movement*.

12. Rugg, *Imagination*.

13. Nina Bull, *The Attitude Theory of Emotion* (New York: Nervous and Mental Disease Monographs, 1951).

14. Edmund Jacobson, *Biology of Emotions: New Understanding Derived From Biological Multidisciplinary Investigation; First Electrophysiological Measurements* (Springfield, IL: Charles C. Thomas, 1967).

15. Jacobson, *Biology of Emotions*.

16. Dale Schunk, *Learning Theories: An Educational Perspective*, 3rd ed. (Upper Saddle River, NJ: Merrill, 2000).

17. Stephen N. Elliott, Thomas R. Kratochwill, Joan Littlefield Cook, and John F. Travers, *Educational Psychology: Effective Teaching, Effective Learning*, 3rd ed. (Boston: McGraw Hill, 2000).

18. Harvey F. Silver, Richard W. Strong, and Matthew J. Perini, *So Each May Learn: Integrating Learning Styles and Multiple Intelligences* (Alexandria, VA: Association for Supervision and Curriculum Development, 2000).

19. Sandra Minton, "Assessment of the Use of Imagery in the Dance Classroom," *Impulse: The International Journal of Dance Science, Medicine, and Education* 4, no. 4 (1996): 276–292.

20. Minton, "Assessment of the Use of Imagery."

21. James Afremoiv, Lynnette Overby, and Eva Vadocz, "Using Mental Imagery to Enhance Sport and Dance Skills of Children," *The Journal of the International Council for Health, Physical Education, Recreation, Sport, and Dance* 33, no. 4 (1997): 45–48.

22. Afremoiv, Overby, and Vadocz, "Using Mental Imagery."

23. Sandra Minton, "Using Movement to Teach Academics: An Outline for Success," *Journal of Physical Education, Recreation, and Dance* 74, no. 2 (2003): 36–40.

24. Lois Ellfeldt, *Primer for Choreographers* (Palo Alto, CA: National Press Books, 1967).

25. Minton, "Using Movement to Teach Academics."

26. Loren E. Bucek, "Developing Dance Literacy: Integrating Motif Writing Into Theme-Based Children's Dance Classes," *The Journal of Physical Education, Recreation, and Dance* 69, no. 7 (1998): 29–32.

27. Stephen Minot, *Three Genres: The Writing of Poetry, Fiction, and Drama* (Upper Saddle River, NJ: Prentice-Hall, 1998).

28. Minot, *Three Genres*.

29. Roger G. Eldridge, "Aspects of Language" (Lecture, University of Northern Colorado, Greeley, May 18, 2004).

30. Eldridge, "Aspects of Language."

31. Eldridge, "Aspects of Language."

32. Eldridge, "Aspects of Language."

33. Eldridge, "Aspects of Language."

34. Eldridge, "Aspects of Language."

35. Desmond Morris, *Body Talk*: *The Meaning of Human Gestures* (New York: Crown, 1994).

36. Ellin O. Keene and Susan Zimmermann, *Mosaic of Thought: Teaching Comprehension in a Reader's Workshop* (Portsmouth, NH: Heinemann, 1997).

37. Betty Edwards, *The New Drawing on the Right Side of the Brain* (New York: Tarcher/Putnam, 1999).

38. Edwards, *New Drawing*.

39. Edwards, *New Drawing*.

40. Fredric Schiffer, *Of Two Minds* (New York: The Free Press, 1998).

41. Schiffer, *Of Two Minds*.

42. Schiffer, *Of Two Minds*.

43. Schiffer, *Of Two Minds*.

44. Edwards, *New Drawing*.

Appendix: Music Resources

COMPACT DISCS

Authentic Israeli Folk Songs and Dances, Legacy International, Box 6999, Beverly Hills, CA 90212.

Bahia Black: Ritual Beating System, Island Records, Inc., 14 East 4th Street, New York, NY 10012.

Blue Man Group Audio, Virgin Records America, Inc., 338 N. Foothill Road, Beverly Hills, CA 90210.

Book of Days by Meredith Monk and Vocal Ensemble, BMG Music, 245 5th Avenue, 8th Floor, New York, NY10016.

Canciones de mi Padre by Linda Ronstadt, Elektra/Asylum Records, 75 Rockefeller Plaza, New York, NY 10019.

Dance Explosion, Volume 1, Pow Wow Records, Inc., 1778 Broadway, New York, NY 10019.

French Playground by Puntumayo for Kids, Puntumayo World Music, 411 Lafayette Street, 4th Floor, New York, NY 10003, www.puntumayokids.com.

International Folk Dance Mixer, RTV Communications Group, Inc., 4375 S. 60th Avenue, Ft. Lauderdale, FL 33314.

Kiss Your Brain by Jean Feldman, 3019 Marsh Haven, Seabrook Island, SC 29455, www.drjean.org.

A Lo Cubano, Compilation, D. V. More Record, Via Quintiliano, 29-20138 Milano, Italy.

Music to Improve Relaxation by Daniel May, Somerset Entertainment, 1110 Lake Cook Road, Buffalo Grove, IL 60089.

A Native American Odyssey: Inuit to Inca, Putamayo World Music, 324 Lafayette Street, 7th Floor, New York, NY 10012, www.putumayo.com.

New Orleans, Puntumayo World Music, 324 Lafayette Street, 7th Floor, New York, NY 10012, www.putumayo.com.

Olantunji: Drums of Passion, originally released by Sony Music Entertainment, Inc., manufactured by Columbia Records, 550 Madison Avenue, New York, NY 10022.

Ole! Ole! Ole! Dr. Jean en Espanol by Jean Feldman, 3019 Marsh Haven, Seabrook Island, SC 29455, www.drjean.org. (This CD contains the English version of songs as well.)

World Playground: A Musical Adventure for Kids by Puntumayo for Kids, Puntumayo World Music, 324 Lafayette Street, 7th Floor, New York, NY 10012, www.putumaykids.com.

TAPES

Breathe: A Relaxing, Meditative Instrumental Journey by Jon Bernoff and Marcus Allen, Dreamweaver Music, Rising Sun Records, P.O. Box 524, Mill Valley, CA 94942.

Drums With Feet and Wings by Mark Berres, Mobile Percussion Productions, P.O. Box 1286, Idyllwild, CA 92349.

Earth Tribe Rhythms: The Primitive Truth by Brent Lewis, Brent Lewis Productions, P.O. Box 428, Joshua Tree, CA 92252.

Earth Tribe Rhythms: The Ultimate Drum Experience by Brent Lewis, Brent Lewis Productions, P.O. Box 428, Joshua Tree, CA 92252.

Journeys: Native American Flute Music by R. Carlos Nakai, Canyon Records, 4143 N. 16th Street, Phoenix, AZ 85016.

Jungle Moon by Brent Lewis, Brent Lewis Productions, P.O. Box 428, Joshua Tree, CA 92252.

Moonrise by Kim Robertson, Invincible Recordings, P.O. Box 13054, Phoenix, AZ 85002.

Planetary Unfolding by Michael Stearns, Sonic Atmospheres, 14755 Ventura Blvd., Sherman Oaks, CA 91403.

Pulse . . . Where the Rhythm Begins by Brent Lewis, Brent Lewis Productions, P.O. Box 428, Joshua Tree, CA 92252.

Rhythm Hunter by Brent Lewis, Brent Lewis Productions, P.O. Box 428, Joshua Tree, CA 92252.

Tibetan Plateau by David Parsons, Fortuna Records, P.O. Box 1116, Novato, CA 94947.

Thunder Down Under: Tribal Drumming and Didgeridoo by Brent Lewis and Peter Wood, Brent Lewis Productions, P.O. Box 428, Joshua Tree, CA 92252.

AB A simple dance form with two sections having contrasting themes.[1]

ABA A simple dance form with three sections having two contrasting themes, A and B, followed by a repeat of the first theme in the third section. The third section may be a shortened version of the first section.[2]

abstract A type of dance that has no message or one that communicates the essence of the real thing.[3]

abstracting Process of condensing something to its essence. One of the thinking tools used by creative people.[4]

abstraction Process of removing, separating from, or condensing something to its essence.[5] Also a method of changing concepts into actions by moving like the basic feeling or essence of the concept. Used interchangeably with *indirect*.

active learning Gaining understanding or knowledge by doing or solving a problem.

Alexander Technique A body therapy system that deals with correcting misalignments in the body and other bad habits.[6]

alignment Placement of body segments so that the ear, shoulder, hip, knee, and ankle are close to a straight, vertical line from a profile view.

analogizing Process of finding a resemblance between two otherwise unlike things. One of the thinking tools used by creative people.[7]

anatomical image Having a picture in the mind that is like a part or parts of the body.

asymmetrical A body shape or grouping of dancers in which the right side does not visually match the left side.

auditory Having to do with the sense of hearing.

auditory literacy Having a sensitivity to or ability to discriminate nuances of sound.

awareness through movement A body therapy system created by Moshe Feldenkrais that deals with creating a heightened sensitivity to body or kinesthetic feelings.

balance To be in a state of equilibrium.

ballet A dance form based on specific steps and body positions, originating in the 16th century.

ballroom dance A couple dance form based on arrangements of specific steps, such as cha-cha or rumba.

basic beat The evenly spaced, ongoing, underlying pulse in metrically organized music. Used interchangeably with *pulse*.

basil ganglia A group of nerve cells located in the inner layers of the cerebrum, or umbrella-like dome of the brain.

bodily-kinesthetic intelligence Having a skilled use of one's body. One of the multiple intelligences.[8]

body attitude Placing the body in a particular pose or position.

body awareness The ability to be tuned into various feeling states of the body.

body feeling A sensation that arises from the body or kinesthetic receptors.

body information Sensations that arise from the body or kinesthetic receptors.

body therapy A system of theories and movements used to rid the body of inefficient actions or positions.

body thinking Using movement to solve a problem.

brain-based learning Lessons based on how the brain/mind functions in organizing and understanding input.[9]

brain hemispheres The two sides of the cerebrum, or large umbrella-like dome of the brain.

brain stem A part of the brain between the cerebrum and spinal cord. It makes up the central nervous system along with the brain and spinal cord.

center The most dense part of the body located slightly below the naval. Can also be the process of becoming aligned and together.

cerebellum Part of the brain lying behind and below the dome of the brain, or cerebrum.

cerebrum The forward and upper part of the brain, which is involved in voluntary movement and conscious thought processes.

chance dance A dance structured by using arbitrary methods, such tossing dice.

choreographer An individual who makes dances.

choreography A fully formed dance. Used interchangeably with *dance*.

circular process Refers to the nature of the creative process in which earlier discoveries are revisited, changed, or used to initiate new ideas.

closure Coming to an ending, as in finding an appropriate ending for a dance.

cognitive structures Relationships that exist between thoughts or mental images.

collapse One of six movement qualities involving downward releasing in response to gravity.

concept An idea or thought, particularly one related to a specific subject.

concept-based movement Movement used to convey a concept or the essence of a concept.

concrete knowledge Ideas based on objects, places, or things existing in reality.

conscious The state of being aware of or knowing what you are doing.

constructive rest A position of the body that reduces muscle strain and aids relaxation.[10]

contextual learning Understanding based on a particular situation, background, or environment.

continuity Having a sense of being connected so that one movement flows into the next one. A basic principle of dance form.

corpus callosum Prominent nerve fibers connecting the two sides of the cerebrum.

cortex The most outer layer of the cerebrum.

creative process A unique way of solving a problem. Usually includes a number of developmental stages.

critical thinking The use of careful analysis of a problem or of the solution to a problem.

cross-cultural A trait or idea related to more than one cultural group.

Culture-Free Self-Esteem Inventory A standardized test measuring the degree to which a person has positive feelings about himself or herself.[11]

curriculum A course of study based on specific goals.

dab A light use of energy performed using short, quick, direct actions in a series.

dance A fully formed choreography. Used interchangeably with *choreography*.

dance making The process of putting choreography together.

deductive thinking Reasoning from general to specific or from known to unknown.

developmental thinking The use of mental processes based on earlier, more basic ideas.

diagram A sketch, drawing, or plan.

dimensional thinking Using mental processes to move from 2-D to 3-D or vice versa. One of the thinking tools used by creative people.[12]

direct A method of changing concepts into actions by moving like a concept or shaping the body like it. Used interchangeably with *literal*.

direct image The process of seeing movement in your mind before performing it.[13]

direction One aspect of the movement element space. One of the movement components.

dopamine A substance that aids in transmission of nerve impulses.

duration One aspect of the movement element time. One of the movement components.

emotional intelligence Being sensitive to your own feelings or the feelings of others.

empathizing Being able to see and understand the world as others see it. One of the thinking tools used by creative people.[14]

energy One of the elements of movement. Energy propels movement.

engaged The act of being focused, involved, or paying attention.

essence The fundamental nature of an object or person.

even rhythm Having movements or sounds organized at regularly spaced intervals.

exploration A process producing spontaneous movement based on suggestions from a leader or from written instructions.[15]

facing The direction in which the front of the body is positioned or to which it is turned.

Feldenkrais Method Body therapy system that increases body awareness to correct movement problems.[16]

felt thought The general body feeling that comes before verbalizing a thought or writing it down.[17]

flash of insight One of the stages of the creative process that occurs suddenly.

flexion A movement in which the space between two body segments narrows.

flick A light use of energy performed using a short, quick, action that follows an upward path.

floor pattern A pathway traced on the floor with locomotor steps.

flow One of the categories used by Laban to describe human effort. Flow can be free or controlled.[18]

focal point The spot where attention is drawn onstage or in a painting.

focus The ability to pay attention.

focused learning Understanding involving paying attention.

form The overall organization and development of a dance.

formation The arrangement of dancers in a space or onstage.

forming patterns Combining two or more structural elements or operations. One of the thinking tools used by creative people.[19] When we form a pattern, a relationship between parts is also created.

framework for creating movement A diagram of the process used for creating movement.

gallop A locomotor movement that travels forward while one foot chases the other.

global Having a sense of the whole.

Golgi tendon organ A proprioceptor that relays information about force or tension in muscles.[20]

group identity The unit or cluster of people with which one associates oneself.

higher brain center Part of the central nervous system that is capable of rational thought.

hop A locomotor movement that pushes off and lands on the same foot.

iambic verse A poetic form in which the emphasis is on the second syllable.

ideokinesis Body therapy system created by Lulu Sweigard in which imagery is important.

image A mental picture or kinesthetic feeling.

imaging Using the imagination to see, hear, or feel something that does not exist in reality. One of the thinking tools used by creative people.[21]

indirect A method of changing concepts into actions by moving like the basic feeling or essence of the concept. Used interchangeably with *abstraction*.

indirect image A movement inspiration that comes from outside the body.[22]

inductive thinking Reasoning from particular facts or cases to generalizations.

input Information, particularly sensory information, that comes from outside oneself.

inspiration The starting point for movement exploration.[23] Used interchangeably with *motivation* and *stimulus*.

interdisciplinary learning Using ideas from different fields to construct meaning or develop understanding.

interlude of giving up Stage of the creative process in which the problem or project is put aside.

interpersonal intelligence Operating primarily through person-to-person relationships and communication. One of the multiple intelligences.[24]

intrapersonal intelligence Having a sensitivity to one's inner states of being through self-reflection and awareness of the spiritual. One of the multiple intelligences.[25]

involvement Having more than a superficial level of attention.

joint capsule receptors A proprioceptor that relays information about exact joint position.

jump A locomotor movement that takes off from and lands on two feet.

kinesthetic The sense that relays information about muscular sensations, position of the body and body parts, movement, and tension.

kinesthetic arts Those art forms that involve movement, such as dance and drama.

kinesthetic feedback The process of receiving impressions and input from the body sense.

kinesthetic image A movement inspiration that describes the body feeling that accompanies an action.[26]

kinesthetic literacy The ability to differentiate between levels of kinesthetic feedback, such as degrees of muscular tension, speed of movement, or the angle at a joint. Individuals who are kinesthetically literate can appreciate subtle differences in movements and understand how actions communicate nonverbally.

kinesthetic sensation The process of receiving impressions and input through the body or kinesthetic sense.[27]

kinesthetic sense Human sense that monitors body position, movement, orientation, and tension.

Labanotation A system of dance notation created by Rudolf Laban. Written symbols are used to describe movement so that it can be reproduced with accuracy.[28]

labeled learning Type of learning based on reading, writing, and talking about information. Includes learning from textbooks, videos, lectures, pictures, and dialogue.[29]

language acquisition Process of gaining the ability to communicate with words.

leap A locomotor movement in which the performer takes off from one foot and lands on the other foot as the body traces an arc in space.

learning style Different ways individuals understand information. Some learn most easily when they see a picture, while others are verbal or kinesthetic learners.

learning tools Cues, strategies, and ideas used to teach information. In the case of this book, movement is a learning tool.

left brain Capacity of the human brain to analyze information step by step, one piece at a time, in a linear manner.

letter blends Pronouncing two adjacent letters such as *bl* or *br* so that their sounds run together.

level One aspect of the movement element space. The three basic levels are high, middle, and low.

level of abstraction The use of a various viewpoints to reveal different qualities of an abstract representation of something real.[30]

line of alignment A straight, vertical line that intersects the ear, shoulder, and hip and comes close to the knee and ankle.

linear pattern A relationship of movements based on their order.

linear process Performing a task in a step-by-step manner.

linear thinking A mental process in which information is digested one piece at a time.

lines of movement Imaginary lines connecting various points on the body. Used in ideokinesis to improve body alignment.[31]

literacy Skilled in reading and writing. In this book, the definition of *literacy* also includes the ability to understand and appreciate visual art, music, and dance.[32]

literal A method of changing concepts into actions by moving like a concept or shaping the body like it. Used interchangeably with *direct*.

locomotor movements Actions used to travel across space.

logical/mathematical intelligence Being skilled in inductive and deductive thinking. The ability to reason using numbers and the recognition of abstract patterns. One of the multiple intelligences.[33]

lumbar Part of the spine that makes up the small of the back.

mental image A picture that can be seen in the mind or a body feeling that can be imagined.

mental model A representation of objects or ideas that can be imagined.

mental picture A visual image that you can see in your mind.

mental rehearsal The act of reviewing movements in the mind without performing them.

metaphor A figure of speech implying comparison by speaking of one thing as if it was another very different thing.

mime A movement art form using realistic gestures and actions to communicate nonverbally.

mind–body split Belief that the mind and body are not connected.

mind's eye Using the mind to imagine visual pictures.

misuse of the body Actions or postures that contribute to misalignment of the body and inefficient movements.

modeling Using the imagination to construct a simulation of objects, actions, or ideas. Models can be a physical or mathematical representation, realistic or not. One of the thinking tools used by creative people.[34]

morphology An aspect of language dealing with the smallest units of meaning, such as words, word endings, and compound words.[35]

motif notation Written symbols used to describe the essence of a movement, not the actual movement.[36]

motivation The starting point for movement exploration. Used interchangeably with *inspiration* and *stimulus*.[37]

motor adjustment Subtle shifts in body posture or attitude in response to one's thoughts.

motor program A central mental structure that defines the details of skilled actions.[38]

movement-based lesson The teaching of concepts and ideas aided by the use of movement.

movement components The essential aspects of movement used throughout this book to transform concepts into actions. Also used to vary movement.

movement discovery The process of creating movement based on an inspiration.

movement efficiency The ability to move without wasted effort.

movement literacy Having the ability to discriminate between slight differences in movements, particularly in terms of nonverbal communication.

movement manipulation The process of creating variations of single movements, particularly by using the movement components.

movement-oriented words Verbal descriptors that create a mental picture of various actions, such as *ooze*, *melt*, and so on.

movement sequence Several actions that are connected and can be performed one after the other without stopping.

movement skill The ability to move the body or its parts effectively and efficiently.

multimodal Relating to more than one sensory modality. Used interchangeably with *multisensory* and *polysensual*.

multiple intelligences A theory of human intellect that challenges the traditional viewpoint by describing diverse ways of thinking and knowing.[39]

multisensory Relating to more than one sensory modality. Using interchangeably with *multimodal* and *polysensual*.

muscle memory The ability to remember and re-create movements based on how they feel in the body.

muscle spindles A proprioceptor that relays information about muscle contraction.

muscular sensation Body feelings arising from the muscles.

musical intelligence Being able to recognize tonal patterns, including sounds from the environment, along with a sensitivity to rhythm and beats. One of the multiple intelligences.[40]

musical motif A germinal rhythmic pattern or patterns.[41]

musical structure The overall form or framework of a piece of music.

mythology A traditional story usually of unknown origin connected to a cultural group.

naturalist intelligence Showing an interest in identifying patterns and classifying things in nature. One of the multiple intelligences.[42]

nerve impulse The transmission of signals along a nerve to other nerves or other body structures.

neuromuscular response A reaction of nerves and muscles to various stimuli.

neuron A nerve cell body and all of its processes.

neuroscience Any one of the branches of study and investigation concerned with the growth, development, and function of the nervous system.[43]

nonverbal communication Sending a message with the body. Communicating without words.

noradrenaline The primary neurotransmitter for arousal of the fight-or-flight syndrome. Also known as norepinephrine.

observing The process of taking in environmental stimuli in an active way. One of the thinking tools used by creative people.[44] When we observe in an active way, we are more likely to notice details and subtle differences.

olfactory Having to do with the sense of smell.

orientation The placement or position of a person or object relative to the surroundings.

outer world The environment, including sensory information, as it exists outside the body.

overall form The structure or pattern of development of a whole dance.

Pacinian corpuscle Proprioceptors located deep in the skin that are stimulated by compression. Primary receptor of compression and touch.

parapsychological The investigation of supernatural phenomena, such as telepathy and apparitions.

pathway Designs traced in the air by moving body parts. Also, designs or floor patterns traced on the floor by moving the whole body across space.[45] One of the movement components.

pattern The organization of movements into relationships that can be described.[46] One of the movement components.

pattern language The arrangement of abstract symbols rather than words into interesting relationships.[47]

pedestrian Movements that are part of everyday life.

percussive One of six movement qualities involving explosive and powerful use of energy.

peripheral learning The taking in and digesting of information that is outside the main area of focus.

peripheral perception Input that is at the edge of the visual field or outside the area of focus.

personal space The area immediately surrounding the body into which one can reach without changing location in space.[48]

phonetics The study of speech sounds.

phonology Small units of sound that make up a language.[49]

pivot point A position without size or shape around which a body part or the entire body turns.

playing Experimenting or fooling around with the elements of what is being created. One of the thinking tools used by creative people.[50]

point of focus A location with size or shape that draws the viewer's attention.

polysensual Relating to more than one sensory modality. Used interchangeably with *multisensory* and *multimodal*.

position The placement of the body or an object relative to other bodies, objects, or aspects of the surrounding environment. One of the movement components.

posture A description of the placement of body segments in relation to a straight, vertical line.

pragmatics An aspect of language that is embedded in a culture and that has a particular meaning for that culture.[51]

preparatory period One of the stages of the creative process in which the creator does research or other preliminary work to get ready for the actual process of creating.

problem-solving dance A dance form in which the choreographer bridges the movement gap between various known elements.

problem-solving learning Understanding achieved by finding a solution or solutions.

progressive relaxation Body therapy system associated with Edmund Jacobson in which a person learns to tune into various states of the body, especially those that are tense or relaxed.

proprioceptor One of several types of sensory receptors that monitor body movement and position, tension, or pressure.

psychoneuromuscular theory The belief that muscles can be innervated by imagining movement.[52]

pulse The basic, steady beat in dance or music. Used interchangeably with *beat*.

qualitative study A research method or process of inquiry that explores social or human problems by building a complex and holistic picture of an issue.[53]

quality The way energy is used when a movement is performed.

quantitative study A research method or process that explores a problem using statistical analysis.

recognizing patterns Identifying relationships between parts of the input from the environment. One of the thinking tools used by creative people.[54]

repetition A principle of choreographic form in which movements are repeated in a dance.

rhythm A structure of patterned movements or sounds occurring over time. One of the movement components.

right brain The capacity of the human brain to analyze information in a global or holistic manner.

righting reflexes A reaction of the body involved in maintaining an upright position. Some aspects of the righting reflexes are found in the inner ear.

role learning Understanding the behaviors required to fulfill a particular function.

rondo A dance form with many sections. There is a return to the original theme in alternation with contrasting themes.[55]

run A locomotor movement in which both feet leave the ground at one point. Faster than a walk.

scaffold A method of learning in which one stage builds on previous stages or pieces of information.

schema Movement structures stored in the brain that are based on relationships between sensory information, memory of previous movement responses, and consequences of performing a movement in a particular way.[56]

self-esteem Having a belief in oneself and self-respect.

self-image How one sees oneself.

self-regulated learning A method of understanding based on the learner's ability to take action, ask questions, make choices, and think critically and creatively.[57]

semantics An aspect of language that conveys subtle shades of meaning.[58]

sensory cue Signals from the environment that relate to the different senses.

sensory modality The different ways in which humans receive information from the environment, such as through vision, hearing, or the kinesthetic sense.

sensory receptor Physical structures in the human body that receive different types of signals from the environment.

sensory stimulation Activation of the physical structures, such as the eyes or ears, by input from the environment.

sequential A method of arranging the same movement so that it is performed by different dancers separated by a certain number of counts.

series A dance form created by finding an order for your movements and determining how many times each movement will be performed.

shape One of the elements of movement. Refers to how parts of the body are arranged or how dancers are placed in a grouping.

simile A figure of speech in which one thing is compared to another very different thing with the use of the words *like* or *as*.

size An aspect of space that refers to the largeness or smallness of a movement. One of the movement components.

skip A locomotor movement that goes into the air from one foot and lands on the same foot. A step-hop.

slide A locomotor movement in which the feet are moved apart and drawn together as the body goes into the air.

social brain The idea that knowledge is learned through interactions with others.[59]

social self-esteem An individual's perception of the quality of his or her relationships with peers.[60]

somatic Having to do with the body.

space One of the elements of movement. Direction, level, size, focus, and pathway are aspects of space.

spatial arrangement The relative position of dancers or objects in a space.

spatial intelligence Knowledge that relies on sight and the ability to create mental pictures. One of the multiple intelligences.[61]

Spatial Kinesthetic Awareness Test A test created by the author and a colleague to assess the accuracy of body position and shape among beginning dancers.

spatial memory The ability to remember the relative location of objects or landmarks.

spatial perception The ability to accurately sense relationships between one's body and the surrounding space.[62]

speed The rate at which movement occurs.

spinal cord A thick length of nerve tissue extending down through the spine. Part of the central nervous system.

split brain patient An individual whose corpus callosum, or connecting link between the right and left brain hemispheres, has been severed surgically.[63]

staccato An action or sound performed quickly with breaks in the movement or sound.

stimulus The beginning point for movement exploration. Used interchangeably with *motivation* and *inspiration*.

study A short dance based on a specific choreographic element.

suspension A use of energy in which movement appears to hover midair.

sustained A use of energy that is slow, smooth, and controlled.

swinging A use of energy in which the body or a part of the body traces an arc in space. It is necessary to give into gravity on the downward part of the swing and apply energy on the upward part.

symbol Something that stands for or represents something else.

symbolic learning theory A use of imagery to rehearse movements before performing them.[64]

symbolize The act of using something to stand for something else.

symmetrical Visually balanced body shape or grouping of dancers.

syncopated Placing accents or points of emphasis where they usually do not occur in metrically organized music or movement.

synesthesia Experiences with one sense that produce imagined sensations in another sense.

synosia A unified way of understanding that links mind and body.[65]

syntactics The rules of grammar or characteristic patterns that are used in a language.[66]

synthesis A putting together of parts or elements to form a whole.

synthesizing The process of creating a whole from separate parts or elements.

tableau A dance form in which different movements or movement sequences are performed in the same space simultaneously. Usually does not make up a whole dance.

tactile Related to the sense of touch.

teaching strategy A plan of action for teaching specific content.

teaching tool A device or idea used to teach specific content. Movement is the teaching tool described in this book.

tempo The speed of a movement.

tendon A fibrous cord that attaches muscle to bone or to other body parts.

tension A state of contraction or tightness in muscles.

text-based dance A dance in which gesture and movement are used to complement spoken text.

texture The density or sparseness of music.[67] Can also be a quality of movement or refer to the tactile quality of a painting.

theme A message communicated in a dance. Also, movements that fit together in a sequence and are repeated and developed throughout a dance.

theme and variations A dance form based on varying a sequence of movements throughout.

thinking tool A strategy for analyzing and coming up with a solution to a problem.

time One of the elements of movement. Refers to the speed of a movement.

time signature Numerical indication of meter in a piece of music.[68]

transform The process of changing concepts or ideas into movement.

transforming The process of changing information represented in one sensory modality into a form represented by another sense. One of the thinking tools used by creative people.[69]

transition An aspect of choreographic form that provides a bridge between movements.

transliminal mind The power of intuition and other unexplained forces that operate during creative work to attract and integrate materials from the unconscious to the conscious mind in order to bring that which is being created into fruition.[70]

trochaic verse A poetic form in which the emphasis is on the first syllable.

unconscious The state of being unaware of your movements or how your movements feel.

uneven rhythm Having movements or sounds organized at irregularly spaced intervals.

unity A principle of choreographic form in which movements fit together in a way that forms a whole dance.

universal language A form of expression that communicates to a variety of cultures. The arts are a universal language.

variation The process of changing movement in terms of the movement components.

variety A principle of choreographic form that presents movements in different ways.

verbal-linguistic intelligence Being skilled with the use of written and spoken language. One of the multiple intelligences.[71]

verification A stage in the creative process when solutions are analyzed and tested.

vibratory A use of energy that involves shaking or trembling.

visual aid A photo, drawing, diagram, or videotape used to enhance the teaching process.

visual arts Those art forms appealing to the sense of sight.

visual field An area that can be observed from one point of view.

visual image A picture in the mind.

visual literacy Having the ability to discriminate between slight differences in line, shape, color, and pattern that can be seen with the eye.

visual-spatial intelligence A way of knowing that relies on the sense of sight. Also the ability to create pictures in the mind. One of the multiple intelligences.[72]

visualize The process of forming a mental picture of an object or activity in the mind.

weight One of the categories used by Laban to describe human effort. Weight can be strong or light.[73]

NOTES

1. Lynne A. Blom and L. Tarin Chaplin, *The Intimate Act of Choreography* (Pittsburgh: University of Pittsburgh Press, 1982).

2. Blom and Chaplin, *Intimate Act of Choreography*.

3. Sandra C. Minton, *Dance, Mind, and Body* (Champaign, IL: Human Kinetics, 2003).